REDEFINING REVIVAL

Biblical Patterns for Missions, Evangelism and Growth

REDEFINING REVIVAL

*Biblical Patterns for Missions,
Evangelism and Growth*

WILLIAM A. BECKHAM

TOUCH PUBLICATIONS
Houston, Texas, U.S.A.

Published by TOUCH Publications
P.O. Box 19888
Houston, Texas, 77224-9888, U.S.A.
(281) 497-7901 • Fax (281) 497-0904

Copyright © 2000 by William A. Beckham.

All rights reserved. No part of this publication may be reproduced, stored in a retrieval system, or transmitted, in any form or by any means, electronic, mechanical, photocopying, recording, or otherwise, without the prior written permission of the publisher. Printed in the United States of America.

Cover design by Don Bleyl
Text design by Rick Chandler
Editing by Scott Boren

International Standard Book Number: 1-880828-26-X

All Scripture quotations, unless otherwise indicated, are from the *Holy Bible*, New American Standard Version, Copyright © The Lockman Foundation, 1960, 1962, 1963, 1968, 1971, 1972, 1973, 1975, 1977. Used by permission.

TOUCH Publications is the book-publishing division of TOUCH Outreach Ministries, a resource and consulting ministry for churches with a vision for cell-based local church structure.

Find us on the World Wide Web at
http://www.touchusa.org

To Mary,

*Who has lived with me in loving community
in places as distant and different as Texas and Thailand.*

ACKNOWLEDGMENTS

Ralph W. Neighbour has been a mentor and friend for three decades. My ministry to this point and this book would have been impossible apart from his unselfish encouragement, sacrificial example and wise guidance. God has used Ralph Neighbour in a powerful way to prepare for twenty-first century revival and God has blessed me because of my association with him.

Also, as my editor, Scott Boren, has patiently guided me through the challenging process of writing this book. He has helped me express the passion in my heart and the pictures in my mind in practical writing that makes this book more readable.

CONTENTS

To The Reader: *Revival Reformation* 11
Foreword 13
Introduction: *A Holistic Definition of Revival* 15

PART 1: REVIVAL CONTEXT
    Chapter 1   The Demographics of Revival 21
    Chapter 2   The Geography of Revival 27
    Chapter 3   The Community of Revival 35
    Chapter 4   The Mathematics of Revival 45
    Chapter 5   The Kingdom of Revival 55

PART 2: REVIVAL ROOTS
    Chapter 6   Jesus' Model 65
    Chapter 7   Christ in the Midst 77
    Chapter 8   Resurrection Power 87
    Chapter 9   Transformation Training 95
    Chapter 10 Jethro Leadership 105

PART 3: REVIVAL PRINCIPLES
    Chapter 11 The Principle of Integration 117
    Chapter 12 The Principle of the Ordinary 129
    Chapter 13 The Principle of Small Churches 137
    Chapter 14 The Principle of Assimilation 149
    Chapter 15 The Principle of Balance 159

PART 4: REVIVAL STRATEGY

Chapter 16 Cultural Strategy 175
Chapter 17 Transplanting Strategy 185
Chapter 18 Indigenous Strategy 193
Chapter 19 Critical Mass Strategy 205
Chapter 20 Step-by-Step Strategy 215
Chapter 21 Curriculum Strategy 227
Conclusion 237
Appendix 245

Notes 249
Index 253

TO THE READER

Some day when we go into the archives of heaven to find a book which expounds the meaning of human history as God sees it . . . that book will be entitled "The Preparation for and the Extension of the Gospel among the Nations.
—George Elton Ladd

The process of writing this book led me to reflect on the New Testament, the Reformation, the twentieth century church, and finally the twenty-first century. In an earlier book, *The Second Reformation*, I sought to apply New Testament theology and church design to the traditional church of the twentieth century. In this book I apply these principles to revival in the twenty-first century.

A brief summary of *The Second Reformation* provides a context for this book.

In 1517, Martin Luther nailed the 95 Theses to the door of the Wittenberg Church as an invitation to debate the theology of the established church. That debate restored some important New Testament beliefs to the sixteenth century church.

Luther realized the need to adjust the Constantine design of the church in order to live out Reformation beliefs. Therefore, early in the movement the reformer of church theology suggested using New Testament house groups to reform church structure. "Those who want to be Christians in earnest and who profess the gospel with hand and mouth should sign their names and meet alone in a house somewhere to pray, to read, to baptize, to receive the sacrament, and to do other Christian works."[1]

For political, personal and practical reasons, Luther failed to implement the small group strategy. Consequently over the past 500 years, God has continued to encourage the church to move beyond Reformation belief to the application of Reformation design.

Prophetic voices have continued to call for the church to complete the Reformation. In the twentieth century Elton Trueblood concluded that changing the church "means, in one sense, the inauguration of a new Reformation while in another it means the logical completion of the earlier Reformation in which the implications of the position taken were neither fully understood nor loyally followed."[2]

In *The Second Reformation*, I suggest that the "logical completion" of the Reformation is to return to the large group/small group design of the church. The fruit of the New Testament and Reformation design of the church will be New Testament revival in the twenty-first century, but revival will be defined in a holistic New Testament way.

FOREWORD

More and more people long to see the Kingdom of God coming alive in the life of the church. Though variously called, it is a yearning for revival.

William Beckham in this compelling study explains how the heart cry for revival can be fulfilled. Avoiding common misconceptions of revival, like some kind of religious extravaganza or emotional high, he interprets revival in its broader New Testament sense as entering fully into the reign of Christ. When Christians embrace this life of authentic holiness, love inevitably overflows in evangelism, church planting and world missions.

To chart a course for us today, the author turns to Jesus, and recognizes in his life a strategy for revival. Our Lord from the beginning, of course, knew that he was sent to die for the world. But before He finished his work at the cross, he prepared the initial members of the first church for revival life in His Kingdom. His strategy did not focus upon methods, materials, or programs. He focused, rather, on disciples, disciples who would become His revival leaders. By involving a few people in His life, He demonstrated and imparted the kind of revival that would spread across the world. All of this without the printing press, television or even the internet. Maybe the church today should consider again Jesus' strategy.

Beckham understands what Jesus did to build His first church. His view provides him with a sharp sword to chip away at accepted paradigms of institutional structures, church planting programs and missionary methods. With disarming sensitivity, he honestly critiques how the church has limited itself. Then he summons us to realize Christ's mandate to disciple the nations. More to the point, he provides a practical way of doing it.

Redefining Revival will not give you more of what your church already has. It will challenge your thinking, test your methods and question your results. Yet if you heed the message of this book, you will seize the call to missions, to church expansion, to evangelism, to the Kingdom of God, and enter into revival.

Robert E. Coleman

INTRODUCTION
REVIVAL DEFINED

*Every generation is crucial;
every generation is strategic.*
—Billy Graham

In the seventh century B.C., God challenged His people to "Look among the nations! Observe! Be astonished! Wonder! Because I am doing something in your days that you would not believe if you were told" (Habakkuk 1:5).

The last several years God has blessed me with the opportunity to "look among the nations" and "observe" what He is doing. I am astonished by what I see. I am filled with wonder at the work of God's hand. I believe that God is doing something in our day that is beyond our wildest hopes and dreams. Our world, exponentially exploding with people, problems and possibilities is beginning to experience the wonder of New Testament revival.

Revival is the state of the New Testament church that is indwelled by Christ, empowered by the Spirit and designed to fulfill God's Kingdom purposes. Revival is first what the church is and second what the church does. Dion Robert of the Ivory Coast explained the nature of revival when he said: "I don't believe in periodic revival. I believe in continuing revival in the church."

Revival Words

The word "revival" is part of a group of words that includes missions, evangelism, church planting, holiness and Kingdom living. Historically these words have been divided but I believe they must be rejoined and redefined. In this book I am using "revival" as the magnet word for the other five. A church of revival is a church of missions, evangelism, church planting (expansion), holiness and Kingdom living.

These "revival" words were interchangeable in the New Testament church. The first century church was missions. It did not just do missions, or pray for missions or send missionaries. It was missions and it was on a mission. It therefore expanded into Jerusalem, Judea, Samaria and the world. The New Testament church of missions was a church of witness and evangelism that began new churches. This church of missions, evangelism and expansion resulted in personal and social holiness and lived out the Kingdom of God on earth.

Jesus built this broad revival mandate into the genetic code of the church. No matter where the church is, what the period of history or the political and social forces around it, the church is a church of revival, missions, evangelism, church planting, holiness and Kingdom living.

Jesus and History

Let me suggest three attitudes that will determine the extent of revival in the twenty-first century. These attitudes represent unprecedented opportunity for harvest, failure or closure and carry consequences of historic proportions.

> Attitude One: The twenty-first century has the greatest potential for expansion and harvest that the church has ever known.

> Attitude Two: The twenty-first century threatens the church with the greatest possibility of decline and failure that it has ever known.

> Attitude Three: The twenty-first century won't be around long enough for the church to harvest because the end is upon us.

I believe the first attitude is the proper historical perspective for the church today. The twenty-first century is the greatest opportunity for revival that the church has ever known.

Revival is possible because of the way God relates to human history. History to Jesus has a heavenly perspective and an earthly application. "Pray, thy kingdom come on earth as it is in heaven." "Whatever is loosed on earth will be loosed in heaven." In John 14, Jesus assures His disciples that He will be in Heaven "preparing a place" for them and at the same time will be on earth "abiding" with them. Paul also connected heaven and earth together in Ephesians. Christ (and the Christian) is seated in the heavens while operating on earth (Ephesians 2:6).

The top and invisible part of holy history is the ascended, glorified and reigning Christ. This means that history moves according to the permission and power of God. The bottom and visible part of holy history is the church living out God's history on earth in every generation.

OUR MOMENT OF HISTORY

Billy Graham opened the World Congress on Evangelism in Berlin in 1966 by stating the responsibility and opportunity of each generation:

> Every generation is crucial; every generation is strategic. But we are not responsible for the past generation, and we cannot bear full responsibility for the next one. However, we do have our generation! God will hold us responsible at the Judgment Seat of Christ for how well we fulfilled our responsibilities and took advantage of our opportunities.[1]

God's story in this century will be your story and my story. You and I will join Peter and Paul, Polycarp and Patrick, Luther and Wesley and the rest of the "great cloud of witnesses." God's history is also the story of your church and my church.

God may use many different historical forces in His Kingdom purposes. However, the church is God's way of living in history, redeeming history, judging history and bringing history to a conclusion. The church is His Bride. The church is His Body. Christ died for the church. The Kingdom is expressed and fulfilled through the church. The church is therefore God's primary agent of revival in every generation.

Billy Graham in his last message at the Lausanne Congress in 1974 reflected upon the future:

> I believe there are two strains in prophetic scripture. One leads us to understand that as we approach the latter days and the second coming of Christ, things will become worse and worse. Joel speaks of "multitudes, multitudes in the valley of decision!" The day of the Lord is near in the valley of decision. He is speaking of judgment. But I believe as we approach the latter days and the coming of the Lord, it could be a time also of great revival.[2]

In conclusion he said: "I am praying that we will see in the next months and years the 'latter rains,' a rain of blessings, showers falling from heaven upon all the continents before the coming of the Lord."[3]

"May you live in interesting times" is a popular blessing for those who appreciate the significance of history. It is an appropriate blessing for the twenty-first century because unique circumstances have merged around the year 2000. As you begin to read this book, I want to bless you with this blessing: "May you be astonished and filled with wonder because of what God is doing in this century through you and your church."

PART 1
REVIVAL CONTEXT

God is a missionary God.
—John Stott

1
THE DEMOGRAPHICS OF REVIVAL

It's easier to grasp the future if you know what it looks like.
—Business Week

The population explosion is the demographic context for worldwide revival in the twenty-first century.

On October 12, 1999 the United Nations celebrated the birthday of the child that pushed the world's population to six billion. The name, sex, place of birth and exact day of arrival of that child are unknown. Kofi Annan, the United Nations Secretary-General, welcomed the symbolic six billionth baby at a hospital in Sarajevo, Bosnia when 29-year-old first-time mother gave birth to a baby boy two minutes after midnight.

Charles Haub of the Population Reference Bureau said, "We've just gone through a demographic century that I don't think will ever be equaled." World population in the twentieth century increased by 4.4 billion. Most of that was during the past three decades when the population increased by one billion in twelve years (1970s), again in 13 years (1980s), and yet again in 14 years (1990s).[1]

The current population figure of six billion is projected to increase to eight billion by 2026 and 9.3 billion by 2050. Many experts believe the population of the world will top out at more than ten billion during the next century. But it could go higher if either the birth rate or mortality rate change slightly.[2]

THE NUMBER OF CHRISTIANS IN THE WORLD

Experts estimate the current number of Christians in the world in different ways. Some experts use cultural counting method and claim that nearly a third of the world's population claims to be His (Christ's) followers. In this method, an entire country or a large portion of a country is automatically declared Christian. Less optimistic numbers result when the more subjective factor of personal commitment is the criteria for determining the number of Christians.

No matter how many Christians we estimate are in the world today, most understand that the twenty-first century is uncharted territory for the church. The church will participate in either an unprecedented harvest and assimilation or the church will suffer a decline in numbers and influence of catastrophic proportions.

Let us suppose the church can even maintain the rate of 1/3 of the population. The number of Christians would be somewhere around 2.7 billion of eight billion in 2026 and 3.1 billion of 9.3 billion in 2050. The most optimistic interpretation concludes that there will be 6.2 billion unbelievers in 50 years.

The figures are even more disturbing if the church maintains its current estimate of two billion Christians. Those who are not Christians would increase from four billion to six billion by 2026 and to 7.3 billion by 2050.

21st Century Population

| | | | Non Christians | |
YEAR	POPULATION	CHRISTIAN	MAINTAIN Number	MAINTAIN 1/3%
2000	6 Billion	2 Billion	4 Billion	4 Billion
2025	8 Billion	?	6 Billion	5.3 Billion
2050	9.3 Billion	?	7.3 Billion	6.2 Billion

The real challenge, and some would say the impossibility, is for the church to successfully reach a significant number of the current four billion unbelievers and to harvest the additional billions that will be born in the next 50 years.

Apocalyptic Paranoia

A portion of the church believes a final apocalyptic solution is the only hope for the church of the twenty-first century. This worldview is driven by "apocalyptic paranoia" that manifests itself in pessimism.

The population numbers alarm them. The evil they see in the world overwhelms them. Technological advances worry them. Future scientific discovers threaten them. The possibility of persecution frightens them. The weakness of the church discourages them. They seek solutions outside the church in politics, the mass media and apocalyptic predictions. They feel that God will remove the church from an impossible, dangerous and potentially embarrassing situation for the church.

I also believe the final solution to history will be apocalyptic when Christ returns in triumph. However, Christians have often made mistakes in interpreting history because of an unhealthy fixation on dates, a narrow view of the world and pessimism about the church. An obsession with evil rather than a passion about Christ's mission in the world always distorts the historical perspective of the church. Therefore, a theology of escape from the world then replaces Christ's theology of Kingdom mission in the world.

A Church Disengaged from History

On the Mount of Transfiguration (Matthew 17:1-13), Peter suggested building three tabernacles because "It is good for us to be here." At that moment, the voice of the Father shook the place, Moses and Elijah disappeared and Jesus led Peter, James and John down from the mountain. Jesus designed His church for ministry in the valley, not for experiences on a mountain. In the valley a father needed help. A young boy needed healing. Demons needed to be confronted. The sheep needed shepherds. Leaders needed to be trained for ministry.

Jesus rejects a *Moses tabernacle*. It is possible to praise the Word, to teach the Word and to study the Word but fail to apply the Word. The church does not impress the world by teaching the Word on one special day. The twenty-first century world will only take note when the church applies the Word in the valley the other six days of the week. "If we ever have to choose between how much Bible is understood or how much Bible is obeyed, my prejudice is in favor of obeyed truth."[3]

Jesus rejects an *Elijah tabernacle*. The temptation is to detach prophecy from life. Jesus applied the spirit of prophecy by caring for the needs of the hurting in the valley. Prophecy has little meaning when enshrined on a mountaintop. God's prophecy is ultimately about people and that is why Jesus would not leave prophecy in a mountain tabernacle. The church is God's instrument for living out His prophetic ministry.

Jesus even rejects a *Jesus tabernacle*. The offer was for the Messiah to be isolated, protected and frozen in time on a mountain of inspiration. What glory that could be! But Jesus fled that place. Would this Jesus in His tabernacle on the mountain have ever been crucified? Holy men in tabernacles are not a threat to governments, societies, religions or the devil. But Christ loose in the world, in the valley, in the temple, in the streets, in the homes and in the lives of people is something quite different. That is a holy man too dangerous to live. That is Messiah.

The twentieth century church continues to build tabernacles to Moses, Elijah and even Jesus. Consequently, the Word, prophecy and Jesus are detached from real life in the valley where the billions live. Christ is recreating His church for revival by creating a church that lives out the Word, prophecy and the sacrificial life of Christ.

Twenty-first Century Revival

In spite of its shortcomings, the twenty-first century church is once more poised for revival. The traditional way of doing church has brought Christianity to a place not only to survive but to harvest in the next century. However, the question is, "Can the traditional approach that brought the church to this point of potential harvest be effective in completing the harvest among the billions born during the decades surrounding the year 2000?"

Most church leaders suspect that the church will need to find a solid New Testament community base in order to participate in twenty-first century revival. Cosmetic changes will not be enough to overcome the population explosion, increased opposition to the gospel and a postmodern philosophy in the West.

Over the past 40 years, God has gradually developed the cell movement as the structural wineskin for revival in the twenty-first century. For the first time since the Wesleyan revival in the eighteenth century, the church has a way to mobilize its members to reach large numbers of lost people and to assimilate them into ministry.

LINE UP ONE BILLION LOST PEOPLE

Most of us cannot even visualize one billion persons, much less conceive of evangelizing them. Larry Stockstill, pastor of Bethany World Prayer Center in Louisiana, uses a dramatic illustration to explain one billion people. Picture a line of one billion lost people starting at your church door and circling the globe. How far will that line stretch? It would circle the globe more than eight times.

Using the current population ratio of Christians to non-Christians, in 50 years more than six billion lost people will inhabit the earth. Six billion lost will stretch around the world and through your church 50 times.

"Like a general plotting His course of battle, the Son of God calculated to win. He could not afford to take a chance. Weighing every alternative and variable factor in human experience, He conceived a plan that would not fail."[4] What strategy does your church have for bringing your portion of these lost people into the Kingdom of God during the twenty-first century?

2
THE GEOGRAPHY OF REVIVAL

*I go forth with the mission to awaken the sleeping China.
Even though in shedding blood, I will never turn back.
I go forth with the vision to see a China for missions
To preach the Gospel to every corner of the world.*
—A recent Chinese hymn

Both evangelized and unevangelized nations are the geographical context for worldwide revival in the twenty-first century.

Peter fell asleep on a rooftop in Joppa and had a life changing vision (Acts 10). A window of heaven opened up and Peter saw a large sheet lowered to the earth. The sheet contained animals that the Jews considered clean and unclean. Three times Peter was instructed to eat of the animals and three times Peter refused. A voice spoke, "What God has cleansed, no longer consider unholy."

Peter was startled out of the vision by three Gentiles knocking at the door below. He immediately applied the vision to the visitors' request to go to the home of a Roman army officer in Caesarea.

Two worlds met at the end of that journey. The Jewish world entered the Gentile world. Israel went to the nations. God's instrument of redemption met God's object of redemption. The church extended the church into foreign territory.

The vision in Joppa was a heavenly window through which Peter saw the need to redefine his priorities. The practical application of the vision was Peter eating with the Gentiles at Caesarea Philippi. Through the window of heaven Peter *saw* the heart of God. Through the door of

Cornelius' home, Peter *demonstrated* the heart of God.

Today, God continues to give the vision of penetrating every geographical area of the world. Flags of many nations are displayed prominently in numerous church buildings, and church bulletin boards are covered with worldwide mission opportunities. In addition, God has provided innumerable support ministries to help reach the "gentiles" in the world.

The church has dreamed with Peter on the rooftop. Now it is time for the twenty-first century church to take a walk with Peter to the home of Cornelius. Visions about the lost are no longer sufficient. The lost need the practical presence of the church so that the windows of opportunity become doors of possibility.

Evangelized and Unevangelized

In the twenty-first century, the church must preach the Gospel to the billions in lands yet to be evangelized while maintaining witness to the billions in countries that have already been evangelized.

The church has learned from painful experience that countries considered Christian are only one or two generations away from dead institutional religion or secular paganism. A revival strategy is ineffective if it wins people in new countries while ignoring those already won.

One geographical area is especially strategic for reaching the billions in the twenty-first century. The term "10/40 Window" was coined several years ago to describe this important geographical area. The 10/40 Window includes all of the countries and people that live between 10 and 40 degrees north of the equator in a band between West Africa and East Asia. Billions of unbelievers reside in this "window" of the world.

The 10/40 Window is the largest and most challenging mission field in the twenty-first century. Therefore, the church needs a strategy for reaching the 10/40 Window while maintaining a vibrant church base in the "post-Christian" West and strengthening the Christian base in South America and Africa. (I have taken the liberty of considering Australia and New Zealand in the cultural sphere of the West even though geographically they represent another important area of the world.)

THE 10/40 WINDOW

The 10/40 Window is the most densely populated area on the planet with four billion plus people out of the current six billion. At least half of these four billion live in two countries: China and India. In 1999 India reached a population of one billion and is projected to pass China in total population within the next 50 years.

Most of the billions in the 10/40 world live in large cities in developing countries that have no Christian roots or that are openly hostile to Christianity. The 61 countries in the area are mostly economically undeveloped and politically, culturally and spiritually anti-Christian.

The region is dominated by three world religions that aggressively oppose Christianity: Islam, Hinduism and Buddhism. In many countries Islamic law forbids a Christian to witness to a Moslem or for a Moslem to convert to Christianity. The penalty is severe punishment often including death. Hinduism controls witness and conversion through cultural and social pressure that sometimes breaks out in persecution and even death to Christians. Buddhism is the most passive of the world religions, but when mixed with political systems that are anti-Christian, it is just as resistant.

Look through the 10/40 Window and you will see massive cities. Some of the largest cities in the world are exploding in this area. In fact, all of the top 50 cities with a population of over one million that are not yet evangelized are in the 10/40 Window.

For more than a decade the 10/40 Window term has helped focus the attention of the twentieth century church on this part of the world. The emphasis on the 10/40 Window has helped the church to gather statistics, set goals, intercede in prayer, promote projects and preach through the mass media. However, as we enter the twenty-first century, awareness about this world is just the beginning. We must have a mechanism through which the church can establish itself within the walls of the countries with few Christians.

Christ is the mechanism that will reach the billions of people who have never heard the Gospel. He claimed this for Himself when He said, "I am the Door" (John 10:7,9), and "I am the Way."

Religions shut the door to witness. Governments close the door to the church. Cultures lock the door to evangelism. Satan slams the door to the Gospel. But "He who is holy, who is true, who has the key of David, opens and no one will shut, and shuts and no one opens" (Revelation 3:7). God can open and close every door.

The door to the nations must be opened from the outside. Jesus designed His church to storm the gates of hell. "I will build my church and the gates of hell will not prevail against it." His church will not only look in through the windows but will storm through the door of opportunity. Therefore, it is not enough just to be a different kind of church in the twenty-first century. The church must also have a different strategy for missions. We will reach the billions in the twenty-first century with first century mission methods, not those of the twentieth century.

THE TWO WORLDS

The yet to be evangelized world and the "evangelized" western world go together. The danger is that the western world will try to do something spiritual in the other part of the world without addressing its own spiritual needs. In truth, God desires to bring about the same revival in both the western world and the world that is not yet evangelized.

Therefore, in characterizing the unevangelized world we must be cautious in properly evaluating the western world. The description of one world can produce a distorted picture of the other. If one world is poor then the other is automatically wealthy. If one is under-privileged the other is privileged. If one is anti-Christian, then the other is pro-Christian. If one is undeveloped economically, then the other is developed economically. If one is uneducated, then the other is educated. Lost is lost whether a person is lost in paganism or in secularism, whether a person is in the jungles of Western New Guinea or the empty church buildings in Western Europe.

Christian philosophers for several generations have referred to the western world as a "cut flower" civilization. By this phrase they meant that the roots of the western world at one time were Christian and produced visible Christian flowers. The flowers still remain to some extent, but according to these philosophers the western world has been cut away from its Christian roots.

God may see far less spiritual difference between the citizens of the 10/40 World and those of the western world than we do. In fact,

Christians in some of the recently evangelized countries view the situation differently. They are now sending missionaries to the United States and Europe.

Both "worlds" are important to God and are inexorably tied together. Jesus' church is the answer for both. In one part of the world Christ and the church must be introduced and established. In the other part of the world the church must be redeemed and renewed.

God wants revival (missions, evangelism, church planting and holy living) worldwide.

Who Completes the Great Commission?

The Great Commission reveals the geographical responsibility of the church to go to Jerusalem, Judea, Samaria and the world. Since Jesus gave the Great Commission to the church He must have designed the church to fulfill that Commission.

Today, the church continues to use the Great Commission to define what it is to do. It is to "go and make disciples of all nations." However, the interpretation of who will complete the Great Commission has changed over the years. Many modern mission strategies reword the Great Commission to say: "the *church* is to go to Jerusalem, Judea and in some cases Samaria and *special ministries* are to complete the Great Commission for the church in the world."

A theological and historical case has been made that the Catholic Orders and the Protestant parachurches represent the mission arm of the church in the world. To make this case, the ministry of the church is separated into two areas: modality and sodality. The modality expression of the church is local, organized as a church and is called "church." The sodality expression of the church is focused on new works out in the world, is not organized as a church and is not called "church." These are special or "parachurch" ministries. In this view, these two structures are necessary to complete God's mission.[1]

I believe that Jesus did not intend to complete the Great Commission through two separate and independent structural expressions: local and mission. Jesus integrated the modality (local) and sodality (mission and ministry) expressions within the large group and small group design of the New Testament church. However, when the church ceases to use small group communities as the ministry and mission expression of the church, separate and independent sodality ministries are necessary to fill the ministry and mission vacuum.

Praise God that the Catholic Orders and the Protestant special ministries filled that vacuum. However, separate ministry expressions, no matter how successful, are God's plan B. In the twenty-first century, God's plan A must be the goal of both the church and special ministries.

The church is more than a local structure that prays for expansion, sends missionaries and supplies money for sodality structures and ministries to do missions. The church in the New Testament and in the twenty-first century is missions and is the redemptive instrument of God to every geographical point of the world. The Great Commission will never be fulfilled until reaching the world is the primary focus of the church and until the church is the primary instrument for reaching the world.

Peter went to Caesarea as a representative and extension of the church. Peter would never have thought of what he was doing as a ministry that was separate from the church. This is also true of Paul and the other apostles who began the expansion of the church. Paul had a missionary ministry team, but that team was directly tied to the church on both ends. Paul went out from a local church and reported back to the sending church, and Paul established local churches wherever he worked. Paul was not doing independent ministry. He was planting churches out from the church.

By necessity the traditional large group based church has depended upon special ministries to do the job of evangelism and expansion. However, a functioning New Testament church is not dependent upon outside ministries to fulfill the sodality ministry. It is designed to operate as God's modality local expression and as God's sodality mission expression. A healthy and functioning cell church doesn't need someone witnessing for it. It does not need someone training its leaders. Nor does it need someone nurturing its new believers. An operational cell church does not need someone ministering for it, nor someone else doing missions for it.

In this century every local church must once again be the pure and blameless bride of Christ that He chose, died for and loves. The local church must attend to all the desires of the Bridegroom. The church can not allow other brides, no matter how effective and beautiful, to take its place. Special ministries can be handmaidens to assist the bride in ministry to Christ, but must never be competing brides.

Instead, sodality ministries must be connected to the church; must have the primary goal of establishing the church and in some cases must become the church in order to fulfill the Great Commission.

THE DOOR OF MISSIONS SWINGS BOTH WAYS

During the 2000 year history of the church, the power center of the church and the direction of missions have shifted several times. Paul's Macedonian call (Acts 16) began the process that moved the Gospel from the East to the West and moved the power center of the church from Jerusalem to Rome. Europe and England were eventually penetrated with the Gospel in this first westward expansion.

The direction of expansion turned back toward the East at the close of the first millennium. Unfortunately, the expansion of the church during the Crusades was driven by political and military considerations that resulted in terrible deeds done in the name of the church.

During the events following the Reformation, the church in Europe followed the westward expansion of civilization into the Americas. After reaching its most westward point of expansion, the church turned its attention to China, India, Brazil and some areas of Africa. However, many other countries such as Australia and New Zealand also participated in the expansion of the church during the nineteenth and twentieth centuries.

The twentieth century church operated from a few political and economic power centers. In the twenty-first century, these mission centers are being replaced with a broad network of power centers. This change is happening because of a more balanced geo-political situation, the integrated worldwide economy, a common language (English), the computer information age and easy travel. Strong church power bases can now develop in many different countries across the world. Even the poorest nations can participate in global evangelization.

Therefore, church expansion in the twenty-first century will change directions. No longer will it flow in one primary direction. Church expansion will move in many different directions: from east to west and west to east, and from north to south and south to north. Some of the traditional church power bases will be evangelized by less economically developed nations. The vibrancy of the church will be a more important factor in missions than the social and economic condition of a country.

A Song of China

Ben Wong of Shepherd Community church in Hong Kong often makes this prophetic statement about China: "The story of China in the twenty-first century will not be outside Christians trying to get in to witness to millions of Chinese but millions of Chinese Christians breaking out of China to evangelize the world."

A group of Chinese Christians sang several songs in Chinese during the Cell Church Mission Network Conference in Colorado Springs, Colorado in May of 2000. An older Christian woman in a house church in inland China woke up one morning with a song on her heart. It has become a mission cry for many of the house churches in that part of China. The title is "The China for Missions" and the last stanza is especially touching and prophetic:

> I go forth with the mission to awaken the sleeping China.
> Even though in shedding blood, I will never turn back.
> I go forth with the vision to see a China for Missions;
> To preach the Gospel to every corner of the world.

The message of this song suggests that God is preparing Christians in formerly unresponsive countries for a special place in twenty-first century revival. The people and countries that have been the recipients of a worldwide missions and prayer strategy will now become a primary force in the implementation of that strategy.

3
THE COMMUNITY OF REVIVAL

*Christianity means community through
Jesus Christ and in Jesus Christ.
—Dietrich Bonhoeffer*

The New Testament cell is the basic community context for worldwide revival in the twenty-first century.

Revival in the twentieth century focused on large group experiences with mass meetings, crusades and large crowds. In the twenty-first century, revival will return to the Pentecost pattern of a local church and small group experiences that breaks out in mass meetings and large crowds.

A church that will impact the twenty-first century world must have a small group unit that is simple, self contained and easily reproduced. The unit must generate fierce loyalty to its lifestyle and must be sustainable during both persecution and prosperity. This basic unit must be able to pass on values, mobilize all members for ministry and produce necessary leaders. It must have the nurturing atmosphere of a family and the commitment and accountability of a squad of soldiers. It must be able to live out holiness and reach out to the world in harvest.

The basic unit of the church is the small group. It was the basic unit in the first century and it must be in the twenty-first century. Christian Schwarz extensively researched what makes the church grow. Of the eight principles of growth he discovered, one is the most important: "If we were to identify any one principle as the most important, then without a doubt it would be the multiplication of small groups."[1]

The practical benefit of groups has become obvious over the past several decades. Small groups can survive extreme political, cultural and social opposition. For example, thousands of groups have multiplied in China during the past 50 years while the number of Christians in China has increased from one million to an estimated 50 million.

CHRIST IS THE "DNA" OF THE CELL

New discoveries about the human cell are a testimony to the creative power and wisdom of God. The cell is God's "universe within." The order and design of the most basic units in life declare the glory of God.

The Human Genome Project is currently charting the entire human gene system. The project has learned that 800 books, each as long as the Bible, would be required to contain all of the information in the gene system of one person. However, nature has a bias toward making things simple and the human gene system has relatively few working parts. These few simple parts fit together in combinations that result in incredibly complex life.

A cell can be a tiny microbe one two-hundred-and-fifty-thousandth of an inch in diameter or it can be the yolk of an ostrich egg which is the size of an orange. An organization of cells can be as diverse as a buttercup, a mayfly, a 125-ton blue whale or a 1000 year-old redwood tree. And yet, for all this diversity, all cells are built according to a fundamental design that provides them with common features necessary for life.

Every cell has an outer wall that makes it a self-contained "room." Within the surrounding membrane is a semi-fluid material in which the life activities of the cell are carried on. At the heart of the cell is the nucleus, a control center that bears within it the cell's hereditary material, ensuring the survival of its line.

The nucleus of a cell contains DNA, which provides the formula for all life and orders the precise functioning of every living thing on earth. The DNA is the blueprint of the cell and conveys the information that tells life how to grow. It is a biological computer that holds the mapping system for life.

RNA is the material that carries the messages of the DNA beyond the nucleus in order to activate and collect new materials that eventually become part of the cell multiplication process.

In a 1998 conference in Londrina, Brazil, Robert Lay, director of TOUCH Brazil, was teaching about the DNA and RNA of the cell. An elderly lady approached him and said, "I understand the teaching about the DNA and RNA of the cell. The DNA stands for the <u>D</u>ivine <u>N</u>ature of the <u>A</u>lmighty. The RNA stands for <u>R</u>elationships <u>N</u>urtured through <u>A</u>mour (love)." This Christian grandmother understood the connection between a biological cell and a spiritual cell. A spiritual cell is about divine relationships of love that operate around the divine nature of God Himself.

The DNA of a cell is Christ in the midst. The RNA represents the individual members of the cell that grow in holiness through the elements of community, equipping, accountability and leadership then multiply the cell by reaching out in evangelism.

A Spiritual Cell Compared to a Biological Cell

The cell is God's way of organizing, sustaining, protecting and reproducing life. Therefore, we should not be surprised that God used this cell principle when He created His spiritual Body. Christ's Body, the church, consists of cells.

Jesus is the nucleus of the church at its most basic unit. Christ in the midst is the DNA of the cell: the genetic code that tells the cell how to grow and what to be. Without Christ at the center, the cells cannot function, and the Body cannot exist as His Body.

The DNA (Christ) instructs the cell in activities that build up the cell and also through the members (RNA) begins new "sites." Edification takes place within the cell for "the building up of the body."

The cell lives to reproduce. One primary requirement for any hereditary material is that it be able to multiply. Information must be passed along from generation to generation. New materials are brought into the cell so that it will have the ingredients to become two cells. Evangelism is the natural process of growth within the spiritual cell. At the right time the cell "unzips" and the stairway of gifts multiplies and becomes two identical cells, each with the nucleus of Christ.

What is the result of this kind of spiritual cell? When Christ is the life source of the cell, the ministry tasks of the church can be fulfilled in the cell. Jesus keeps His promise to abide with His followers in His church and to empower it. He begins to direct the cell as the Head, to gift it with spiritual gifts and to fill it with His power. Genuine edification, fellowship and evangelism take place. It is His presence that activates leadership, music, gifts, materials, Bible study, fellowship and warm relationships. Jesus Himself is the one essential factor in the life of His community on earth.

FIVE BASIC ELEMENTS OF CELL LIFE

Scientists use five letters for the five basic elements that are used to build the genetic code of a person. These basic elements are arranged in different combinations and sequences and account for the complexity of life on earth.

The spiritual cell also has five important elements that make up the life of the cell. The hand helps us understand the uniqueness of the working elements in a cell: equipping, accountability, leadership and evangelism all work in relationship to community. These elements flow out of the heart of God and are extensions through the cell of who God is.

This hand illustration is simple enough for a child to understand but profound enough to contain the very life of the omnipresent Christ in community. Christ is in the midst of the cell. As such, the fullness of the Trinity is there — the Father, the Son and the Spirit.

THE THUMB REPRESENTS COMMUNITY

The hand is a marvelously designed instrument. The arrangement of the four fingers with the thumb makes the human hand special. Each finger operates in relationship to the thumb. All the fingers work independently but also interdependently with the thumb.

Just as all of the fingers operate in relationship to the thumb, every element in the cell operates in relationship to community. Christians must be in community with each other before the other elements can be lived out. Equipping (discipleship), accountability, leadership and evangelism fit together as a whole when activated in community. However, none of the elements will unite the others. For instance, a focus on equipping often neglects evangelism. The element of accountability may become legalistic and restrictive while focusing in upon itself. Integrating the work of the church around leaders often focuses on the particular gifts of the leader and neglects the other important elements. Evangelism as the integrating element often neglects the other four.

But New Testament cell community integrates all of the elements and allows them to operate in the proper way at the proper time.

"Abiding in Christ" (John 15 and 1 John 1) best sums up the New Testament meaning of community. In His discourses in the Gospel of John, Jesus explains His relationship with His followers. He abides with and in them and they abide in Him. Abiding in Christ and Christ abiding in a group of Christians is the place of community worship, prayer and the Word.

The thumb represents the cell meeting that is the most basic unit of the life of Christ. But the thumb also represents the spiritual aspect of cell life that unites the life of all the members into the life of Christ. Together, in the most basic unit of the Body of Christ, Christians live out the practical implications of the great doctrines of the church.

THE LITTLE FINGER REPRESENTS EQUIPPING

The little finger represents the equipping of babies: the new believers and the "little ones."

The power-centers of the hand are found near the thumb and the little finger. These power centers work in tandem and allow the hand to grip objects tightly. The strength of the church comes from the spiritual babies nurtured to maturity (represented by the little finger side) and productivity in community (represented by the thumb side).

The inability of the church to care for new believers is one of the great tragedies of the twentieth century. Large numbers of new Christians have been birthed over the last decades but have been neglected and lost to meaningful ministry within the traditional church system.

The world knows the best way to care for a baby is in a family context. After the fall of the "iron curtain" it was discovered that some Eastern European countries attempted to care for large numbers of children institutionally. Pictures and accounts of children who were emotionally and physically damaged shocked the world. No matter how good the institutional care, it falls far short of the care of children within a family. Warehousing God's spiritual children produces equally horrifying results.

Christ provided for the care of His spiritual babies in spiritual families. Churches that lack a small group family structure must try to care for the spiritual babies in a more sterile institutional setting. New Christians are placed in a warehouse environment in the Sunday structure. We should not be surprised that the church has been less than effective with this approach.

New believers in a cell church are cared for in a small group family setting. The cell leaders are spiritual parents to new believers. The other members of the cell are the older brothers and sisters who help guide the steps of the new babies. The activities for the little finger are the equipping track for new believers and special encounter events through which they are nurtured.

THE RING FINGER IS ACCOUNTABILITY

On August 3, 1963 Mary Harrison and I exchanged rings as a symbol of our commitment to each other. We pledged to be responsible for each other, to be accountable for each other, to support each other and to love each other. Within cell life the same commitment associated with New Testament marriage is lived out in the spiritual realm.

In cell life the ring finger represents accountability. The New Testament concept of accountability is taught in the "one another" passages. "And be kind to one another, tender-hearted, forgiving each other" (Ephesians 4:32). "And be subject to one another in the fear of Christ" (Ephesians 5:21). "Bearing with one another, and forgiving each other . . ." (Colossians 3:13).

When understood correctly, this is one of the most precious elements of cell life. However, accountability today may be the most misunderstood and feared element in church life. I have found that Christians in all countries and cultures react negatively to the word "accountability." One must look long and hard to find any practical application of the concept in the twentieth century church.

One of the names Jesus uses for the promised Spirit explains the meaning of accountability. The Spirit is the Advocate: "the one Who comes alongside" (John 14:16). This is a beautiful picture of the work of the Spirit and the spirit of accountability. The Holy Spirit comes alongside of and cares for the Christian.

How did the disciples know what Jesus was talking about when He said the Holy Spirit would "come alongside" of them? In their relationship with Jesus the disciples had experienced spiritual accountability in its intended meaning. He had walked with them, encouraged them, supported them and had been their advocate and friend. Jesus promised that the Holy Spirit would continue this relationship.

This work of the Spirit is multiplied in a cell as the Spirit enlists each member to share in His work of "coming alongside" every other cell member. The Holy Spirit through me "comes alongside" you and supports and encourages you. Then, the Holy Spirit through you "comes alongside" me and supports and encourages me. This beautiful ministry destroys the harsh pictures many have when they think of accountability.

Activities associated with the second finger in a cell church begin with a mature Christian mentor for each new believer. Members in a cell who are not mentoring a new believer will partner in support pairs, men with men and women with women. This finger also represents the accountability relationships among leaders who support each other in mentoring relationships.

Accountability between leaders moves back and forth between submission and authority. Each leader submits to another leader and in turn cares for and serves a different leader. Consequently, leadership moves back and forth between overseeing as a servant and submitting as a servant.

THE LARGE FINGER STANDS FOR LEADERSHIP

The middle finger is significant because it is the most prominent finger, representing the strong and mature people who are fathers and mothers. God as Father is one of the most basic truths of leadership. The heart of God is to father and to parent. This is why Christ calls and prepares leaders. His leaders are to care for the spiritual babies and to lead His flock.

God's trinitarian nature best explains the concept of cell leadership. Christians experience the fatherhood of God, the brotherhood of Christ and the parenting of the Holy Spirit. Parents have great control over children. However, in the morning a father may be seen on his knees before a squirming two-year old helping put socks and shoes on. Jesus built His church around leaders who would be able to be responsible for other members. Leadership grows out of the heart of God as Father. In 1 John, the writer separates this mentoring process into fathers, young men and children. Fathers (and mothers) are mature Christians. Young men (and women) are growing Christians. Children are new believers. Fathers mentor the young men and the young men mentor the children.

Jesus demonstrated the warm, loving relationship of the Father in His relationship to His followers and to the children in the crowds. Mature members in a cell live out the love and life of Father God. God the Father parents His spiritual children in the spiritual family of the cell.

Fatherhood implies reproduction. The object of the cell is to reproduce itself. This reproduction must first take place at the point of leadership. Only then can the cell reproduce numerically. Every cell has a leader and is developing at least one other to be a leader. In addition to leadership in the cell, this finger also represents training for cell leader interns, the coordinating meetings for leaders and the Jethro structure through which the cell church coordinates the work of the ministry through its leaders.

THE FIRST FINGER REPRESENTS EVANGELISM

The index finger is good for pointing, directing and picking things up. This finger represents evangelism because the cell exists to point out toward the lost, to direct the cell members toward the lost and to "pick up" those who are separated from God.

Jesus came "to seek and to save the lost." It is Christ's eternal purpose to draw all men unto Himself. Because He is the center of the cell, this desire is fulfilled through the cell. Jesus promised, "If I am lifted up, I will draw all men unto myself." Evangelism begins when Christ is lifted up in the cell. Christ then draws the lost to Himself.

A cell relates to its spiritual society much like a nuclear family. At the smallest level we see the immediate family. Then comes the "extended" family of other Christians in other cell families. For those living in cell life another type of family will be the "adopted" family. Ben Wong explains this "adopted" family concept. He has no trouble with large cells; in fact, he wants his cells to be large. For Ben a cell might have only ten Christians but really has 100 members. Ninety people are lost and just don't yet know they are part of the cell. The cell includes them in the family of God and believes and prays for their salvation.

Evangelism in a cell church is varied, creative and comprehensive. Through cells a cell church throws out different evangelism nets. Relationship evangelism is the basic form of evangelism in a cell church. In order to enlarge the *oikos* (extended contacts) of a cell, a cell church will evangelize through special groups that target unbelievers who are outside the relationship sphere of cell members. Cell churches also plan harvest events from time to time so that the cells can come together and bring their cell and group contacts to a special event.

THE HAND TEST

Can you remember the five essential cell systems? Look at your hand and name them. Begin with the thumb, then the small finger, the ring finger, the large finger and finally the pointer. This is a simple picture of how Christ, through the Spirit, expresses His life through the most basic unit of His Body . . . the cell.

The heart of Christ is to abide with His followers and for His followers to abide in Him. Therefore the cell lives out the very life of

Christ as He abides in the cell and as the cell abides in Him (thumb). The heart of Christ is to care for the babies. Therefore, through the cell Christ cares for the new believers (small finger). The nature of Christ is to come alongside and to care for His followers. He does this in the cell as more mature members care for new believers and as the other members support each other (ring finger). God reveals Himself as a Father who loves and leads. Leaders are assigned to every cell and leaders are identified and raised up because this is the very heart of God (large finger). God so loved the world that He died in order to draw all men to Himself. This is Who He is. The cell is an extension of the love and ministry of Christ to reach out to the lost and hurting (index finger).

Now with your hand you carry a picture of the cell wherever you go. Every time you look at your hand you can remember the dynamic life and ministry of Christ through your cell.

The Cell is the Basic Context for Revival

Revival in the first century was expressed in and supported by cell community. The first thing the Holy Spirit did when revival broke out of the upper room and spread into the temple compound was to contain the revival in the homes (Acts 2:42, 46). The Pentecost revival was nurtured, explained and passed on within a small group context.

Cell community is the context for revival because of the relationship the cell has with Christ. Christ is present in the cell, His power flows through the cell and His purpose is fulfilled in the cell. Revival is a result of the life of Christ expressed in a practical way. No lasting revival is possible without New Testament cell community. Revival is lived out in community, birthed by caring for new believers, maintained in accountability relationships, protected by servant leaders and fueled by community evangelism.

4
THE MATHEMATICS OF REVIVAL

†

*The epidemic ends not for lack of susceptibles
but for the lack of infectives.
—John Hayward*

Personal and group evangelism is the witness context for worldwide revival in the twenty-first century.

During a conference in Wales, a man offered me a paper called *The Mathematics of Revival*. My schedule was heavy and I was busy with other projects so I referred him to Lawrence Singlehurst, the director of YWAM for England, who was teaching a session on evangelism.

Lawrence accepted the paper and discovered that it was an intriguing study of revival. John Hayward, a professor of mathematics at the University of Glamorgan in Wales, wrote the paper. His field of study calculates the factors and chances of epidemics. As a committed Christian he compared the factors necessary for revival with factors used to predict the spread of a disease.

Professor Hayward concluded that epidemics (and revivals) end "not for lack of susceptibles but for the lack of infectives."[1]

This means that epidemics end when those infected with the disease are reduced in number or in intensity of contagion. The infected persons (believers) determine the intensity and length of an epidemic or revival, not those yet to be infected (unbelievers). Revival ends not because of the lack of unbelievers who will respond (susceptibles) but because of the lack of believers (infectives) who are infected with a strong enough dose of the Gospel to witness.

LIFE AND DEATH QUESTIONS

Several important questions must be asked and answered in determining the seriousness of an epidemic.

1. How serious is the disease? This addresses the ultimate consequence of the disease. Is it the inconvenience of a common cold or the consequence of a life threatening disease such as AIDS or cancer?
2. How contagious is the disease? This is about the transmission of the disease. How easy is it to catch? Is it passed on by a sneeze or sharing body fluid?
3. How long will the person be infected? The duration of the infection determines how many others will be infected. Will the infection period hang on for a long time and thus increase the number of people infected?
4. How infected is the person with the disease? Does the individual have a mild case? Does the person have a virulent dose of the disease?
5. How many people come into contact with the disease? This is about exposure. How many people are in danger of being exposed to the disease?

Experts have reduced these questions to factors and then to a mathematical formula. These factors for predicting an epidemic were used in 1998 to estimate the danger of a strain of flu that was breaking out in Hong Kong. It was called the "fowl flu" because birds such as ducks and chickens were carriers of the disease.

After applying the epidemic factors to Hong Kong, the authorities became alarmed. The disease was very serious. People died from it. The disease was very contagious. It could be caught through the air like a common cold. The persons with the disease were very infected, with full-blown cases of the disease. The infectious period of the flu was long enough to provide multiple exposures. And Hong Kong is the most densely populated place on the face of the earth. Without even trying, the carriers would come into contact with hundreds of people in a day who would in turn contact hundreds of others. This is the classic meaning of an epidemic.

Consequently, upon the recommendation of epidemiologists the authorities killed every chicken and duck in Hong Kong at great financial loss. Their swift action probably prevented an epidemic of major proportions.

EPIDEMICS AND EVANGELISM

Let us apply these factors of an epidemic to revival at the point of the problem (sin) and at the point of the cure (the Gospel).

The consequence of sin is very serious because people die and go to hell because of it. Sin is very contagious because it is both an inherited congenital disease (I am a sinner) and a learned acquired condition (I do certain sins). Sin also infects a person totally. It is like pregnancy. There is no such thing as being partially pregnant. You either are pregnant or you are not. Man is completely and hopelessly infected with sin. That is a total reality. Finally, people influence each other to sin through hundreds of human contacts that are part of the normal course of life.

Now lets apply these epidemic factors to the spiritual cure. The Gospel is a very costly antidote for the disease of sin. God Himself died on a cross in order to provide this antidote. The Gospel can also be very contagious because it spreads by contact and word of mouth. The Gospel spreads more quickly when the Christian (the carrier) has a good dose of the Gospel. It is helpful if the Gospel infection lasts all of the life of the Christian. The speed with which the Gospel spreads is directly related to how many contacts the carriers of the Gospel have with other people.

Only God can do anything about the deadly and contagious nature of sin. However, God uses the church to affect several factors for revival. The church can make sure that a Christian has a good dose of the Gospel (holiness) that results in a passion to witness for a long period of time. And the church can also have a system through which Christians multiply contacts with lost people (harvest).

Revival: A Work from Without or Within?

The conclusions of Professor Hayward address the long-standing question about revival. Is revival a result of external or internal forces? Does revival fall down from heaven or explode out from the church?

In one sense revival is a total work of God. God anoints people, places and the church with His Spirit and revival is the result. The danger in the outside theory of revival is that the church will sit back and wait for revival to happen through external circumstances. Revival is seen as something that comes upon a place and time because of an outside and independent work of God. This partial truth leads the church to wait for that special moment in history and special place on earth when God miraculously produces revival. Most of the time, a sitting and waiting church will be unprepared when revival finally falls.

Professor Hayward concludes that the condition of Christians in the church is more important to revival than the condition of the lost in the world. Outside forces don't guarantee or stop revival. God initiates revival through the church. And revival is stopped when the members of the church no longer pass along the infection. If the members of a church continue to be passionate in holy living and faithful in harvest witness then revival will be maintained.

The first church witnessed God's power fall and great masses responded. Some conclude from Pentecost that when the power of God falls upon the lost, great harvest will result and the church will be built. However, we must remember that the power of God first fell upon the church. Then the power touched the lost through the proclamation of the Word and the demonstration of the presence and power of God in the followers of Christ (the church). "The Lord added daily to the *church* those who were being saved."

Revival Formula

This epidemic analogy suggests the following "formula" for revival. This "formula" is obviously not mathematical or scientific and could be written in several different ways. It is my attempt to put the major elements of revival together in a form that can be remembered.

Formula for Revival

Prayer X Enthusiasm X Contacts + Assimilation X Cells = REVIVAL

Prayer multiplied by the intensity and duration of enthusiasm, multiplied by the number of contacts, added to assimilation and multiplied by the number of cells equals revival. This "formula" implies that for the church to participate in revival it must magnify God through prayer, mobilize its followers for passionate and lifelong witness, multiply the number of personal contacts, maximize the assimilation process and operate in community cells.

PRAYER AND REVIVAL

Prayer is the first element in the revival formula. Prayer prepares the church for revival and sets revival in motion. Prayer taps into the presence, power and purpose of God. Therefore, prayer is the initial element in revival.

Formula for Revival

PRAYER X Enthusiasm X Contacts + Assimilation X Cells = REVIVAL

The catalyst for revival is found within God and His people. "If my people, who are called by my name, will humble themselves and pray and seek my face and turn from their wicked ways, then will I hear from heaven and will forgive their sin and will heal their land" (2 Chronicles 7:14 NIV).

The New Testament church spent more time praying for the church than for the lost. Jesus saw fields that were already "white unto harvest." He told the disciples to pray for "laborers." Jesus knew that laborers would pray for the church and witness to the lost out in the "fields." Obeying Jesus' command, the New Testament church directed its praying for revival more toward the church than toward the pagan world and the lost in it.

God produced the harvest at Pentecost through the church when it was all in one place praying. Jesus prepared the church and then

Pentecost revival fell upon the lost. From Pentecost we learn that the church as designed by Christ participates in preparing the climate for revival, the act of revival and the fruit of revival.

Prayer is not just an evangelism activity. Prayer *is* evangelism for both a Christian who offers a prayer and for the unbeliever for whom the prayer is offered. Praying opens a spiritual door in the heart of unbelievers and is the first step of evangelism. Prayer is also a work of evangelism in the life of the Christian who prays. Prayer is the first step of evangelism in the life of a Christian and the church.

THE INTENSITY AND DURATION OF ENTHUSIASM IS IMPORTANT

According to John Hayward the intensity and duration of enthusiasm is one of the most important factors in maintaining revival response. He maintains, "If enthusiasm is not limited in duration, religious belief spreads along the line of classic social diffusion and eventually covers the entire population. It is the limitation of enthusiasm that prevents the whole susceptible population being ultimately converted."[2]

Formula for Revival

> Prayer X **ENTHUSIASM** X Contacts + Assimilation X Cells = REVIVAL

If a church wishes to begin and maintain revival, members must have a passion to witness for the duration of their life.

The enthusiasm of those trying to begin revival is much more important than the number of people trying to begin revival. "Growth is more sensitive to changes in effectiveness than it is to the initial number of infected believers."[3] One of the most important factors in revival is increasing the quality of witness of the individual believer. "The benefits from doubling the effectiveness of an individual believer is to more than double the growth rate of the church."[4]

Revival ends because of waning enthusiasm for the Gospel.

> Another significant result is that the revival is ending due to dynamical effects dependent on its initial intensity, and the fact

that a believer's enthusiastic phase is limited. It is not ending due to any change in spiritual conditions such as the revival work being hindered in some way. Given that infected people are only effective for a fixed period then, with a given number of susceptibles, only a certain number of conversions become possible before the number of susceptibles an infected person is likely to meet in that time period is too small to keep the revival going. Of course the believer may still be involved in conversions after their infectious period ceases, but this is at a much lower level and does not give "revival-type growth."[5]

Professor Hayward suggests that at present the best the church can hope for is that a Christian is infected with a good dose of the gospel for the first two years after conversion. This two-year duration of passion and enthusiasm to witness will not result in infectious "revival-type growth" that we need in the twenty-first century. This means that keeping the fire of enthusiasm burning in every Christian is vital for revival.

REVIVAL IS RELATED TO THE NUMBER OF CONTACTS

In his study Professor Hayward concludes: "The growth in the church is proportional to the contacts between an active believer and non-believers, just as the spread of an infectious disease is proportional to the number of contacts between infectives and susceptibles."[6]

Formula for Revival

> Prayer X Enthusiasm X **CONTACTS** + Assimilation X Cells = REVIVAL

The more contacts, the greater the chance for response and revival. The number and quality of contacts determines the number and quality of conversions. Contacts can happen in several venues: one on one, small group or large group. These contacts can be made in homes, at work, during leisure or at a church building. The secret to revival is to multiply as many quality contacts as possible between believers and unbelievers.

Groups are an excellent way to multiply the number and quality of contacts. Through sub-groups the church can increase the number of contacts that passionate Christians have with the lost. These contact groups, bridge groups, interest groups, share groups and target groups have been one of the most successful tools for evangelism over the past several decades. Churches of all kinds have reached lost people through such groups.

Bill Hybels built Willow Creek Community Church in Chicago by mobilizing his members to reach seekers who were willing to become part of a group. Lyman Coleman has developed scores of booklets that assist Christians in contacting and building relationships with friends and neighbors. The International Charismatic Mission in Bogota, Colombia has been very successful in mobilizing its members to contact the lost with evangelism groups. Alpha is an eleven-week group experience that was developed in England; it is a non-threatening investigative Bible study built around personal relationships and group experiences.

Ralph Neighbour began his journey into cell church life by using share groups and interest groups. West Memorial Baptist Church in Houston reached hundreds of people in a brief period of time by mobilizing its members to contact their lost friends and neighbors through these kinds of groups. He has continued to challenge the church to use these types of contact groups.

These groups are not cells but sub-groups. They are groups for increasing the contacts between Christians and unbelievers. The method can be applied and adapted to every culture and people group. Through an outreach group, a Christian infected with the Gospel can infect numerous lost people over a period of several weeks. This in turn exposes an exponentially growing number of unbelievers to the Gospel while increasing the possibility of them "catching" Christ's message.

Assimilation Must Be Added

The fourth key to revival is the ability of your church system to assimilate the new believers so that they in turn will be infected with a passion for the Gospel that will last all of their lives. Revival is never possible until these new believers are assimilated into the church. This assimilation process cares for the new believers and prepares them for holy living and passionate witness.

We will consider this important element of revival in more detail in Chapter 14, *Strategy Key: Assimilation*.

Cells are the Place of Passion and Contact

The cell is designed to maintain the passion for holiness and to multiply contacts for harvest. Within community, believers are continually exposed to the presence and power of Christ that results in believers participating in the purpose of Christ to reconcile the world to Himself.

Cell groups are a witnessing training ground. They provide a place to nurture the passion, to share the gospel and a place to plan for contact with unbelievers. Within cell life every Christian catches a good dose of the Gospel which means the Christian will grow in holiness. As a natural result, the believers will be more effective in witnessing.

Formula for Revival

> Prayer X Enthusiasm X Contacts + Assimilation X **CELLS** = REVIVAL

The concluding question of every cell meeting should be, "How does God want to use me to touch the hurts and needs in the world?" This kind of intense commitment to seek and save the lost is caught from Christ and from the group.

A personal equipping track promotes evangelism by helping a new Christian grow in maturity. Life-changing encounters rearrange the actions and attitudes of new believers and prepare them to witness. More mature Christians grow in cell life and continue to have a passion for evangelism.

The cell church design provides a way to plan for maximum exposure of the Gospel to the maximum number of people with the maximum amount of commitment and the maximum length of duration for the passion to witness.

Your Church and Revival

What are the mathematical chances that your church will participate in New Testament type revival? Your chances for growth and revival are directly related to the five key elements in the revival formula.

Formula for Revival

Prayer X Enthusiasm X Contacts + Assimilation X Cells = REVIVAL

First, revival depends on the commitment of your church to pray for revival. Second, revival depends upon the intensity and duration of enthusiasm that your members have for sharing the Gospel. Third, revival depends upon the number of contacts your members have with unbelievers. The more contacts, the more chance for growth and revival. The fourth key to revival is the ability of your church system to assimilate the new believers into the life of Christ and the church. And finally, revival in your church depends upon a basic unit of church life that can be the context for revival: the cell.

5
THE KINGDOM OF REVIVAL

✝

The early church . . . saw itself as . . . an "eschatological community."
—John Bright

God's kingdom is the spiritual context for worldwide revival in the twenty-first century.

An often-told story has a philosopher lecturing on the solar system. An old lady in the audience dismisses the philosopher's scientific theory and confidently declares that "the earth rests upon a large turtle." "And what does this turtle stand on?" the philosopher needles. The old lady replies, "A far larger turtle." As the scholar persists, the old lady retorts, "You are very clever but it is no use, young man. It's turtles all the way down."

The old lady was correct about one thing. If our paradigm is correct, then it is correct "all the way down." However, if our paradigm is flawed, then it is flawed all the way down as well.

During the past 2000 years, the church has tried many different paradigms: economic, political, cultural, social, educational and religious. However, the purpose of the church is not to expand economic prosperity, to introduce a better culture or to teach morality. The purpose of the church is to be the earthly expression of the Kingdom of God. When the church lives out the Kingdom, then economic hope will result, cultures will change and religions will be replaced as a by-product of redeemed lives. That is a Kingdom definition of revival.

In order to reach the twenty-first century world, God's people must live in and establish His Kingdom. God's revival work in the world is His Kingdom "all the way down."

THE KINGDOM IN THE NEW TESTAMENT

Jesus established God's Kingdom during His earthly ministry. His message was about the Kingdom. He operated in the power of the Kingdom. The followers of Jesus became citizens of that Kingdom.

In his book, *The Work and Words of Jesus*, Archibald M. Hunter gives the following six characteristics of Jesus' teaching about the Kingdom.[1]

1. The Kingdom of God "is essentially God's Kingdom and not ours."
2. The Kingdom of God "is something which God gives, not something which men build."
3. The Kingdom of God "is not a Utopia or new social order."
4. The Kingdom of God "is not a mere disposition within men's hearts."
5. The Kingdom of God "is an act of God himself."
6. The Kingdom of God "is His initiative in breaking the power of evil."

God's Kingdom is present and future, earthly and heavenly, physical and spiritual. The trick is for the church to balance these two expressions of the Kingdom and to teach them in their proper proportion. The promise of participation in the future Kingdom is one of the most cherished doctrines of the church. However, in this chapter I want to focus attention on the earthly expression of the heavenly Kingdom.

Out of 27 primary references to the Kingdom of God in the New Testament, 18 imply a kingdom that is already present. For example: "For I say to you that many prophets and kings wished to see the things which you see, and did not see them, and to hear the things which you hear, and did not hear them" (Luke 10:24).

Paul clearly saw the power of the Kingdom of God operating in the here and now. "For the kingdom of God does not consist in words, but in power" (1 Corinthians 4:20). Paul declared the Kingdom truth that God has already "transferred us to the Kingdom of His beloved Son" (Colossians. 1:13).

THE ROLE OF THE CHURCH IN GOD'S KINGDOM PLAN

Alfred Loisy, a radical Catholic theologian who was excommunicated in 1908, observed that "Jesus foretold the kingdom, and it was the church that came."[2] While it is possible to elevate the church over the Kingdom, it is also possible to lose the importance of the church in the midst of Kingdom theology and prophecy.

God's church is not just a footnote or parenthesis in God's Kingdom history. The church is more than God's "plan B" for redemption. The church is the fulfillment of God's Kingdom on earth and the instrument for ushering in the final Kingdom. God is writing His kingdom history in and through His church.

John Bright argues that the early church "understood itself as the successor of Israel, true Remnant and people of the New Covenant."[3] He taught that the early church saw itself as the people of the Messiah living in the last days, an "eschatological community."

The Bible sees the church in a cosmic perspective. Howard Snyder declares that the church is "the earthly agent of the cosmic reconciliation that God wills. God is bringing about his cosmic purpose through the instrumentality of the church." Snyder adds, "The kingdom of God is coming, and to the extent this coming takes place in space-time history before the return of Christ, it is to be accomplished through the people of God."[4] Living out the Kingdom in space-time history is one definition of revival.

THE KINGDOM IN THE FIRST CENTURY CHURCH

Most of the uses of the word "Kingdom" in the New Testament are in the Gospels. In fact, it is somewhat of a shock to realize how few times the word is actually used in the book of Acts and the remaining books of the New Testament. If the Kingdom was the primary message of Jesus why was the word not used as often by His followers?

The concept of the Kingdom is used by the disciples of Jesus even if the word itself is not. The followers of Christ saw the church as the expression of the Kingdom of God in history. Therefore, the concept of the Kingdom is equated with the ministry of the church. Christians are "citizens" of what must be a kingdom (Ephesians 2:19 and Philippians 3:20).

Believers are part of God's "household" (Ephesians 2) which implies a family Kingdom. Throughout the book of Ephesians words are used for the church that are associated with the Kingdom. The church is the Body of God, the wisdom of God, the power of God, the glory of God and the Bride of Christ.

God's Kingdom on earth cannot be separated from the church. The very glory and greatness of the heavenly Kingdom gives glory and greatness to God's earthly Kingdom, which is lived out within the context of the church. Of course, the earthly expression of the Kingdom is only a shadow of the heavenly expression. However, the future glory of the Kingdom does give a degree of glory to the present Kingdom. Therefore, the Kingdom in its present expression through the church must be taken seriously in light of the importance and the glory of the Kingdom in its future expression.

Even in all of its weakness, the church in the present age is still the earthly expression of God's eternal Kingdom. This places the church at the very epicenter of God's Kingdom history that He continues to write in the twenty-first century.

The church has often made the mistake of connecting the heavenly Kingdom and the earthly church at the point of authority. The New Testament church connected the heavenly Kingdom and the earthly church at the point of mission and life. Revival happens when the church leaves more of the authority in Heaven with God and applies more of the Kingdom life on earth.

Revival will come in the twenty-first century as the Kingdom of God is lived out through the church. In Colossians 3:12-17, Paul pictures this practical Kingdom lifestyle that Jesus taught about in the Sermon on the Mount. The admonition is to "God's chosen people, holy and dearly loved." These titles can certainly apply to Kingdom people and the words that follow suggest practical living that is associated with the heavenly Kingdom. "Clothe yourselves with compassion, kindness, humility, gentleness and patience. Bear with each other and forgive as the Lord forgave you. And over all these virtues put on love which binds them all together in perfect unity.

"Let the peace of Christ rule in your hearts, since as members of one body you were called to peace. And be thankful. Let the word of Christ dwell in you richly as you teach and admonish one another with all wisdom, and as you sing psalms, hymns and spiritual songs with gratitude in your hearts to God. And whatever you do, whether in word or deed, do all in the name of the Lord Jesus, giving thanks to God the Father through him" (Colossians 3:12-17; NIV).

The Kingdom is God's Historical Tide

Peter Wagner describes a series of "waves" that have rolled across the church in this century. The First Wave Wagner identifies as the rise of Pentecostalism, which sprang up in the early 1900's and emphasized the baptism of the Holy Spirit and speaking in tongues. The Second Wave developed in the 1960's and 1970's as the growth of the charismatic renewal movement among Protestant mainliners and Catholics. They adopted spiritual healing and other Pentecostal practices in their churches.

Wagner identifies the more recent Third Wave as the supernatural manifestations that appeal to a significant number of fundamentalists and conservative evangelicals. Previously, these Christians tended to deny modern-day faith healing and doubted "prophetic gifts" on theological grounds.

Wagner has correctly identified important factors in the history of the church during the last half of the twentieth century. However, I believe these factors originate from another more basic force at work. There is something greater than the historical "waves" that seem to periodically flow over the church. Trends, new programs, different methodology and materials have driven the history and ministry of the church. Political waves, social ministry waves, Sunday School waves, doctrinal waves, busing waves, edifice waves, reformation waves, denominational waves, second coming waves, TV waves, prayer waves and "refreshing" waves roll upon the shores of church history.

Many of these "waves" are heralded as a Kingdom force that will prevail and remain. These waves, however, beat upon the shores of history for a brief moment and then ebb away. Some are more powerful than others, but they still have their day and their time. The danger is that we will mistake the historical "waves" for the Kingdom tide that causes them. These "waves" are not true revival and will not sustain revival. New Testament revival flows out of a Kingdom "tide" that is more basic and powerful.

THE KINGDOM TIDE

The New Testament church was a Kingdom church with a Kingdom design that originated out of the nature of God. The practical expression of the Kingdom through the church grows out of the experience of the church with God in His transcendence and immanence. God's nature is the center of gravity that flows like a tide through God's Kingdom on earth and in heaven.

This tide was set into motion by Christ in the first century. He designed His church to express His nature in a counter-balance between the large congregation and the small community. God's Kingdom is expressed on earth as it flows between these two. Just as the force of gravity pulls the sea back and forth between shorelines in its ebb and flow, God moves His church within the counter-balance of the large community (ebb) and small community (flow). This is how He expresses Himself, where He meets His people and how He expands His Kingdom. This is the root and source of revival!

Revival is the church living out God's transcendent and immanent nature in practical everyday community both in the church and in the world.

This ebb and flow moved across the Old Testament. The transcendence and immanence of God was the source of that tide. God, the "most high" and the "most nigh" resided eternally above man and abided personally in the midst of man. God declared Himself on top of the sacred mountain with smoke, thunder and lightening. God revealed Himself in His "shekinah" glory in the midst of the "Tent of Meeting" and the Holy of Holies within the Tabernacle.

The birth of Jesus was a result of this tide of transcendence flowing into the tide of immanence The incarnation tide left the transcendent shores of heaven and ended at the shores of the Mediterranean as a young Jewish girl gave birth to Immanence, the Son. For 33 years the transcendent and immanent tide built up force in the life of Jesus until it shattered death at the tomb.

The transcendent and immanent nature of the Triune God met at the point of 120 disciples in an upper room in the city of Jerusalem on the fiftieth day after the resurrection of the Transcendent-Immanent Jesus. The wind, fire and sounds signaled the presence of God on earth in a new way. Jesus had prepared His community to be the dwelling place of the

Triune God. "In whom (Christ Jesus Himself) you also are being built together into a dwelling of God in the Spirit" (Ephesians 2:22).

This is what Jesus had been talking about all along. This is what He meant when He promised they would do "greater things." His final words "I am with you forever" were spoken in light of this incarnation fact. "Where two or three are gathered together in my name, there I am in their midst" describes the powerful community context in which this movement flows.

No wonder the tide came with such force and power. What else can we expect when the nature of God as the eternal God and the nature of God as the incarnate God meet at the very point of His people? That place is the epicenter of the presence, power and purpose of the living God. Transcendence meets immanence. The great God comes near.

GOD'S TIDE MOVES TODAY

Christ designed His church to move with His Kingdom tide in every generation, not just in the first. Unfortunately Satan deceived the fourth century church into forsaking the design that Jesus had so carefully built. The small community aspect of the church was ignored. Operating with only the large group dimension of the church is like the tide operating with only the ebb and not the flow. The power is lost. The counterbalance is neutralized.

Today God is restoring the flow of His church by recreating the small group to once again work in tandem with the large-group meeting. The result is the release of a spiritual force more powerful than the tide that moves in the ocean.

How can the addition of the small group element make so much difference? The reason is that it releases the power of the Spirit to operate between the two poles of the nature of God. Transcendence and immanence arc at the point of Christ and His church.

Waves have come and gone and repeated themselves again and again, but the tide remains the same. It is the same tide set into motion in the first century that swept cultures and nations before it. It is the force designed by God to be the "power in the church." Even the gates of hell will not prevail against this tide.

Revival happens when God's transcendent and immanent nature flows out from His church into the world. That spiritual tide purifies, waters and sweeps before it all that stands against His Kingdom.

PART 2
REVIVAL ROOTS

In Scripture the earthly and heavenly sides of the Church fit together in one whole and do not leave us with two incompatible Churches or with a split-level view of the Church.
—Howard Snyder

6

JESUS' MODEL

†

*The Gospels are the only textbook the
Christians after Pentecost had on the Church.*
—Robert Coleman

Returning to Jesus' church model in the Gospels is a biblical root for worldwide revival in the twenty-first century.

A spiritual sonogram of the church during the last days of Jesus' ministry would reveal a small but perfectly formed church body. All of the essential organs, appendages and functions of the church were operating as it approached Pentecost. At Pentecost the church reached viability outside of the womb when the Spirit breathed into it and the new church responded with its first cry of life and witness.

Jesus' ministry is the conception and gestation period for the church that was birthed at Calvary, empowered at Pentecost 50 days later and reproduced in church plants in countries around the world by first century converts. Without Jesus' three and a half years of church formation and preparation, Pentecost has no context, the church has no roots and the sheep have no shepherds.

The connection between the Gospels and Acts is evident in the thinking of Luke, whose two-volume work on the origins of Christianity constitutes approximately one quarter of the New Testament. Luke ties his Gospel of the life of Christ and his history of the church together with a connecting summary in the first verses of his second volume (Acts 1:1-11).

"The contrasting parallel [Luke] draws between his two volumes was not between Christ and his church, but between two stages of the ministry of the same Christ."[1]

THEOLOGICAL AND INSTITUTIONAL LEVELS OF THE CHURCH

The embryonic elements of the church that we see in the book of Acts (leadership qualifications, rituals and creeds) formed around the life and nature of the church that Jesus established in the Gospels. These elements are the "wineskins" of the church.

These institutional wineskins have continued to develop over the course of church history into programs, boards, committees, buildings, denominations and independent ministries. Some institutional elements have remained true to the original life and nature of the church. Others have not. Therefore, the modern institutional elements of the church must always be judged against the original life and nature of the church as seen in Christ.

The danger is that the historical additions of the church will be stacked one upon the other until the life and nature of the church is so cluttered with institutional forms that the original life and nature is hidden.

Kevin Giles explains the wine and wineskin elements of the church in his excellent book, *What on Earth is the Church?* He describes the development of the church in two levels: the theological level and the sociological level. The theological level of the development of the church is the original idea, life and dynamic of the church that Jesus established. The sociological level is the institutional elements of the church that began to develop in Acts and that continued in the course of church history. He suggests that "the continuity to be seen lies at the theological level, not the sociological."[2] The life of the church must be maintained by returning to the theological level that is seen in the life of Christ in the Gospels.

John Wesley saw his movement in the eighteenth century as a return to New Testament life (the theological level) established by Jesus. Michael Henderson observes that Wesley "did not view church history as the progressive unfolding of God's plan, but rather as deviations from the correct model of Christianity followed by occasional returns to it."[3]

Does Jesus Know Any Thing about the Church?

When I went to Thailand as a missionary in 1975 I overlooked the importance of the Gospels for understanding the church. During the first half of my 15 years as a church planter, I focused on learning how Paul did church. I suppose my neglect of the church in the Gospels is understandable, if not excusable.

I followed the accepted approach. Study the Gospels in order to understand the life of Christ and then go to Acts and the Epistles in order to understand the church. Focusing primarily on the church in the Epistles produces an incomplete view of Jesus' ministry and of the church. It implies that the church at Pentecost emerged full-blown and independent of what happened in Jesus' life. This approach suggests that Jesus was waiting around during His years of ministry until the authorities get mad enough to kill Him. Then the church could begin to operate.

About half way through my time in Thailand the question came to me: can I learn anything about the church by studying how Jesus began the first church? Jesus said, "I will build my church." Did Jesus' church starting strategy influence how His followers, including Paul, started churches?

These questions drove me to study the church in the Gospels. To my surprise, I discovered a rich resource of church principles and methods. Out of that study I concluded that all of the churches in the New Testament, including Paul's, were directly linked to the church seen in the Gospels. Jesus' ministry is the key to understanding the church at Pentecost, the church during its early formative history and the church in the twenty-first century.

Stages of the Church in the New Testament

Expansion of the church in the New Testament is best understood as a process of several stages that flow out of the Gospels into the book of Acts and the Epistles. These stages overlap and build upon each other.

Stage 1: Jesus established the DNA of the first church. Through His public and private ministry Jesus modeled the design and nature of the church.

Stage 2: The Holy Spirit was the mid-wife at the birth of the church at Pentecost and formed the new believers into basic home units.

Stage 3: After Pentecost the first wave of new believers returned home. The Pentecost converts began Jesus' kind of church in their own cultures.

Stage 4: Early church leaders went to areas surrounding Jerusalem. Philip, Peter, John and undoubtedly others seeded the church in cities in Judea and Samaria.

Stage 5: Persecution resulted in expansion of the church in "all the world." The church leaders (except those apostles who remained in Jerusalem) extended the church.

Stage 6: Churches such as Antioch sent out church planters. Barnabas, Paul and Mark established churches that were linked to Jesus through Antioch back to Jerusalem.

Stage 7: Churches spread into Europe. On the prompting of the Spirit, Paul and his disciples extended the church into the "West."

Stage 8: Regional churches, such as Ephesus, became centers of area church expansion.

The church at each of these stages carried the imprint of Jesus' church in both its essential nature and basic design. Let us consider the development of Jesus' church in this birthing process in five situations: Jesus' own ministry, the work of the Spirit at Pentecost, the lives of the Pentecost converts, Jesus' core leaders and the ministry of Paul.

JESUS MODELED THE CHURCH

Jesus' three and a half years of ministry were well known to the early Christians as well as the first century world. In a court appearance Paul later said, None of this happened in a corner (Acts 26:26). The authorities evidently knew the basic facts about who Jesus was and what had happened to Him. The New Testament Christians certainly knew the details of how Jesus lived out the church with His disciples.

However, it is not surprising that twentieth century Christians who define the church in terms of geography and buildings overlook the church in the Gospels. Jesus never stayed in one place long enough to model church in our geographical paradigm. Jesus' church moved across Galilee, Judea and Samaria with Him. Therefore, it is difficult to fit Jesus' kind of church into our geographical box. He modeled the first church, but not in a building or in one city. The church in the Gospels is a mobile experience centered around Christ as He modeled His church on the road.

Seventeen hundred years of experiencing church in large groups in buildings has blinded the traditional church to the small group community life found in the New Testament. Furthermore, we don't have a detailed explanation in the New Testament of the large group structure we have used for centuries. It is a huge jump from Peter's sermon at Pentecost to what happens on Sunday morning in most churches today.

But it is fair to ask the question, "Why don't we have a systematically organized small group explanation in the New Testament?" The New Testament writers and first century Christians were all living in the context of small groups and so did not explain their natural habitat in detail. The habitat of the New Testament church was small-group theology, culture and structure. Every day of Jesus' ministry was in one way or another lived out in small group community. Small groups were the center of gravity for the first century church; the air they breathed, the atmosphere in which they lived, the organizing principle of their lives.

Back and forth between the cities of Galilee, Judea and Samaria over a period of more than three years, Jesus lived out the community nature of the church. When we cut through our geographical paradigm, we can see Jesus forming the church around Himself in the Gospels and then establishing the church around the Spirit at Pentecost. As Jesus moved toward Jerusalem that last time, His church was not yet fully birthed (that would happen at Calvary), empowered (that would happen at Pentecost) or planted (that would happen during the next phase). But the characteristics of the church were set in Jesus' DNA and would be passed on in both a universal and local expression.

The Spirit Continued to Establish Jesus' Kind of Church

Through the Holy Spirit, the enthroned Christ led the first Christians into the same kind of church life He had shown them as the incarnate Christ. "Thus Jesus' ministry on earth, exercised personally and publicly, was followed by his ministry from heaven, exercised through his Holy Spirit by His apostles."[4] Jesus promised that "the Spirit will teach you all things." Does the Spirit know anything about how Jesus formed His church? Certainly the promised Spirit continued the same kind of church and church planting as Christ the Son. "Christ institutes the church, the Spirit constitutes it."[5]

The work of the Spirit at Pentecost took place through six important events that accompanied the birth of the church: prayer, power, preaching, harvest, community and expansion. Countless sermons and books devoted to the initial events of Pentecost typically cover the first four experiences of Pentecostal prayer, Pentecostal power, Pentecostal preaching and Pentecostal harvest.

But is this all of Pentecost? What about the period of time (Pentecostal community and Pentecostal expansion) that immediately followed these initial stages?

Pentecost Miracles

1. PRAYER
2. POWER
3. PREACHING
4. HARVEST
5. COMMUNITY
6. EXPANSION

PENTECOST

The danger is that churches will either deny the power of Pentecost or neglect the community design of Pentecost. Without the power of Pentecost all church structures are ineffective. Without the community design of Pentecost, its power is ineffective. "If you put new wine into old wineskins, both are ruined." Either way, the church can miss important aspects of the Pentecost experience essential for living out the New Testament church. All six of these experiences were Pentecost miracles in the first century, and all six are necessary for the church in the twenty-first century. Community in the homes was the Pentecost miracle most often neglected in the twentieth century.

THE PENTECOST CONVERTS TRANSPLANTED JESUS' CHURCH

An academic analogy helps us to understand Pentecost. The school was God's "church," the subject matter for this school was Jesus and the head teacher was the Holy Spirit. "One might perhaps say that the Holy Spirit opened a school in Jerusalem that day; its teachers were the apostles whom Jesus had appointed; and there were 3000 pupils in the kindergarten."[6] After graduation the Pentecost converts returned home and started the first new churches.

How did this first wave of new converts begin these churches? Did every believer create their own theology of the church and new patterns of church design?

Every principle of logic suggests that the Pentecost converts began the same kind of church in their own cities that they had experienced during those exciting weeks/months in Jerusalem. Their only example of the doctrine and design of the church was Jesus' model. Therefore the new converts returned home after Pentecost and implemented the principles, experiences and basic design of church they learned during their Pentecost training.

One can only marvel at the incredible results seen in the Pentecost church. Jesus rooted His church in the soil of His ministry, fertilized it with His blood at Calvary, germinated it in the ground for three days and rejoiced as the church blossomed into full flower at Pentecost. Then the Holy Spirit sowed the Pentecost converts like seeds into the fertile soil of the Mediterranean world.

The church Jesus planted had the genetic make up to take root in new places and to grow through ordinary Christians. Who did the planting was not as important as what was being planted. Our problem today in church expansion may not be the quality of the church planter as much as the DNA of the church we are beginning. The traditional church design does not easily take root in other places. For this reason we need to return to the original Gospel model of the church and rediscover the principles that Jesus built into His church.

The experience of the New Testament Christians confirms that church expansion is not dependent on professionals. This does not discount the work of "professional" church planters; It merely suggests that Jesus designed the church with a simplicity that can take root in new places by non-professionals as well as professionals. Benjamin Franklin's observation also applies to the followers of Jesus: "One man of reasonable ability may work great change."

JESUS' CORE LEADERS CONTINUED HIS KIND OF CHURCH

Luke records in Acts that Peter, John and Philip began new churches soon after Pentecost. However, the organizational structure and methodology they used is not clearly explained. What kind of church did they begin?

The earliest church planters had only two common church sources: first, what they saw Jesus doing during His ministry when the church formed around Him and second, what they saw happen in Jerusalem when the church re-formed at Pentecost around the Holy Spirit. Jesus' core leaders planted the same kind of church they experienced with Him before Pentecost and with the Holy Spirit during and after Pentecost.

Still the question remains: Why aren't more details given about the nature of the church immediately after Pentecost? Chapters 9 - 12 in Acts reveal more about certain individuals and groups (Samaritans and Gentiles) than about the structure and life of the church.

The answer: When Luke wrote the early chapters of Acts, he did not consider it necessary to explain in detail what was already carefully recorded in his earlier book (Luke) or in the accounts of Matthew and Mark. The Gospels clearly show that Jesus lived in community. The context for His teaching, His works, His miracles, His training and eventually His preparation for death was the community of twelve. Jesus' small group/large group wineskin was the environment for the life in both the Gospels and Acts.

Several phrases are used to explain what is happening in these early accounts. After Pentecost, those who left Jerusalem were "preaching the word" (Acts 8:4). Philip went down to Samaria and was "proclaiming Christ to them" (Acts 8:5). After checking up on the revival in Samaria, Peter and John returned to Jerusalem and along the way "preached the Gospel" to villages in Samaria (Acts 8:25). When Paul believed he began to "proclaim Jesus" in the synagogues (Acts 9:20).

All of these early accounts use words about preaching the gospel, not planting the church. What do these phrases mean to them? Can the Gospel be preached without the church being planted?

First century Christians used the word "gospel" or "good news" in a more inclusive way than we now use it. To modern day Christians the "good news" is almost exclusively about personal salvation or biblical truth. To the first century Christians "good news" was also about a community. To use the phrase "preached Christ to them" was not only a reference to preaching salvation through Christ, but also preaching about living in a community with Christ.

It is dangerous to assume that the Gospel can be preached without the church being planted; to Jesus and the New Testament Christians preaching and planting went together. During His public and private ministry, Jesus proclaimed and taught the Gospel from a community perspective, and wherever Peter, John and Philip "preached," Jesus' kind of church sprang up.

PAUL PLANTED JESUS' KIND OF CHURCH

Paul did not begin his extraordinary missionary career in a church vacuum but was linked to the kind of church and church planting that preceded him. "St. Paul's missionary method was not peculiarly St. Paul's, he was not the only missionary who went about establishing churches in those early days."[7]

While Paul was persecuting the church and while he was being prepared in obscurity to serve the church, the church was being planted. In fact, the time between Paul's conversion and his first missionary journey was as long as seven to nine years. This much time is needed to account for Paul's experiences in Damascus, Jerusalem, Arabia, Tarsus and Antioch.

Paul's ministry provides strong supportive evidence that Jesus was the first and greatest church planter and that all other churches in the first century followed His pattern. Paul is linked to Jesus' type of church through his two primary mentors: Ananias and Barnabas. If Ananias, Paul's first mentor, was not at Pentecost, he must have come into contact either with Jesus Himself or with Christians who were at Pentecost. Therefore, Ananias only knew about the church modeled by Jesus and continued by the Spirit at Pentecost. Ananias nurtured Paul in Jesus' kind of community.

Barnabas, Paul's mentor in the ministry, was either a follower of Jesus himself, at Jerusalem during the events of Pentecost or in contact with the Jerusalem Christians soon after Pentecost. We know that he sold a piece of property in order to support the needs of the first Christians in Jerusalem. Barnabas understood Jesus' kind of church design because he was connected to it personally through his relatives, John Mark and his mother whose home was a center for Jesus in Jerusalem.

The churches Paul experienced at Damascus, Jerusalem, Tarsus and Antioch were all patterned after Jesus' first model in Jerusalem. Therefore, Paul's importance to the New Testament movement is not found in the nature and design of the church he planted but in the number of churches he planted and where he planted them. Also, Luke the historian accompanied Paul and recorded in detail the story of his church planting. With his church planting team, Paul planted scores of Jesus' kind of large-group/small-group churches throughout key cities of Asia and Europe.

LIVING OUT THE EVIDENCE

The evidence in the New Testament supports a link between Jesus' small-group approach to church in the Gospels and the church in the rest of the New Testament. Despite all of this supporting evidence, the small-group approach to the church has still found no permanent place in the theology and structure of the traditional twentieth century church. Many New Testament theologians see small groups in the New Testament but fail to give adequate attention to small-group *ecclesiology* in their theological books.

Pastors may see the practical benefits of the small group for church growth, but too often they do not operate groups out of a passionate theological conviction. For many pastors, groups in the church are just one more church-growth method.

Church members are caught in between. Their practical theology tells them that they need small-group life in order to experience New Testament fellowship, care, accountability and ministry. However, they fear that church leaders will expect them to maintain all of the old programs while adding on small-group life. Or they fear their pastor will get their hopes up one more time and then abandon the vision when the next attractive church-growth fad comes along. In spite of these concerns, God is restoring first century community in the church today and revival always follows the restoration of Jesus' New Testament wineskin.

7
CHRIST IN THE MIDST

✝

As a body without breath is a corpse,
so the church without the Spirit is dead.
—John Stott

Experiencing Christ in every cell is a biblical root for worldwide revival in the twenty-first century.

On a recent holiday in Israel, the omnipresence of God came alive to me. The insight began at the Wailing Wall in Jerusalem and climaxed in a nearby excavation that is called the Rabbi's Tunnel. The tunnel has been cut deep under a Muslim neighborhood of Jerusalem, exposing the whole length of the foundation of the western wall of the Temple for the first time since its destruction in A.D. 70.

On our way to the entrance to the Rabbi's Tunnel, my wife, Mary, and I passed by a mass of Orthodox Jews milling around the Wailing Wall. All were dressed alike in knee length black coats and wide brim hats with uncut beards and long side curls. Some covered themselves completely with their prayer shawls and mumbled portions of the Old Testament while swaying and jerking.

This was a scene of religious zeal, national pride, mass chaos and ancient ritual. The 3000 years of history contained in the tunnel we were about to enter had witnessed this same scene many times.

Esther and the Holy of Holies

Our group, consisting mainly of American Jews, had made appointments in advance with an authorized Israeli agency. We were permitted to follow Esther, our guide, through the almost concealed gate and a tight security system. Soldiers with loaded assault weapons guarded both ends of the tunnel against terrorist attacks.

Layer by layer our group passed through thousands of years of history in a little more than two hours. We saw the impressive ruins of the Ottoman Empire and the destruction and construction of the Crusaders. We observed the ruins of fourth century buildings that were present when Helena, Emperor Constantine's Mother, visited Jerusalem. We walked on a first century street that Jesus might have traveled.

Descending through the maze of tunnels and cisterns, we finally arrived at the foundation stones of the impressive wall built by King Herod. These huge stones, some weighing more than 90 tons, rest upon a foundation believed by our guide to have been laid by David for the original wall of his city.

Walking along the wall in single file we came to a small room and a door sealed up in the ancient wall. Esther, who had helped excavate the tunnel, informed us that we were standing as close as we could to the Holy of Holies. On the other side of that door was the very place on Mt. Moriah where Abraham had taken Isaac as a sacrifice 4000 years before. For as long as Abraham's descendents controlled Mt. Moriah, the High Priest came to this spot on one day of the year to make sacrifice for the sins of the people. Today the area on the other side is covered by the Dome of the Rock and controlled by Moslems.

We listened to Esther as she encouraged, even pled with evangelistic zeal for the Jews in our group, especially the children, to go to that sealed stone door to pray and to think about that place. She declared with the conviction of an Old Testament prophet, "It is not the building on top of the site that is important. That is a Moslem building. It is the site, the place where Abraham took Isaac bound that is important."

Christians and the Holy of Holies

However, another event that had taken place at this same spot occupied my mind. The heavy veil that surrounded the Holy of Holies was split from "top to bottom." That alone was an event of monumental religious and political significance. However, it is the timing of the exposure of the Holy of Holies that was of even greater significance. At that exact moment a man died on a cross between two thieves on a skull shaped hill outside the city wall. The sign over his head identified him as "Jesus of Nazareth, King of the Jews."

The rest of the group prayed to a Messiah yet to come, a sacrifice yet to be offered and a presence yet to be. The Christians in that tunnel prayed to Messiah revealed, crucified, buried, resurrected and present in our lives.

There in the bowels of Jerusalem the omnipresence of God came alive for me. Everyday of the week, every hour of the day and on any place on the planet Christians experience what before only one priest experienced, on only one day of the year and at only one special place. Through Jesus Christ, every Christian becomes the Temple of the Holy Spirit, the Holy of Holies, everyday of the year and in every place on earth.

THE PLAN

Fifty days after the "wall of partition" in the Holy of Holies was split from the top to the bottom, God poured Himself out upon 120 followers waiting in the second story of a nearby house. Eventually 8000 experienced the presence and power of Christ in the early weeks of the church.

Upon the shoulders of the 8000 new Christians at Pentecost rested the hope of beginning God's church among their families, cultures and nations. Indeed, the hope of the New Testament movement depended upon whether or not they could pass on the dynamic experience in Jerusalem.

The Pentecost converts were quickly prepared and returned home carrying the DNA of church with them. How can this be? Their teachers remained in Jerusalem so the new converts were completely on their own. Since they only had the Old Testament Scriptures how much could they possibly know about this new way of life? How could they be trusted with this new movement? Who guided the explanation of their experiences? How did they know what to say and do? What theological concepts could they teach?

Jesus himself provided the plan for church formation. Jesus preached and taught publicly to large numbers. Out of the multitudes He chose a select few to be with Him. Through these first core followers Jesus carefully set a predictable and transferable pattern for His community. He endured the cross and overcame sin and death. Then Jesus returned to the Father and "another one like Him" came, forming His followers into His spiritual Body on earth. They were indwelled, empowered and directed by the Spirit. "Thus before ending his personal ministry on earth, Jesus deliberately made provision for its continuance, still on earth (through the apostles) but from heaven (through the Holy Spirit)."[1]

That was the special secret: "Christ in you." Through the ministry of the Holy Spirit, Christ continued to be among them. The plan introduced the first converts to the Holy Spirit who would be their companion, teacher and advocate. They returned home with the indwelling presence, power and purpose of the One who met Abraham on Mt. Moriah. No wonder the plan worked!

OMNIPRESENCE IS "CHRIST IN THE MIDST"

"Christ in the midst" is the practical expression and application of the doctrine of the omnipresence of God, and God's plan for His church rests upon His omnipresent nature. Omnipresence means that God isn't limited by time or restricted by space. This does not mean that God is "in" everything as taught in Hinduism. However, as creator of time, space and all things God is present in time and space, as He desires.

God's plan was to prepare a people who could participate in His omnipresent nature as a normal way of life. The Spirit would live with each Christian personally and do the same things Jesus did with only a few. This is what Jesus meant when He said, "Greater things shall you do." "Greater things" are possible because of the multiplication of the presence of Christ through the Spirit. "They needed an experience of Christ so real that their lives would be filled with His Presence."[2]

When the first century Christians began to live out church in their own homes, Christ was alive among them and they learned to abide in Him constantly. God's omnipresence is personal and caring. It is not some kind of surrounding force or indwelling energy. This is omnipresence of Person. God is not in the world as a substance, a principle, or law. God is personal Spirit.

Christ created the cell as the basic unit of His spiritual body on earth. It is the building block for the expansion of His life in every generation and every country. Christ in the midst of every group in every part of the world is the way Christ lives in His church.

CHRIST SHOWS UP

In discussing the characteristics of community we must begin with Christ. His presence is the key to spiritual community. Unless we start with Christ we will end up with something other than Christ and New Testament community. Without Christ at the center of cell life, other tasks and activities will become primary, and Christ will be a secondary influence upon what happens in the group.

Christ is the center of every cell meeting, every leadership meeting and every celebration. I was delighted when I finally found the essential element in the life of the cell was Christ Himself!

While living in community in Germany under Hitler, Dietrich Bonhoeffer learned the relationship of community to Christ.

> Christianity means community through Jesus Christ and in Jesus Christ. No Christian community is more or less than this. Whether it be a brief, single encounter or the daily fellowship of years, Christian community is only this. We belong to one another only through and in Jesus Christ. What does this mean? It means, first, that a Christian needs others because of Jesus Christ. It means, secondly, that a Christian comes to others only through Jesus Christ. It means, third, that in Jesus Christ we have been chosen from eternity, accepted in time and united for eternity.[3]

My wife, Mary, compares small group community with what she experiences in her personal devotional time with the Lord each morning. She calls the cell meeting "a group devotional with the Lord."

OMNIPRESENCE IS THE WORK OF THE SPIRIT

Jesus taught about the promised Spirit with childlike anticipation. He could not wait until the Spirit came. Things would be so much better after He returned to the Father. Jesus had been restricted in the time/space continuum of the world because of His human incarnation. The Holy Spirit would be omnipresent in God's spiritual time matrix on earth. Jesus knew that through the omnipresent Spirit He would be able to be with every Christian, in every place at all times. "Jesus was God in revelation: but the Spirit was God in operation."[4] "God sent the Spirit at Pentecost as the outworking of Christ's completed work."[5]

The Spirit operates in omnipresence at the intersection of divine immanence and transcendence. Divine immanence is God's caring presence in space and time with His people. Divine transcendence means that time and space do not limit God. God is greater than all other created forces.

Omnipresence is the truth underneath Jesus' teaching in John 14. Christ is transcendent in heaven preparing a place for His Followers, but through the Spirit He is also immanent with them on earth. Because of God's omnipresent nature expressed through the Spirit, He can never be thought of as an absentee God. "I will not leave you as orphans. I will come to you."

The cell as the Body of Christ is the secret to the life of the New Testament church. The cell is the divine system through which Christ, through the Holy Spirit, delivers His life to His spiritual Body on earth. Then, through that Body He multiplies His life into the world.

Through the Holy Spirit the essential tasks of the church are integrated in Jesus' self-contained community system. Fellowship, edification, sanctification, nurturing, accountability, leadership training and evangelism are all integrated through cell groups in the homes. Consequently, each cell is an extension of the life and ministry of Christ Himself. Together, the cell components receive a divine synergism as Christ lives and ministers through cell life. Omnipresent God indwells, empowers and uses the cell to express His life between the time of His ascension and His second coming.

FAITH IS THE KEY TO EXPERIENCING CHRIST IN THE MIDST

The relationship of the disciples with Jesus during the 50 days between the resurrection and the ascension helps us understand our relationship with Him today. During this time, Jesus' followers were challenged to exercise new faith every time He revealed Himself to them.

When they saw the resurrected Jesus, the disciples often responded, "It's a Spirit." I can understand this reaction the first time they encountered the resurrected Christ. After all, they had seen Him killed on the cross and buried in a tomb. They knew He was really dead. But what about the third and fourth times the disciples encountered Christ? If they saw Jesus alive on one occasion, wasn't that sufficient proof to confirm His resurrection? But it seems the disciples were dumbfounded all over again every time Jesus manifested Himself to them. What is going on here?

Wasn't He physical? Yes, He was everything He had been physically and more. Evidently there was a spiritual quality that He manifested in resurrection in addition to the physical quality that He had acquired at the incarnation. The disciples could only see Christ from the eyes of faith. They could touch Him physically because He was flesh. But they had to exercise faith in order to experience Him spiritually.

This is why during the previous years He devoted so much time to teaching them about faith. He sought to instill in them the kind of faith that would be necessary to experience Him as the resurrected Christ and as the ascended Christ. He taught them about the Holy Spirit who would be with them after He returned to the Father. The disciples would not see or touch the Holy Spirit but He would be real and present.

In the upper room during one of His post-resurrection appearances Jesus said, "Because you have seen me, have you believed?" (John 20:29). Believe what? Just believe that Jesus had been resurrected? They were not dealing with the theological or scientific facts of resurrection at that point. They were trying to make sense out of the fact that Christ, who had been dead, was now standing among them.

Jesus was saying, "Blessed are those who have seen me physically present in their midst as the resurrected Christ and who believe." "But more blessed are those who have not seen and yet believe." Extended further, Jesus was saying, blessed are those who have not seen Me physically present in their midst, but who believe that the resurrected Christ is living and present.

The issue is the presence of the resurrected Christ rather than a doctrine about the resurrection of Christ. A doctrine of the resurrection brings understanding but an experience with the resurrected Christ brings life. This phenomenon is not so much about the physical and spiritual makeup of Jesus' resurrected body as it is about how we relate to Him after His resurrection. The issue is not the molecular makeup of the resurrected Christ but the spiritual makeup of the faith of Christians today who meet the resurrected Christ through the Holy Spirit.

I believe these post-resurrection appearances of Christ in the last pages of the Gospels are the closest to how we relate to Him today. While on earth, Jesus was physical just like us. After the resurrection, Jesus was physical but with a spiritual dimension that had not been evident before. Today, Jesus is no longer physically present but through the Spirit He is spiritually manifested to His followers. Faith is the lens through which we see the resurrected Christ.

Christians exercise this resurrection faith when gathered together in small groups. Through faith Christians of every age experience Christ in their midst. This corporate resurrection faith builds up the faith of the individual and the larger Body.

We Must Expect Him

God has formed thousands of groups over the past several decades. Unfortunately, these groups have for the most part been Bible study groups, task groups or care groups and have often lacked a sense of His presence, power and purpose. However, I believe He has been in these groups all along, and we just have not recognized Him in the same way as His followers in Acts and the Epistles.

Is it really possible to have Christ with us without experiencing His living presence in the way He promised?

Two disciples returning from the events of the crucifixion walked with Jesus for four miles to Emmaus without knowing He was the risen Christ (Luke 24:13f). He had promised that He would be with them after the cross but they did not recognize Him. Only when He broke bread at the evening meal and they saw the nail prints in His hands did they recognize Him. He had been with them all along, but they had not known it.

Cleopas and his companion could have walked those four miles from Jerusalem to Emmaus knowing it was the resurrected Christ. What a blessing that would have been! However, their faces were "downcast" and they did not look closely at Him. They did not expect to see Him. They talked about Him in the past tense. Later they remembered that their hearts "burned within them" as they walked with this stranger, talked about Jesus and listened to Him teach.

It is possible for a group to walk with Him, to receive His teachings and to talk about Him without recognizing Him. These groups vaguely experience Him as a "burning" in their hearts instead of knowing Him as the risen Christ. He is a strange presence who creates a sentimental feeling.

Talking about the details of Christ's life may be good, but it is inferior to experiencing Him. Instead of having conversations about Him, Christ wants us to look at Him, recognize Him and experience the reality of His presence.

We need to open our eyes in our groups so that we can recognize Him when we pray, when we experience His power and when He works through His spiritual gifts. In order to do this we must believe that He is alive in our midst. We must acknowledge His presence and welcome Him into our groups so that by faith we may experience Him at the center of our community. Experiencing Christ in the midst revives the cell and revival in the cells will revive the Body. Revival of the Body (local church) will result in New Testament revival in the world.

8
RESURRECTION POWER

✝

*The believers in miracles accept them (rightly or wrongly)
because they have evidence for them.
The disbelievers in miracles deny them (rightly or wrongly)
because they have a doctrine against them.*
—G. K. Chesterton

Operating in God's resurrection power is a biblical root for worldwide revival in the twenty-first century.

A Pope once said while looking at the grandeur of Rome, "No longer can it be said of the Church: 'silver and gold have I none.'" A nearby cardinal responded softly, "But neither can it be said, 'take up thy bed and walk.'"

A great move of God in the twenty-first century is unlikely if it must be driven out of the physical treasures or political power of the church.

The church today needs more power and less pomp. The multiplication of evil in personal and national behavior suggests that only a fresh release of God's spiritual power can break the cycle of evil. The sickness of twentieth century society flows through the bloodstream of the twenty-first century. Sophisticated intellectualism, impressive church buildings, powerful institutions, dramatic television programs and carefully formulated doctrines are powerless to heal the systemic evil.

Hope for healing and harvest in the twenty-first century increases when the power of God is available to confront cultures, religions and the power of the evil one. The church must access God's power in order to combat the world's evil and must live out God's holiness in order to give integrity to the power.

IS NEW TESTAMENT POWER STILL POSSIBLE TODAY?

As the catchy phrase of a once popular hamburger commercial asked, "Where's the beef?" so must the church confront itself with a similar question: "Where is this promised power?" Is resurrection power still possible today?

Intellectualism says, "NO!" Man cannot conceive any spiritual power that is outside his mind.

Science says, "NO!" Scientific laws rule the universe and will not accept the intrusion of spiritual power.

Humanism says, "NO!" Man is the center of the universe and spiritual power is not possible in man's world.

Secularism says, "NO!" Power is in the marketplace, in the inventions of man and in the things that man possesses.

Hedonism says, "NO!" Power lies in the experience of pleasure and self-gratification.

Religion says, "NO!" Man's task is to search to know God by man's own efforts and by knowledge.

The Bible says, "YES!" Jesus said, "All power is given to me in heaven and earth." "The gates of hell will not prevail against my church." "Greater works shall you do."

John Stott argues,

> As Campbell Morgan put it, "granted the truth of the first verse in the Bible, and there is no difficulty with the miracles." Moreover, since we believe that the miracles recorded in the Bible, and not least in the Acts, did happen, there is no *a priori* ground for asserting that they cannot recur today. We have no liberty to dictate to God what he is permitted to do and not to do. And if we have hesitations about some claims to 'signs and wonders' today, we must make sure that we have not confined both God and ourselves in the prison of Western, rationalistic unbelief.[1]

Personal Discoveries about God's Power

During the 1980's, I was determined to come to a biblical understanding of the work of God's power in the modern world. Over a period of several months, I once again studied the passages in the Bible related to God's power and gifts. This study revealed more about myself than about a new doctrine of His power and changed how I view God's power.

First, I discovered that I believed in the greatest miracles: creation, incarnation and resurrection. If these miracles were true, then why doubt God's power to perform lesser miracles?

Second, God had personally spoken into my life in such a powerful way that I could not deny His work in the twentieth century. I had two options about believing in God's continued work in the present age: either God continued to work and speak personally today, or I was crazy.

Third, it became clear to me that I was reacting to God's power instead of acting upon what I read from Scripture. I was more influenced by how others were interpreting God's power than by how it was presented in Scripture. I had allowed those I saw as my theological "enemies" to distort my theology of God's power.

Fourth, I had come to believe that knowledge was closer to faith than experience. In fact, I now know that the intellect can be just as much a hindrance to faith as the most superficial spiritual experience.

Fifth, I realized that I was enslaved to an academic worldview. I had confined both God and myself in the prison of western, rationalistic unbelief.

Sixth, I was embarrassed by the emotion that is often connected to God's power. I could show uninhibited passion during a sporting event, but Christianity had to be formal, restricted and controlled. This did not square up with the passion I saw in Scripture or the passion I felt in my personal relationship with Christ. I realized that I was not embarrassed by excessive spiritual deadness, I was embarrassed by excessive spiritual life!

Dragging Dead Horses

During this study of power and gifts, God gave me the picture of two men, one chasing a runway horse and another dragging a dead one. The conclusion I drew from the picture was this: "It is better to hold a live horse than to try to drag a dead one." This picture changed how I now relate to His power. Expressions of God's power can be as frightening and unpredictable as a runaway horse. However, holding a runaway horse is better than trying to drag a dead one.

God was saying to me that I must react positively to His power rather than reacting negatively to how others use or abuse God's power. Between extreme life and extreme death, I must choose extreme life. Christ can not abide in deadness. C. H. Spurgeon stated the danger of this passionless expression of Christianity when he said, "I would sooner risk the dangers of a tornado of religious excitement than see the air grow stagnant with a dead formality."

The church in the twenty-first century must rediscover a New Testament doctrine of God's power. Without such a doctrine of omnipotence, the church emerging out of the twentieth century will be ill prepared to face the challenges of the twenty-first century world. The church desperately needs a New Testament theology of expectancy in which Christians expect Christ to indwell, to empower and to use His church in the twenty-first century.

Reasons We Need God's Power

Reason 1: The church and the world desperately need the gifts and fruit of the Spirit. Spiritual gifts and spiritual fruit only work in relation to spiritual power. It is impossible to have one without the other. "[The church] will never again affect the world as it did in the first century until individual Christians begin to utilize the gifts God has given them in the power of a resurrected Lord."[2]

Reason 2: God's church cannot be effective apart from prayer, and prayer is not effective apart from God's power. Elton Truebood explains,

> Though they are usually handled separately, prayer and miracles are both better understood if they are handled together. Every prayer of petition is really a request for a miracle. When I pray

for the recovery of my sick child, I am asking God to bring to bear upon the concrete situation something more than what is provided by antibiotics, however valuable these may be and however grateful we may be for their invention. Prayer is, in its very essence, supernatural.[3]

It is difficult to participate in meaningful prayer if God's power is restricted to what happened in the pages of the Bible. Why pray if the power can only be expressed in some vague manipulation of medical science, in the releasing of natural healing processes, in positive thinking or in celebrating what He did in the past?

Reason 3: The church needs God's supernatural power in order to witness to the lost and change society. Francis Schaeffer argues, "If the church does not show forth the supernatural in our generation, what will? The Lord's work done in the Lord's way does not relate only to the message, it relates also to the method. There must be something the world cannot explain away by the world's methods, or by applied psychology."[4]

Reason 4: God's power is necessary for the church to participate in the ministry of Christ. Human ministry applied in human ability is no longer able to deal with the hurts and pains of society (if indeed it ever could). The church desperately needs God's power to complete Christ's mission statement: "heal the broken hearted, bind up the wounded and set the captives free." The power that the church needs is not just the power to impress but the power to show forth compassion, the power to enter into spiritual healing and the power to love, forgive and live together in unity.

Reason 5: The church needs the power of God to proclaim His personal nature. If God only intervened personally in the physical world of the Bible then our generation loses something of the personal nature of God. Again, Trueblood helps clarify, "If God is, as Christ affirmed, then it is wholly reasonable that He should design events which constitute special revelations of His personal activity, in the long fulfillment of His purpose. A miracle is not a mystery but a revelation. Miracles do not contravene the laws of nature, but reveal the Lawgiver."[5]

Reason 6: God's power is necessary to put the universe in proper perspective. "[Miracles] are an offense only to those who place things above persons, the mechanical order of nature above the moral order. The doctrines of Fatherhood and grace are far from complete without them. They vindicate the conception of the universe as a family, in which persons are bound together by love, over against the conception that the universe is merely a cosmos bound together by physical force."[6]

Reason 7: God's power is needed to break through modern religious humanism that invaded the church of the twentieth century. The church needs resurrection power to break into the sophisticated scientific mind of man that refuses to acknowledge the spiritual. "Such a naturalistic dogmatism is nothing but disguised atheism, for belief in a God who cannot affect events in the world is really worse than no belief at all."[7]

Reason 8: God's power brings the Scripture to life. God's power is essential in saving us from dead intellectualism. Without the expectancy of God's power we are left with a secondhand academic understanding of God. Scripture is intellectualized instead of being experienced and applied. A closed canon and closed physical world ultimately produces dead legalism.

To claim that the Word is living in a spiritual way but is no longer operative in a physical way is to deny full participation in the life of the resurrected Christ. God operates in our world in both spiritual and physical realms; He works in the realms with power, not just with knowledge.

Jesus was not just raised "spiritually," he was also raised physically. "Put your fingers into the nail prints. Thrust your hand into my side." Part of the twentieth century church worshipped and served a resurrected Christ whose power was relevant only to spiritual needs. Christ's resurrected power could spiritually save and spiritually intervene into daily life; it could heal spiritually and emotionally. However, they denied Christ's power to touch the physical.

Reason 9: The church in the twenty-first century must rediscover the New Testament way of living out the doctrine of God's presence, power and purpose in a balanced manner. In order to reach a healthy balance, God's power needs to be exercised by all streams of the church. The evangelical stream of the church must develop a doctrine for the gifts, miracles and God's power so that the Spirit can operate in the world today. The experiential stream of the church must insist upon the Reformation principle of scripture alone *(sola Scriptura)* not experiences as the guide for God's gifts, power and miracles.

GOD'S POWER FLOWS THROUGH THE CHURCH

The working of God's power is expressed best within the church as He designed it. The small-group context is therefore essential for living out New Testament resurrection power. Everything we see in the New Testament suggests that personal gifts of power will be exercised normally within a community group context. In a small group, prayer can focus on practical needs, gifts can operate naturally to edify the group, the spirit of Simon the Magician can be minimized and honest verification can be applied to the genuine works of God's power. The small-group dimension of the church is essential for the manifestation of God's promised power on earth.

9

TRANSFORMATION TRAINING

✝

*People are looking for a demonstration,
not an explanation.*
—Robert Coleman

Training through transformation encounters is a biblical root for worldwide revival in he twenty-first century.

On public television I recently saw the birth of a baby wildebeest. The wildebeest is a cow-sized African animal with small, curved horns, high shoulders and low narrow hindquarters. They eat grass, run in herds and are a favorite food of lions.

As soon as the newborn calf touched the ground it was struggling to stand. When it stood it began to nurse. Within minutes it was running around its mother. An hour later when the herd was startled and began to run, the calf was able to keep up.

The newborn babies of grazing wild animals on the plains of Africa must be able to stand, eat and survive within minutes of birth. Otherwise, they become lion food.

New believers must also be able to eat and become mobile very quickly if they are to survive the early moments of Christian life. The continuance of a movement is directly related to how well the movement can protect its new converts, provide them with survival skills and prepare them to live out the basic truths of the movement. Satan is a roaring lion constantly on the prowl to find and devour the weak.

In this chapter, I want to explore the special training approach of Jesus and the first century church. New Testament training depended heavily upon transformation encounters and life experiences through which new believers absorbed and internalized great theological truths. In the Jerusalem homes, the Pentecost converts were transformed from raw recruits into trained soldiers with spiritual survival skills. They went back home with the Holy Spirit as their teacher, with a new community as their context for life and with a reproducible transformation training system as their method for protecting and preparing converts.

GRADUALISM: FLAT-LINE EQUIPPING CONTRAST

The traditional church operates within a cognitive-based system that puts a premium on information. This information system uses a type of training I call "gradualism." New believers are taken through a drawn-out study of materials. Seven weeks of one study, then ten weeks of another study and then twelve more weeks of yet another study. If the new believer has the discipline and cognitive skills to survive all of this study, somewhere in the process he or she has probably disengaged from a large part of the information. Even some of the most well-known training systems that use this approach admit to a high drop-out rate for Christians in the early stages of discipleship.

The traditional church has used the same approach to train leaders. Years of theological education are required to pastor a traditional church. This is "flat-line learning." If this kind of learning could be monitored on a heart machine, the patient will show few signs of life. This is frog-in-the-warm-water training. Place a frog in a pot of warm water. Gradually increase the water to the boiling point, and the frog will die in the pot. The frog will remain in the pot because there is not enough change in temperature for the frog to register the increased heat and jump out.

Information-based training is often boring, academic and unrelated to life. It doesn't register enough change in intensity to cause significant reaction. Consequently, new believers become comatose in the warm, cognitive pot because their spiritual senses are never activated. Transformation training is just the opposite.

A Description of Transformation Training

Children who attend a Christian camp may learn as much about God in one week as in the other 51 weeks of the year in church. Why? The experience is focused, intensive, concentrated and comprehensive. Adults also respond positively to this kind of learning in retreats, revivals, crusades and encounters.

It is not uncommon for a Christian to come to faith through one or a series of events that bring them to a point of crisis and decision. Unfortunately, this transformation approach is seldom used within the traditional church itself to assimilate new believers or to train leaders.

Many cell churches schedule transformation encounters on the yearly calendar. These encounters are developed for maximum impact. Normally an encounter will last for twelve to 15 intensive hours in a retreat setting. The goal is to change attitudes and values more than to impart knowledge.

"Transformation training" is the experience and internalization of truth in a series of intensive life experiences. Transformation training gets attention, confronts with clear choices, provides spiritual power and changes lives while raising the level of commitment and dedication. This kind of New Testament training expands understanding, intensifies relationships, transforms lives and accelerates growth. It compresses discipleship into a time frame that results in optimum growth.

I am not using the word *experience* as an emotional or theoretical concept but as a learned skill that grows out of practical knowledge and is lived out through spiritual power. That is what the Pentecost converts returned home with. Once back home they could duplicate what they had learned. Knowledge would be difficult for them to pass on quickly, and emotional experiences alone would lack credibility. However, they could reproduce practical experiences like prayer or living together in community, skills they had learned.

Transformation training has the following benefits for the church:

1. Follows Jesus' pattern of intensive encounter training
2. Develops productive Christians, not consumers
3. Counteracts Satan's assault on the new believer
4. Incorporates all aspects of learning
5. Facilitates personal holiness and group edification
6. Accelerates the discipleship process

Follows Jesus' Pattern of Intensive Encounter Training

Jesus understood the importance of learning through life experiences. He moved His disciples from one encounter to another, giving whatever information was necessary but always applying that information in life transformation encounters. If normal events would not produce encounters, Jesus created them Himself. Let us consider several of these encounters in order to illustrate Jesus' philosophy of equipping.

The Sea of Galilee was the backdrop for much of Jesus' training. Jesus called the twelve (Matthew 4:19) in a dramatic encounter by the seaside; in full sight of their boats and nets, Jesus asked them to follow Him. Jesus' call did not happen as an intellectual exercise or academic teaching about the Kingdom and the Messiah. Jesus called the disciples in an encounter in which their old life was placed before them in contrast with His life. Do you love me "more than these" . . . these boats and nets, these friends and family.

The storm was an encounter of faith (Matthew 8:23). On a mountain slope overlooking the Sea of Galilee, Jesus taught about faith, but the disciples learned faith in a real storm. Faith may be defined on hillsides but is exercised on stormy seas. Faith may be described while sitting in the safety of a church pew, but it is experienced sitting in a tossing boat out in the storms in the world.

Jesus sent 70 of them out two-by-two into the world. They encountered the forces of Satan and saw demons "fall from the sky."

Jesus used the events leading up to His last days on earth to complete the training of His disciples. "Jesus set His face toward Jerusalem." Every step on the last journey brought the disciples face to face with the depth of their loyalty to Jesus as the Christ. At the vortex of danger in Jerusalem they internalized the lessons that Jesus had been trying to teach them for three years.

This last journey to Jerusalem had exposed the pettiness of position and pride that was boiling among them. When no disciple was willing to serve in the menial task of washing the dirty feet of the others, Jesus seized the opportunity to teach one of His most profound lessons. With an ordinary towel and basin, Jesus showed them the actions and attitudes of a real leader. His disciples were transformed by the powerful image of Christ on His knees washing their feet.

The resurrection encounters had a surreal quality to them. When Christ met them after the resurrection they acted confused, frightened and perplexed. "No man dared ask who he was?" "Are you the same?" "Are you a ghost?" "Are you touchable?" "How do you appear and disappear like that?" Every resurrection encounter was a transformation event that shook them to the roots of logic and drove them to the foundation of faith.

The Ascension was an encounter designed for maximum impact. Jesus could have quietly gone to be with the Father. However, He chose a dramatic parting to transform their hopes and expectations and to establish a pictorial and theological bridge between heaven and earth.

Finally, Jesus promised the disciples an encounter with the Holy Spirit and instructed them to wait in Jerusalem. Ten days later the dramatic Pentecost encounter with the Spirit transformed their lives.

See chapter 21 for a more detailed explanation of a planned encounter.

Develops Productive Christians, Not Consumers

In China, many ducks and geese are force-fed. A long funnel is inserted into the mouth of a duck or goose and pushed into the gullet. Then grain is poured directly into the funnel. These ducks and geese grow very large. But if you ever stop force feeding one of these ducks or geese, food can sit all around them but they will die from starvation.

The church has been force-feeding members for years. Cognitive facts are poured into the minds of Christians who sit and receive all of the teaching they can absorb. Unfortunately, these Christians seldom learn to feed themselves. They are dependent upon professional teachers who must always "give a fish." The New Testament approach was to teach a man to fish by introducing every new believer to the Holy Spirit.

The Pentecost converts had human teachers in the homes of Jerusalem. But, they were not force-fed Christians. The Pentecost converts were introduced to a teacher who would return home with them and reproduce the same kind of transformation training through them.

COUNTERACTS SATAN'S ASSAULT ON THE NEW BELIEVER

A Texas farmer once bragged about his very obedient mule. His friends gathered one day for a demonstration. Just before he gave a command to the "obedient" mule, the farmer stepped in front of the mule, looked it in the eyes and hit it between the ears with a large pole. Then he gave a command and the mule obeyed. He repeated this several times. Finally, one of his friends raised the logical question: "We are very impressed with the obedience of your mule. But why do you hit him between the ears just before you give a command?" "Well," the farmer explained, "he is a very obedient mule, but you must first get his attention."

For most of us, learning only begins after someone gets our attention. Teachers and parents depend upon attention-getting phrases, "Let me have your attention." "Pay attention." "Look at me."

Someone is going to get the attention of the new believer. It will be either the church or the "unholy trinity" of the world, the flesh and the Devil. New believers often come to Christ out of some kind of transformation experience. God gets their attention with a crisis or some other life-changing event. Then the traditional way of training kicks in and the new believer moves into flat-line learning.

A mule doesn't respond to begging, pleading, singing or calm teaching. It has to be confronted with the expectation and reality of its life. The "old man" within a new believer is like that mule. Calm and lengthy reasoning does not often change the old nature.

Be assured that the Devil will get the attention of new believers. He will not approach deserters from his ranks with a drawn-out reeducation program. When unable to keep a lost soul from being saved, the Devil will try to keep the new believer from being of any use in God's Kingdom. He will hit the new believer between the ears with every weapon in his arsenal . . . past hurts, guilt, habits, attitudes and strongholds.

What is our natural instinct when hit from the back? We turn in the direction from which a blow is struck. When assaulted by the past the new believer automatically turns toward it and begins to live in it once again. This means the new believer is turned in the wrong direction and cannot possibly walk forward into a new life in Christ. It is impossible to walk in the light while turned toward the darkness. Mature Christians must provide new believers with spiritual encounters that will keep the new believer facing in the right direction . . . toward God.

INCORPORATES ALL ASPECTS OF LEARNING

One axiom of education has remained constant over the years: learning is processed through cognitive, affective and psychomotor experiences. Mankind learns from information, influences and experiences. Christians learn in one additional way: from revelation. Learning takes place through the head, the heart, the hand and the Spirit.

Christian Learning Grid

		I	II	III	IV
	FUNCTION	**COGNITIVE**	**AFFECTIVE**	**PSYCHOMOTOR**	**SPIRITUAL**
1	**ANATOMY**	Head	Heart	Hand	Spirit
2	**PROCESS**	Information	Relationship	Application	Revelation
3	**METHOD**	Teaching	Situations	On-the-Job	God
4	**MEANS**	Teacher	Model	Coach	Holy Spirit
5	**EXAMPLE**	Sermon on the Mount	Andrew & Peter	Blind Man Healed	Peter's Confession
6	**WEAKNESS**	Data Base	Social Influence	Subjective Experience	Human Opinion

Oswald Chambers used the terms "common sense and revelation sense" to explain the relationship between physical and spiritual learning.

> Faith in antagonism to common sense is fanaticism, and common sense in antagonism to faith is rationalism. The life of faith brings the two into right relation. Common sense is not faith, and faith is not common sense; they stand in the relation of the natural and the spiritual; of impulse and inspiration. Nothing Jesus Christ ever said is common sense, it is revelation sense.[1]

Learning through spiritual revelation does not reject the three traditional ways of processing knowledge. In fact, because God created us with these three capacities of learning, we can better receive revelation truths about God. Jesus uses all of these types of learning. Jesus' Sermon on the Mount gives a large body of information (cognitive learning) about Kingdom living. Peter learns from his brother Andrew about the Messiah (affective learning). The blind man experiences healing but admits he doesn't know that much about Jesus (psychomotor learning). Peter's confession does not come from human understanding but from revelation (revelation learning).

Information indoctrinates. Relationships and attitudes influence. Experience excites. Revelation inspires. Any one of these aspects of learning is inadequate and even dangerous by itself. Each sphere of learning has its own potential weakness when it stands alone. By itself, purely academic knowledge becomes a dead database. In the affective realm, relationships can impose social and group influence that corrupts truth. Psychomotor experiences can become subjective events that distort or even replace truth. Even truth received from revelation alone is subject to human interpretation and therefore may be flawed. God's holistic learning process comes from Scripture and gives the church a check and balance system for discovering, evaluating and teaching truth.

Information was not the power that fueled Jesus' movement and cannot explain Pentecost or the transplanting of the church in the first century. The Pentecost Christians experienced a person, a community and a way of life, not just theology, doctrine and a system of belief. "Jesus did not urge His disciples to commit to a doctrine, but to a Person Who was the doctrine, and only as they continued in His Word could they know the truth."[2]

FACILITATES PERSONAL HOLINESS AND GROUP EDIFICATION

The first century church used transformation training to radically change new converts. An impressive number of these new believers quickly moved past their old habits and pagan cultures to become productive Christians. Paul continued this focus on changing lives. All of his letters include sections about personal behavior. In Ephesians 4:17-29 Paul contrasts the new life of the Christian with past behavior. Paul encouraged the

Christians "in reference to your former manner of life . . . Lay aside the old self, which is being corrupted in accordance with the lusts of deceit, and that you renewed in the spirit of your mind, and put on the new self, which in the likeness of God has been created in righteousness and holiness of the truth. Therefore, laying aside falsehood, speak truth, each one of you, with His neighbor, for we are members of one another. Be angry, and yet do not sin; do not let the sun go down on your anger, and do not give the devil an opportunity. Let him who steals steal no longer; but rather let him labor, performing with his own hands what is good, in order that he may have something to share with him who has need. Let no unwholesome word proceed from your mouth, but only such a word as is good for edification, according to the need of the moment, that it may give grace to those who hear" (Ephesians 4:22-29).

Application of the Word, not information, cleanses. In fact, information without application is always in danger of slipping into legalism, institutionalism or intellectualism. Man can teach an information system but transformation is a work of God.

John Wesley's movement in eighteenth century England had a training system that was designed to transform rather than inform. "Wesley designed a system for correcting behavior first."[3] His strategy was: "To spread scriptural holiness throughout the land." So effective was Wesley's training that even the mules had to be retrained to obey instructions that were not profane. "For Wesley the locus of activity relevant to the gospel of Christ was the experience or behavior of a person; to most of the reformers the locus was in verbal or printed statements . . . books, pamphlets, creeds, confessions, catechisms, and other doctrinal formulations."[4] Wesley's objective was to change lives.

ACCELERATES THE DISCIPLESHIP PROCESS

Transformation training shortens the time between conversion and meaningful ministry, while the traditional church training system lengthens that time. Certainly, in an information system new believers can't be trusted with doctrine and theology. While we instinctively know that new believers have important truth related to their experience with God, we are cautious about turning the untrained loose in the "theological" realm. Consequently, years are required to prepare someone to pass the orthodoxy litmus test.

Because of the time factor, information training could not have been the training method used at Pentecost. There simply was not enough time to transfer sufficient doctrinal information to the Pentecost converts before they returned home. But the Pentecost converts were able to go home quickly and help "turn the world upside down" because they were trained in life experiences.

The objective of the first century church was to prepare witnesses to go home and tell, not to train theologians to explain. In a transformation training system, new believers don't have to be taught interpretation or the intricate details of theology before they share the gospel, disciple new Christians or even begin new churches.

Exit Poll of Church Youth

In spite of the use of informational church training, many church members today are still biblically illiterate and functionally pagan. Fifty-two weeks of Bible teaching and sermons has not transformed lives.

Conduct an exit poll with 16-25 year olds who grew up in the church. This important age group matriculates through our religious information system, but then largely abandons the church upon leaving home. Recent surveys reveal that young people who grow up in the church in the United States have essentially the same value systems as their pagan peers. For example, the same percentage of young people believe in sexual purity outside of marriage whether they attend church or never attend church.

Why is the church losing the hearts and values of young people? The Word is just as relevant to the modern world. The problem is the system used to teach the Word. Information is no longer enough to attract or keep those raised in a world that rejects absolute authority. The Word must be taught through transformation encounters in order for information, relationships, experiences and revelation to be internalized and applied.

Information cannot maintain orthodoxy. Influence will not control orthodoxy. Experiences, no matter how impressive, will not protect orthodoxy. Even revelation will not guarantee a living orthodoxy. Ultimately, orthodoxy must be validated by transformed lives.

10
JETHRO LEADERSHIP

†

The time which Jesus invested in these few disciples was so much more by comparison to that given to others that it can only be regarded as a deliberate strategy.
—Robert Coleman

Empowering leadership is a biblical root for worldwide revival in the twenty-first century.

After finishing a cell church conference and packing up my equipment, I hurried to catch a shuttle bus that would take me to Midway Airport in Chicago.

The bus driver recognized my Texas accent when I said "hello" and began to quiz me about my reason for being in Chicago. I was exhausted from talking and answering questions for two straight days, so I gave a polite answer that I thought would bring an end to the conversation.

The driver maintained eye contact with me through his large rear-view mirror and kept demanding more information as he expertly negotiated the evening rush hour traffic. Finally, I began to explain to this Catholic bus driver what I had just spent two days explaining to 100 pastors. I told him about a different kind of church that worked through small groups in homes.

I was somewhat taken aback when he brusquely responded, "How can that work?" I knew I had to think of a good answer so he wouldn't ask questions for the rest of the trip.

I responded, "It works because of its leadership structure." Then I explained the Jethro leadership approach in which different types of leaders function in a military-like leadership system. My answer seemed to satisfy this critic.

In that forced conversation God gave me an answer to a key question about the cell church. "How can it work?" Of course, the ultimate answer is that the cell church works because of God's power. My answer to that bus driver explains why the design of the cell church works. It works because of its leadership.

Through its leadership the cell church is able to coordinate, support, supervise and implement basic holiness and harvest tasks. This results in revival. In order for the church to experience revival in the twenty-first century, the leadership of the church must experience revival. The leadership of the church cannot experience holistic revival unless it operates in the New Testament cell-based design.

MOSES' LEADERSHIP OPTIONS

As Moses surveyed the multitudes of people surrounding him, he must have thought, "What kind of mess have I gotten myself into? How am I going to lead these people?"

He had to mold a mob of former slaves into a travelling nation and to lead them to the land God had promised. Moses was the best-educated person in that crowd. He had been trained in the best schools of Egypt while his followers were slaving to make bricks. How would Moses organize this mob into a functioning nation?

Moses had several organizational options. He could govern with the *Pharaoh Model* that he had learned during the first 40 years of his life. This is a model of dictatorship based on absolute authority enforced through absolute power. This model is excellent for coordinating. However, people rebel against absolute authority. In fact, Moses was the leader of such a rebellion, which brought him to his present leadership quandary.

Moses learned another organizational model in the desert of Median. For 40 years Moses operated with the *Shepherd Model* where the shepherd cares for each sheep individually and provides personal attention to every detail. This is an excellent model for a limited number of sheep, or people. Feed the sheep, lead the sheep, care for the sheep and provide for the sheep. This leadership model eventually breaks down because of the pressure placed upon one caring person. Evidently Moses was trying to use a variation of this model at the time of his conversation with Jethro.

Moses could have chosen the *Prophetic Model.* Moses had successfully used this model of leadership to secure the release of the children of Israel from Egypt and had brought them to the desert. This model depends upon awe and reverence for God's prophet and the recognition that the prophetic figure has received a special word from God. The problem in this model is sustaining the awe. Paul says that Moses would place a veil over his face so that the people would not "look intently at the end of what was fading away" (2 Corinthians 3:13). The glory of prophetic leadership fades and the leader must either hide his humanness or fake the glory of God.

He could have used a *Tribal Model.* This model had been used to organize the children of Israel before they were slaves in Egypt. It would again be used when they moved into the Promised Land. The twelve tribes would be assigned geographical areas and each tribe would be divided into basic family units. The Tribal Model depended upon a sense of kinship as one family and was excellent for administrating geographical areas. This model developed into the King Model that Israel used for a large portion of its history. The strength of this model is also its greatest danger. The people see themselves as separate tribes and clans and set up their own kingdoms. This eventually happened with the forming of the Northern and Southern Kingdoms of Israel.

WISE COUNSEL

Jethro, the father-in-law of Moses, suggested an *Empowering Model* of shared leadership to Moses. It included some of the strengths of all the other models. Jethro suggested that Moses organize the nation of Israel around four different types of leaders: leaders over tens, fifties, hundreds and thousands. These numbers represent four universal principles of leadership essential to the successful operation of any organization: coordinating, supporting, supervising and implementing. These leaders share the burden and blessing of leadership. Each leader empowers the unique function of other leaders so that all contribute to the successful implementation of the vision.

Every military since the time of Moses has used this leadership approach in one way or another. The military has divisions made up of battalions (thousands), companies (hundreds), platoons (fifties) and squads (tens). World War II historian, Stephen Ambrose, explains the organization of the military from the perspective of the squad. "The social bond within the Army was like an onion. At the core was the squad, where bonding could be almost mystical. After the squad came succeeding layers, the platoon, company on up to division, all covered by the loose outermost layers of corps and army."[1]

Successful businesses are organized along this same basic leadership structure even though different titles may be used. A company will have CEO's, vice presidents, mid-management leaders and working teams.

Even Jesus used a multi-level system of empowering leadership. The Master modeled the implementing role in His relationship to the twelve and early in His movement chose Peter, James and John to be sub-leaders at the level of supervision. After three and a half years of on-the-job training, Jesus installed a leader to coordinate His movement (Peter) and instructed the others in appropriate leadership roles.

Every leader (coordinating, supporting, supervising and implementing) uses all four of these leadership qualities to some extent. For instance, each leader will be functioning in the principle of coordination to some degree. In the broader picture of leadership, however, each one of the four leaders will be associated primarily with one leadership quality. Empowering leaders operate as a team because each leader is dependent upon the unique gifts and roles of the other leaders for success.

RESULTS OF USING
THE JETHRO APPROACH

Jethro told Moses that two things would happen if he organized the children of Israel into functioning groups. First of all, Jethro assured Moses that "the people will go home satisfied." That is the goal of a good leader. The people are satisfied in the vision, the purpose, the ministry, the direction and the administration of the church. I must confess that as a leader my followers have not always returned home satisfied.

Pastor Elias leads a Baptist church in Jales, a city of 100,000 in Brazil. In 1997 the church of 600 members began the transition to a cell church structure and over a period of three years grew to 1200. Pastor Elias was part of a year of training that mentors pastors in the process of transition into a cell church. He shared the following testimony: "For 28 years I pretended I was able to pastor my flock and my flock pretended that I was able to pastor them. Since I died to my old pastor paradigm I am now in a joyful time of ministry. I no longer have a make-believe ministry. I can now truly pastor my people through my cells."

Other models will not satisfy the people. The people may fear the Pharaoh but they will not be satisfied. The people may love the Shepherd as long as the Shepherd is able to give individual attention, but eventually the sheep will not be satisfied. The people may be in awe of the Prophet as long as the prophetic messages are pleasing and the miracles are beneficial. Tribal Kings are praised until they impose taxes to pay for their palaces and privileges of power.

The old paradigms of ministry always result in a gap between the leader and the people. No matter how hard the leader tries to fill the gap between leadership and ministry it still exists.

With what is the gap filled? In the past, leaders have attempted to fill the gap with authority and power, personal care giving, reverence and respect or strong government. The Jethro approach establishes an empowering model that fills the gap with leaders. Paul describes this leadership approach in Ephesians 4. God gives gifted leaders to the church in order to "equip the saints for the work of ministry." When this leadership system is working then the church "builds itself up in love."

In addition to the people "going home satisfied," Jethro assured Moses that with this delegated approach he "will be able to bear it."

I asked the pastor of a Baptist church in northern Denmark about her ministry, "How are you doing? How are you feeling?" After a moment of honest reflection the pastor replied with tears in her eyes, "Tired."

The organizational systems used by the traditional church often result in this feeling among pastors. Pastors are weary in "well doing." Jesus promised that His "yoke is easy and His burden is light." Jethro promised Moses that "you will be able to bear it." This is not true of many organizational leadership models.

Take this simple test for the effectiveness of your organizational leadership structure. Are the people satisfied? Are you able to bear the burden of leadership? Are you experiencing leadership burn out?

JESUS AND THE JETHRO PRINCIPLES

Robert Coleman's book *The Master Plan of Evangelism* is a classic on the ministry of Jesus. In the book Coleman returns to the theme of leadership over and over because Jesus' ministry cannot be understood apart from understanding His leadership approach. "Men were to be His method of winning the world to God."[2] This meant that Jesus' concern "was not with programs to reach the multitudes, but with men whom the multitudes would follow."[3] "Though He did what He could to help the multitudes, He had to devote Himself primarily to a few men, rather than the masses, in order that the masses could at last be saved."[4]

Coleman saw the dynamic tension in Jesus' ministry between the multitudes and the leaders. He declares that "victory is never won by the multitudes."[5] On the other hand, he asserts that "everything that is done with the few is for the salvation of the multitudes."[6] "Jesus had already demonstrated by His own ministry that the deluded masses were ripe for the harvest, but without spiritual shepherds to lead them, how could they ever be won?"[7]

Jethro and Jesus Leadership

JETHRO	ARMY	PRINCIPLE	JESUS	QUALIFICATIONS
1000	Battalion	Coordinate	3000	Elder 1 Timothy 3:1-7
100	Company	Support	120	
50	Platoon	Supervise	70	Deacon 1 Timothy 3:8-13
10	Squad	Implement	12	

Jesus' leadership strategy follows the Jethro principles even though the exact numbers are different. The Master modeled the basic unit with the twelve disciples, who relate to the tens (implementing). Jesus tested His model with 70, which corresponds to the fifties (supervising). Jesus established His model with 120, which represents the hundreds (supporting) and the base church. Jesus reached the thousands (coordinating) and anticipated large numbers being part of His movement. He thus provided a way to lead at the thousands level. These levels of leadership were necessary for Jesus to model leadership for His church.

The key to the New Testament system is the cell leader who facilitates the implementing groups in the homes. Once the implementing unit is in place, the other principles of leadership operate naturally as a means of supporting the basic unit.

THE PRINCIPLE OF COORDINATION

A leader (or team of leaders) coordinates the overall vision and directs the total project. This is the primary role of a leader over thousands, the gathering of all members and units. Remember the numbers represent a type of leadership and not just a number of people. A church of 75 members also needs someone to coordinate.

The leader who coordinates a cell church must:

1. Coordinate the administration of the church
2. Cast the vision
3. Birth the concepts
4. Model the basic task
5. Mentor the leaders of the hundreds
6. Have vision for growth
7. Facilitate the five-fold gifts
8. Oversee celebration

The coordinating and supporting roles are linked together in overseeing larger areas of the work. They work to give direction to the coordinating units of the church, congregations. But, the two roles differ in the number and nature of people they oversee. The coordinating leader can oversee numbers in the thousands and works through leaders over hundreds. The support leader oversees numbers in the hundreds and works through leaders over fifties and tens.

THE PRINCIPLE OF SUPPORT

Leadership is also required at the level of hundreds. This level of management interprets values, applies strategy to a designated geographical or people area, trains leaders and sees that all support resources are passed to the basic point of implementation. This area of leadership is often associated with a congregation. The congregation has been traditionally identified with worship and a building. However, in a cell church, "congregation" is a unit for planning, coordinating, counseling and training, not primarily for worship. Unfortunately, this word often confuses those trying to understand a cell church and so must be redefined.

The size of the area task unit (congregation) ranges from six to 25 cells (70 to 250 people) depending upon the phase of development of the area unit.

The support leader must:

1. Lead the flock
2. Plan for expansion in an area
3. Counsel leaders and members
4. Train leaders
5. Equip members (special equipping encounters)
6. Shape growth in the designated area
7. Mentor the leaders over fifties
8. Administrate the five support systems
9. Serve as a link to the whole church

THE PRINCIPLE OF SUPERVISION

A leader is needed to supervise the implementation of the basic task, to monitor quality control and to mentor leaders of the basic task unit, the cell. This is mid management level leadership and is represented by the leader over fifties (three to five cells or 15 to 70 members). The profile for the supervising leaders requires:

1. Shepherding two to five cell leaders
2. Quality control for cell life and ministry
3. Trouble shooting

4. Being the eyes and ears for leaders of hundreds
5. Mentoring leaders of tens
6. Affirming the selection of cell assistants

The leaders over fifties and tens operate as a team that focuses on the basic cell unit. The supervising leader is responsible for the overall direction of two to five basic units, while the cell leader is responsible for the specific tasks of one cell.

THE PRINCIPLE OF IMPLEMENTATION

A project must have leadership at the fundamental level of implementation so the basic task can be completed. The leader over tens oversees one unit of five to 15 adults that implements the basic task of holiness and harvest, edification and evangelism.

The basic unit of the squad in the military helps illustrates the uniqueness of the cell. Stephen Ambrose saw the squad (cell) as the most important unit in the military. In his book *Citizen Soldiers* he explains the uniqueness of the squad: "In assessing the motivation of the GIs, there is agreement that patriotism or any other form of idealism had little if anything to do with it. The GIs fought because they had to. What held them together was not country and flag, but unit cohesion."[8]

"Organization for a common and concrete goal in peacetime organizations does not evoke anything like the degree of comradeship commonly known in war. At its height this sense of comradeship is an ecstasy. Men are true comrades only when [each member of the squad] is ready to give up his life for the others without reflection and without thought of personal loss."[9]

We see this level of community and commitment to one another in the New Testament movement. As in the military, the groups (squads of ten to twelve adults) in the New Testament produced this kind of commitment.

The profile of the implementing leader includes:

1. Following the model of Aquila and Priscilla (Romans 16:3-5)
2. Shepherding Christ's sheep
3. Tending Christ's lambs
4. Facilitating community
5. Mentoring an assistant
6. Referring to support leaders
7. Monitoring spiritual growth
8. Bringing cell members into the presence of Christ

All other leaders exist in order to support the leader over tens. If the leader over tens is successful, the leader over fifties is successful. If the leader over tens is successful then the leader over hundreds is successful. If the leader over tens is successful then the leader over thousands is successful. The leader over tens makes sure that the basic tasks of the church are completed.

THE JETHRO APPROACH STILL WORKS

Every successful cell church uses some variation of the Jethro model. These cell churches may use different names for the leaders and have slightly different job descriptions but they have leaders who coordinate, support, supervise and implement.

From time to time a cell church model claims to use a new leadership approach different from the Jethro structure. I believe this is a misunderstanding of the Jethro approach and an unnecessary distinction. With new models we must carefully watch for "unofficial leaders" and "unofficial leadership structures" that are not taught but that are present in the working structure.

Leadership will not work properly without each of these roles functioning in one way or the other. Thousands of years of management confirm this conclusion. The proper functioning of these four leadership roles is essential for worldwide revival in the twenty-first century.

PART 3
REVIVAL PRINCIPLES

*Through the purging of revival,
God's people will be brought to the true beauty of holiness.
—Robert Coleman*

11

THE PRINCIPLE OF INTEGRATION

†

The system must provide the predictability.
—*Michael Gerber*

Integrating the systems of the church is a principle for worldwide revival in the twenty-first century.

The biblical account of creation confirms that God is a God of systems. In the beginning, the earth was "formless and void, and darkness was over the surface of the deep." The Spirit of God "moved over the waters" and brought order, form, and system out of the chaos. The creative power of the Spirit always moves toward system.

That is why man calls everything God has created a "system:" the solar system, the nervous system and the cell system. Throughout history, God has organized and implemented His vision through practical systems. The books of Numbers and Leviticus explain God's system for living out His holy life as a nation. Thus, we should not be surprised that when God created the church, He designed it as a system.

"Systems theory looks at the world in terms of the inter-relatedness of all phenomena, and in this framework an integrated whole whose properties cannot be reduced to those of its parts is called a system."[1]

The church is an extension of a system Jesus carefully built during the last years of His life on earth. Jesus knew that the wine of the church had to have a wineskin system.

Paul's picture of the church in Ephesians 4:16 describes this integrated system. "From whom the whole body, being fitted and held together by that which every joint supplies, according to the proper working of each individual part, causes the growth of the body for the building up of itself in love." That is a classic description of systems integration.

FEAR OF SYSTEMS

Some in the church believe systems to be unspiritual because they are often associated with dead programs and rigid institutions. However, the opposite of system is chance, randomness and chaos. A system gives freedom while chaos restricts, limits and distorts. Satan loves chaos and fragmentation and causes it at every opportunity. God unifies, integrates and systematizes everything that He touches. We should not fear systems, but the lack of spiritual life in a system.

The traditional church has an elaborate and complex system for operating as church. Think about all of the administration, organization and systems required for a typical traditional church to operate just one day of the week. However, the traditional church lacks an effective system for functioning the other six days of the week.

The church in the twenty-first century must find a way to operate an effective seven-day-a-week system. This does not mean that the church will have meetings seven days a week. But, the church will have a system through which the members can function as the Body of Christ beyond the meeting on Sunday.

A SYSTEM MODEL

In the eighteenth century, God developed a church system through John Wesley that dramatically changed the face of England and set into motion one of the greatest modern revivals. Wesley's followers were called "Methodists" because Wesley had a systematic method of doing every aspect of church. He left nothing to chance.

The gear that moved Wesley's system was holiness. Wesley's cry was "to spread scriptural holiness throughout the land." Secular historians credit Wesley's movement for saving England from a bloody revolution like those in France and other European countries during the eighteenth and nineteenth centuries.

To live out holiness, Wesley developed what Michael Henderson calls "an interlocking group system." This system was made up of three different types of groups that resulted in holiness and harvest, Wesley's definition of revival.

Wesley's Interlocking Group System

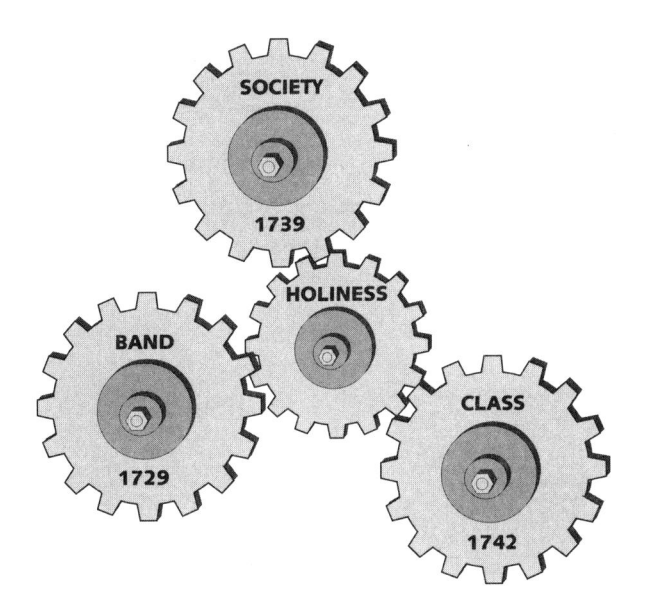

[Diagram: Four interlocking gears labeled SOCIETY (1739), BAND (1729), HOLINESS, and CLASS (1742)]

Wesley called his three interlocking groups — bands, societies and classes. In modern terms Wesley's groups were leadership and accountability groups (bands), large group worship (society) and cells (classes). Wesley put the three groups in place over a period of almost 15 years.

He began with a leadership accountability group in 1729 while at Oxford University. In the bands, mature members and leaders were accountable to each other for living a holy life. Wesley understood that holy living developed out of a heart of holiness. His bands promoted this kind of holiness, especially among leaders.

Wesley also knew that holiness depended upon a conceptual understanding of it. Ten years after starting his bands, Wesley began large group meetings on Sunday nights to teach holiness. He chose Sunday night instead of Sunday morning for this large group meeting so as not to conflict with the Church of England. The first society met at a building in London formerly used as an ammunition foundry.

After developing the band and the society, Wesley was still frustrated by the lack of close pastoral oversight, especially for those who were recent converts. Later, Wesley admitted that the solution to this problem was discovered quite by surprise. "At length, while we were thinking of quite another thing, we struck upon a method for which we have cause to bless God ever since."[2]

"This is the Thing We Have Wanted So Long"

On February 15, 1742, John Wesley was in Bristol, England with the leaders of that Society (organized Methodists in that area). They were searching for a plan to pay the debts of the Bristol Society. Captain Foy, a leader of the Bristol Society and a former ship captain, suggested collecting a penny from every Methodist in the area. Wesley himself relates that moment:

Captain Foy: "Let every member of the Society give a penny a week, till all [debts] are paid."

Another answered: "But many of them are poor and cannot afford to do it."

Captain Foy: "Then, put eleven of the poorest with me, and if they can give nothing, I will give for them as well as for myself; and each of you call upon eleven of your neighbors weekly; receive what they give, and make up what is wanting."

Wesley then describes what happened. "It was done. In awhile some of them informed me they found such and such a one did not live as he ought. It struck me immediately, 'This is the thing, the very thing we have wanted so long.'"[3]

Wesley then called together all the leaders and asked them to "make a particular inquiry into the behavior of those whom he saw weekly." Wesley observed that many "disorderly walkers" (backsliders) were identified and commented that some "turned from their evil ways, and some were put away."

Think about this first week of the "penny collection" in Bristol. The leaders met with eleven members for the practical purpose of collecting a penny from each one of them and community broke out. Members began to confess failures and needs in their lives. The leaders naturally prayed for those needs and restoration was experienced. When Wesley heard about what was happening in the "penny collecting" groups, he realized that this was the missing piece in his interlocking group system. In his own words, "This is the thing, the very thing we have wanted so long."

Up to that point, his system only had a way to teach holiness in the large group meetings and a way to help mature Christians and leaders internalize attitudes of holiness in the bands. The "penny collection" revealed the way for his members to encourage each other to live out holiness. Wesley saw this and reorganized his entire movement around these basic units (cells).

Within the month, the "penny collection groups" in Bristol became intimate groups of ten or twelve people who met weekly for personal supervision of their spiritual growth. Two months later in April, the plan was applied to the Foundry Society in London and from there was quickly applied to all the other Societies across England.

When the Foundry Society in London was organized into classes it consisted of 426 members plus 201 waiting for membership. They were divided into 65 classes. 18 months later (December of 1743), the membership in that one society had grown to 2200 people and all were members of classes (cells).

Henderson concludes, "The 'class meeting' turned out to be the primary means of bringing millions of England's most desperate people into the liberating discipline of Christian faith."[4]

WESLEY'S HOLINESS RESULTED IN HARVEST

Wesley's three interlocking group systems resulted in harvest. The more his societies, bands and classes lived in holiness the more impact the movement had on England. Wesley went into the Cornwall region of England and found only 16 Christians. It is said that when Wesley left the area that only 16 were not Christians.

Wesley's effectiveness in harvest was not just at the point of winning converts. After Wesley added his classes, his movement was able to assimilate the converts that were won. This assimilation accounts for the uniqueness of Wesley's movement. (See chapter 14.)

Wesley built his evangelism efforts around his classes or cells.

Wesley's Interlocking Group System

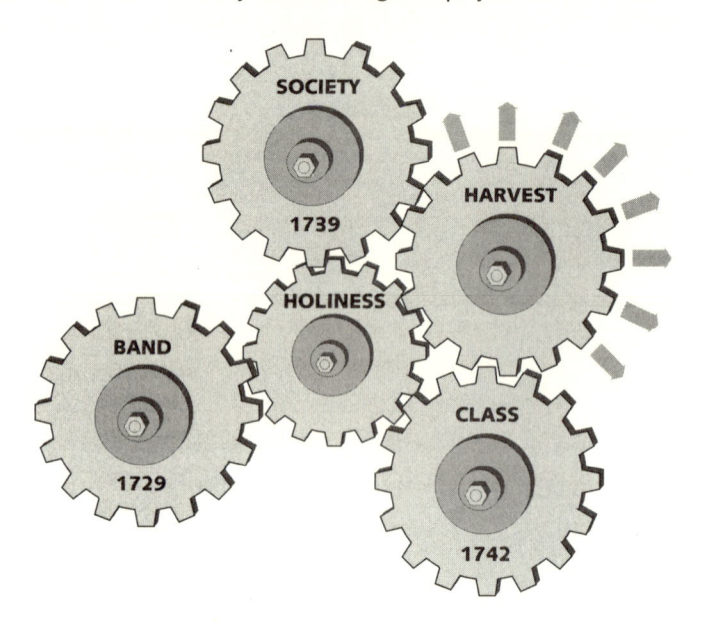

- SOCIETY 1739
- HARVEST
- BAND 1729
- HOLINESS
- CLASS 1742

On one occasion Wesley was asked why the Methodists could not content themselves with preaching and letting God look after the converts instead of going to all the trouble of forming them into societies and classes and bands. Ever pragmatic, Wesley replied, "We have made the trial in various places; . . . but in all (of them) the seed has fallen by the highwayside. There is scarce any fruit remaining."[5]

There are seven benefits for following Wesley's example and adopting a systems approach to church structure.

FIRST BENEFIT OF A CELL SYSTEM: IT FULFILLS VISION

A cell system is a structure for implementing vision. God told the prophet Habakkuk to "write the vision down" so that those who "hear the vision can run" (Habakkuk 2:2). God's vision can be written down. Vision can be expressed in a strategy and a system, which allows people to understand and participate in the vision.

"Vision has no force, power or impact unless it spreads from the visionary to the visionless. One mark of a great leader is the ability not only to capture the vision, but also to articulate it and to cause people to fully embrace it. Because vision concerns action, it is imperative that the vision be cast in such a way that people understand and can respond to it."[6]

Wesley's implementing system grew out of and fulfilled his vision of holiness and harvest, resulting in revival.

SECOND BENEFIT OF A CELL SYSTEM: IT ORGANIZES AROUND PRACTICAL FUNCTIONS

A cell system organizes around practical functions rather than personalities. Wesley was successful because he was practical. Ben Wong, pastor of Shepherd Community Church in Hong Kong, often uses the quote of Chairman Mao. "I don't care if it is a white cat or a black cat. Will it catch rats?"

People are important but personalities do not make a system successful. In developing a system the "who is going to do it" is secondary to "what is going to be done." If functions are the centralizing focus then many different people can do the functions. If a person or several people are the center, then when those people are no longer actively involved, the functions are compromised.

Churches and ministries are tempted to organize around personalities rather than functions. This was one of my frustrations as a missionary. Mission strategy was often developed around available personnel rather than biblical functions that needed to be implemented. It is easier to move personnel around than to stop and consider the basic tasks and functions that the personnel should be doing in the first place.

Wesley focused on functions but understood that people are important both to develop and to implement an effective system. Wesley's bands and leadership structure mobilized each person in the system to live out the vision of holiness and harvest. That vision and system flowed down from the leaders to the members.

THIRD BENEFIT OF A CELL SYSTEM: IT INTEGRATES ALL ESSENTIAL PURPOSES

A system integrates all essential purposes into a practical process so that the pieces and parts work together rather than stand alone as separate tasks. Wesley's system eventually organized all tasks around his small group classes and large group societies.

Wesley never fell into the trap of preaching purposes without an integrating system to implement them. Without an implementing system, the purposes continue to be fragmented. Some excellent books teach us about these purposes of the church, but identifying those purposes does not guarantee that a church will effectively live them out. The important question is: "What mechanism will I use to live out the purposes?" Many churches are still trying to accomplish their purposes through the same old systems.

The essential purposes of a church fall into two categories: implementing horizontal purposes and supporting vertical purposes. The implementing horizontal purposes are community, accountability, equipping, leadership and evangelism. The supporting vertical purposes are prayer, worship, the Word, authority and spiritual gifts. These vertical purposes support the five implementing purposes. Fit together as a system, these implementing and support purposes result in holiness and harvest. Integrating these ten purposes around Jesus' large-group and small-group design results in divine synergism, another descriptive term for revival.

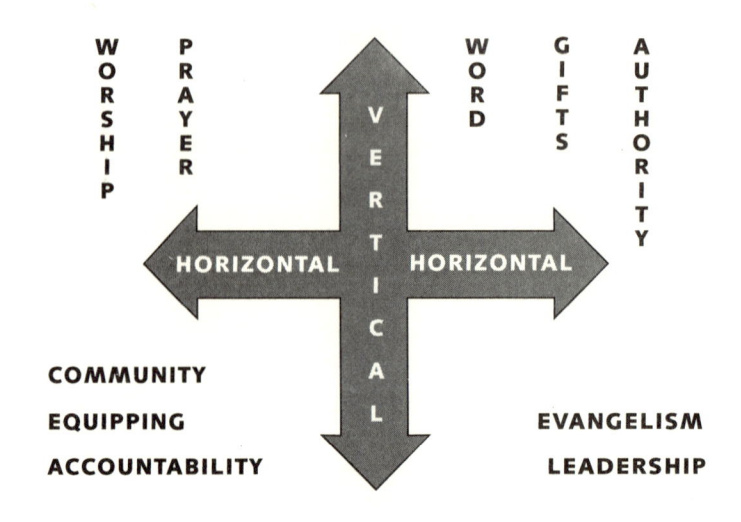

Ten Church Purposes

WORSHIP PRAYER VERTICAL WORD GIFTS AUTHORITY

← HORIZONTAL   HORIZONTAL →

COMMUNITY   EVANGELISM
EQUIPPING
ACCOUNTABILITY   LEADERSHIP

Fourth Benefit of a Cell System: It Is Predictable

A cell system is built upon predictable components that will work no matter what. Gerber states the importance of predictability for successful implementation of vision: "For your business to be predictable, your people must be. But if people aren't predictable, then what? The system must provide the predictability."[7]

Wesley reproduced the same system in every area of England. The components he discovered that worked and fulfilled his vision of harvest and holiness were used in every situation.

Dion Robert leads a church of more than 100,000 members in the Ivory Coast. When Pastor Dion meets one of his members on the streets of Abijaan, he may ask the member, "How long have you been part of our church?" If the member says, "Five months," Dion Robert then knows exactly what that member has experienced as a Christian for the past five months. How? Pastor Dion Robert has a predictable system in place that works.

This is the genius of a system that operates around one simple basic unit for production. If the cells operate properly, then everything else within the system will work with predictability.

Fifth Benefit of a Cell System: It Is Intentional

After listening to an explanation of the cell church, a leader of a network of churches made this comment to me. "In this movement we always embraced the values of groups, equipping and evangelism. However, we did not have an intentional way to implement those values." A core characteristic of a cell church will be intentional systems for completing the basic tasks.

A system gives intentional direction by integrating the three practical elements of methods, mentors and materials. A method provides a way to do a task. A mentor sees that a task is done. And materials are the tools required for doing a task. These three elements work together in an integrated system.

Elements in a System

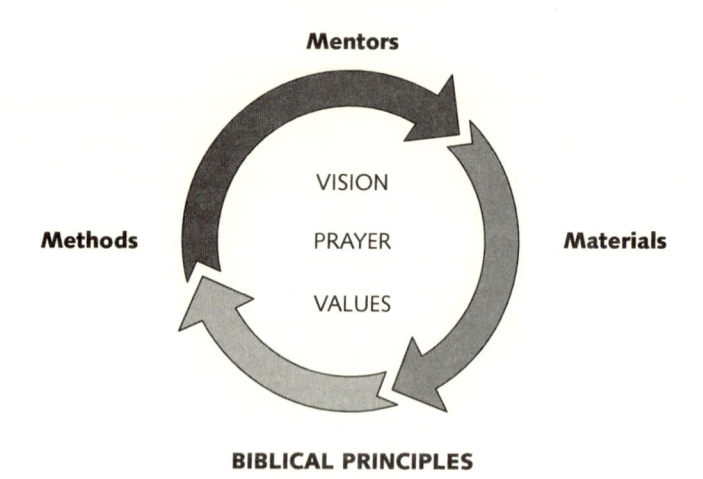

Mentors — **Methods** — **Materials**

VISION
PRAYER
VALUES

BIBLICAL PRINCIPLES

Different models of cell churches emphasize these three elements in slightly different degrees. For instance, some models will have weaker materials but will make up for this weakness by having very strong methods and mentors. All successful cell church models use these three elements in one way or another to develop intentional implementing systems.

Sixth Benefit of a Cell System: It Is Simple in Operation

It took Wesley almost 15 years to discover the basic class or cell unit. Once he discovered it, however Wesley made the class (cell) the primary unit of the movement. Everyone was expected to live in a basic cell unit. Membership in the Societies (large group worship) was determined by membership in the basic units (classes).

The cell church appears complex to those studying it as a subject but it is simple to those who have learned to operate it. The illustration of an automobile may help us understand how the cell church functions. A car consists of hundreds of working parts and is extremely complex. Consequently, a garage needs the latest equipment, experts and manuals to repair a car. However, an automobile is simple to operate because it has a relatively small number of working parts necessary for the car to run.

The same is true of a cell church. There are only a few simple working parts that must be operating before the cell church will work. You don't need to be a trained professional to make it work.

The cell unit is the frame that integrates every other part of the cell church. As a car has a basic form that gives it identity, so the cell gives the cell church its identity. If it does not work right here, at its most basic level, then the cell church will not work at all. Without this priority, the cell will become just another attached program, not the integrating element of cell church life.

Seventh Benefit of a Cell System: It Is Reproducible

McDonald's is a prime example of how a reproducible franchise system works today. The fast food chain markets a certain kind of "turnkey" business franchise (a system) that works each time it is reproduced. McDonald's sells a system for selling hamburgers.

The dictionary definition of franchise that relates to this subject is "the right to sell a product or service." Jesus set into motion a dynamic Kingdom system that exploded in different countries, cities and cultures across the world. How? Jesus' predictable system could be franchised in its essence in other cultures and places. His franchise has survived in good times and bad times, in persecution and prosperity.

Wesley desired to franchise the wine and wineskin of New Testament life and community. He believed that the church in every age could be remade into the pattern of the New Testament church. Wesley meticulously duplicated and monitored his system in every city, town and village in England. The same system was exported to other countries such as the United States of America.

After Wesley's death, the Methodist Church continued to have a significant impact on church history, but somewhere along the line the unique power and life associated with Wesley's movement was lost. What happened?

At some point, Wesley's followers ceased to franchise the New Testament pattern. Changes were made. The interlocking group system ceased to be the center of the movement. Nineteenth and twentieth century embellishments replaced Wesley's operating system of cells.

Wesley's movement did not stop because Christ's New Testament franchise stopped working; it stopped working because Wesley's followers stopped working Wesley's system after a certain point. Wesley's system will work today because it was patterned after Jesus' franchise.

12
THE PRINCIPLE OF THE ORDINARY

✝

All the links were weak, yet the chain survived.
—*Elton Trueblood*

Maximizing the ministry of ordinary leaders is a principle for worldwide revival in the twenty-first century.

Dave pastors a large, fast-growing church in Asia. The success of his church can be attributed to his preaching ability, his motivational skills, his management, his passion for reaching the lost and the responsiveness of the lost to the Gospel in his country. While a strong Sunday service has continued to be a central focus of his ministry, Dave reorganized his church into groups in order to promote more growth.

To say that Dave has an on-hands management approach would be an understatement. He promotes and motivates his leaders to reach out and grow with the fervor and skills of the president of a successful company, which he once was. Each day he reads reports on the growth of his groups. Praise God for Dave and his church.

Dave was in a meeting that included pastors of smaller and less dynamic churches. The subject of developing equipping and leadership training systems was being discussed. Dave wasn't interested in developing such systems, but the other leaders were. Dave had a simple solution to church growth: preach passionately, promote evangelism, work hard and manage efficiently.

The reactions of the other pastors surprised me. Even with the success of Dave's approach, the other pastors were interested in developing equipping and leadership systems. The leaders of the smaller churches realized that they could not successfully use Dave's approach. They had already tried it in one form or the other. They knew what Dave had not realized. Dave *was* his system.

These ordinary leaders realized that they needed support systems to help them be effective even if Dave didn't. In this chapter we will consider how Jesus leveraged ordinary people into extraordinary leadership. Ordinary leaders are a key factor for revival in the twenty-first century.

THE OLD CHURCH STAR SYSTEM

During our last term in Thailand, a man who had been educated in America was discussing "religion" in America. He was greatly impressed with the Christian leaders he had seen on television. In our discussion he could not think of the term in English for pastor. Finally he used the Thai word for movie star to refer to the pastor. "You know the star of the show." This was probably an accurate impression of how someone from another culture views church leadership in the United States in its most visible expression.

Depending on extraordinary leadership goes contrary to the best management principles. Michael Gerber categorically claims, "It is literally impossible to produce a consistent result in a business that is created around the need for extraordinary people."[1]

Professionals and the most gifted leaders are required to make the traditional church system operate successfully. This kind of leader must have a combination of administrative gifts, salesmanship, entertainment skills, political acumen and natural self.

For decades denominations have lifted up extraordinary leaders and their churches as the latest and greatest church success story. All leaders have been exhorted to pattern their ministry after these extraordinary leaders. This invariably results in frustration and guilt for those ordinary leaders who cannot produce similar results.

Such successful pastors represent a small percentage of church leaders blessed with extraordinary leadership gifts. Like Dave in the earlier illustration, these leaders can make almost any system work because in essence they *are* the system.

EXTRAORDINARY LEADERS

- Motivational Skills
- Communication Gifts
- Administrative Know How
- Promotional Ability

Limited in Number

ORDINARY LEADERS

Most Leaders are Ordinary

Many dynamic leaders begin businesses that fail as soon as the founder is out of the picture. Why? The business is built around them. The extraordinary leader is the scaffolding of the building and is built into the major support beams. When the scaffolding is taken away then the business collapses upon itself.

A system that is tailor-made for one leader is seldom transferable to other leaders. It would help the wider church family if these extraordinary leaders would do what Christ did: develop systems that others can successfully understand and implement, instead of teasing ordinary leaders with systems that only extraordinary leaders can implement.

Like Dave, few extraordinary leaders can get outside of their own ministry long enough to develop a transferable model. The church needs to return to the system modeled by another great leader: Jesus. His system leveraged ordinary leaders into extraordinary leadership. Only in this way can God mobilize, maximize and multiply His leaders for the challenge of harvest and holiness in the twenty-first century.

WEAKNESSES OF THE "STAR LEADERSHIP" APPROACH

The "star leadership" approach has several weaknesses that hinder revival and exponential growth in the church. First of all, few extraordinary leaders exist. Therefore, to depend upon them to provide the vision and initiative for every church will limit the places where a reproducing church can be established.

Second, identifying leaders in the early stages of a movement can be a hit and miss proposition. A Saul, Absalom or Judas can look very attractive in the beginning. And even the best leaders can be killed, jailed or neutralized. In Chile I heard a fascinating story about the only Indian tribe in the Andes Mountains never subjugated by the government. Why was the government unable to control this group? The unique leadership structure of the tribe thwarted the authorities. All of the other tribes had a chief or king who was easily identified by rank, uniform or deference shown by other members of the tribe. With these tribes, the government would single out the chief, capture or kill him and subdue the tribe. The tribe that was never subjugated had a broad leadership base. Any member of the tribe might be the leader at any given time. No special rank, insignia or deference was associated with the leader. The government could never identify the leader of the tribe, and even if they did capture or kill the current leader, another one would immediately fill the vacancy.

Third, pride is always a problem in a star system. Followers tend to give these star leaders an unhealthy adoration that should be reserved only for Christ. Extraordinary leaders may begin to believe their press clippings and accept honor due only to God. In the New Testament we see respect for leaders but not undue adoration that exempted them from humility and death.

The fall is great when an extraordinary leader fails . . . especially in this day of investigative reporters and television. The star leader system of the church has not served the cause of Christ well. Time and time again extraordinary celebrity leaders have brought reproach upon the name of Christ because of a lack of accountability. These celebrity leaders often become "a law unto themselves" and lose touch with the ordinary.

Fourth, dependence on extraordinary leaders kills the initiative of ordinary leaders and members. "I can never lead like that person." "Look at all of the gifts of that leader." Dependence on extraordinary leaders paralyzes action at the grass roots level. Followers sit around and wait for the dynamic leader to do it for them.

A System that Leverages Ordinary People

Paul described the leaders of the New Testament church: "For consider your calling, brethren, that there were not many wise according to the flesh, not many mighty, not many noble; but God has chosen the foolish things of the world to shame the wise, and God has chosen the weak things of the world to shame the things which are strong, and the base things of the world and the despised God has chosen, the things that are not, that He may nullify the things that are, so that no man may boast before God" (1 Corinthians. 1:26-29).

Why is Paul's ordinary leadership system better than the star system? Gerber explains why: "If you intentionally build your business on the skills of ordinary people, you will be forced to ask the difficult questions about how to produce a result without the extraordinary ones. You will be forced to find a system that leverages your ordinary people to the point where they can produce extraordinary results."[2]

While, extraordinary leaders were important in Jesus' approach (after all, He was one), it was His ordinary leadership system that caused growth and multiplication. Jesus' system leveraged ordinary people so that they could produce extraordinary results. Jesus' system was better than his leaders.

Jesus carefully developed His system to work after He returned to the Father. The New Testament design integrates the five ministry systems below (community, equipping, accountability, leadership and evangelism) around the life of a small group. These ministry systems are implemented by an appropriate method, an experienced mentor and value designed materials.

EXTRAORDINARY LEADERSHIP

- Community
- Equipping
- Accountability
- Leadership
- Evangelism

SYSTEM

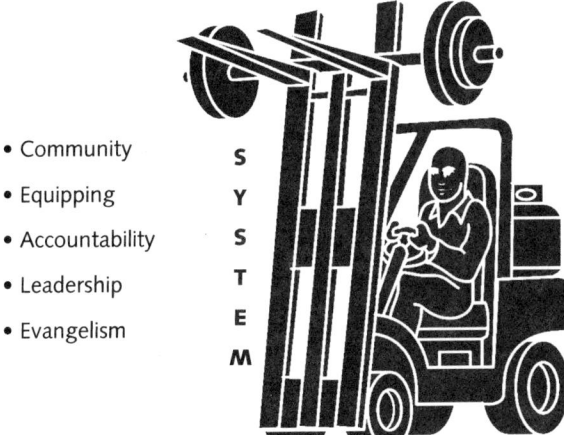

- METHOD
- MENTOR
- MATERIALS

A Divine System Results in Divine Synergism

Elton Trueblood understood the uniqueness of the New Testament system and described it as spiritual synergism: according to our common proverb, a chain is no stronger than its weakest link. The aphorism may be true, when applied strictly to the realm of the mechanical, but it is absurdly untrue when applied to a social organism such as the church of Jesus Christ. "All the links were weak, yet the chain survived!"[3] In another book Trueblood elaborated on this phenomenon:

> How then would the work go on? He did not leave a book; He did not leave an army; He did not leave an organization, in the ordinary sense. What He left, instead, was a little redemptive fellowship made up of extremely common people whose total impact was miraculous. Though the members were individually unworthy, the fellowship which they came to share was so far superior to the sum of its parts that it was not only able to survive and endure, but finally to dominate and save.[4]

Synergism is the universal truth that "the whole is greater than the sum of its parts." One horse can normally pull about two tons. Two horses together can sometimes pull up to 23 tons. That's synergistic horsepower.

The ancient world understood the principle of synergism. The writer of Ecclesiastes stated the principle in terms of relationships. "Two are better than one because they have a good return for their labor." That is what synergism is all about. "A good return on the labor." "If either one falls, the one will lift up his companion." "If two lie down together they keep warm, but how can one be warm alone?"

The writer of Ecclesiastes also explained the principle of synergism in physical terms. "A cord of three strands is not quickly torn apart" (Ecclesiastes 4:12). Individually the cords of rope can be easily broken, but together their holding power is much greater than the strength of each strand.

Pentecost is another example of this principle at work. The spiritual power that the 120 followers of Christ experienced after the Spirit had fallen was much greater than if they had been 120 individuals sitting in

120 separate upper rooms all over Jerusalem. God could work a greater power through them because they "were all together" and "of one mind."

Spiritual community provides a context and atmosphere where spiritual synergy can be powerfully experienced. Christ multiplies Himself in the midst of His spiritual Body and the whole church then becomes greater than the sum of its individual members.

Once again consider Ephesians 4:16. "From him the whole body, joined and held together by every supporting ligament, grows and builds itself up in love, as each part does its work." The parts are fitted together in such a way that the whole becomes greater than the sum of each part. That is dynamic community synergism.

Elizabeth O'Connor wrote about this phenomenon in *Call to Commitment*, a book detailing her early journey into community.

> Have you ever been with a group of people and guessed that they must be very extraordinary people because of their excitement and wonder? And then have you considered that group person by person and found that each was very ordinary, though very beautiful: one a clerk, another a bricklayer; then you remember that one was a fisherman and one was a tax collector, and another . . . He was the Son of God. The Christian community knows this. That which makes it more than it is, is the gift of the Holy Spirit.[5]

Christ Makes the Ordinary Extraordinary

Small groups and their leaders seem so ordinary. How can groups of ten to 15 adults be the organizing principle for worldwide revival? It is evident in the New Testament that the small groups of "two or three" provided a place for a special relationship between Christ and His ordinary followers. "Where two or three gather together in my name, there I am in the midst." Jesus did not say 200 to 300 or 2000 to 3000. Jesus said "two or three," the designation for a small group. This kind of small group is extraordinary because Christ manifests Himself within the group in a spiritual power that results in community synergism.

In a cell, spiritual synergy works itself out in several ways not seen in secular small groups. First, Christ's presence in the life of each individual gives a starting point. The Christ in me is the same Christ that is in you.

Christ in each Christian creates a point of contact that opens up the possibility of new depths of relationship with Christ and with each other.

Second, when Christians gather in a cell more happens than just Christ indwelling each individual Christian. Christ is also *with* the group that gathers in His name as the indwelling, incarnate and resurrected Christ. Through the Holy Spirit, He comes into the midst of the group and sets up His presence as an active participant. Together, the group enters into community with Him and becomes His spiritual body at that place and time. Christ abides in the group and the group abides in Christ. The life of Christ flows through the branches. That also is powerful synergism.

Third, synergism takes place in the tasks that flow out of the group. The tasks are extensions of His person, power and purpose . . . of Who He is. Therefore in a cell, synergism of purpose takes place and gives power to ministry. All of the individual ministries are united as His ministry. Christ in the midst sets into motion spiritual fellowship, edification, sanctification and community. It can be described as love in action.

In this community, all of the "fullness of the Godhead bodily" is expressed. He operates and ministers through the varying gifts as "everyone has a hymn, or a word of instruction, a revelation, a tongue or an interpretation." That spiritual synergism releases the presence, power and purpose of Christ through His spiritual gifts in his church. The cells become the life of Christ.

Divine synergism also results in witness, expansion and evangelism. What happens is far greater than individual Christians witnessing. Christ draws all of the witnessing together within Himself so that multiplication synergism results.

Fourth, the church experiences synergism as a whole. The cell parts are integrated into a local corporate body. Then each local corporate church is integrated into the universal corporate body of Christ. In heaven the "great hosts" is a picture of divine synergism in its greatest expression.

The ordinary becomes extraordinary in God's hands. This kind of cell system leverages ordinary leaders into the kind of extraordinary leadership necessary for revival in the twenty-first century world.

13

THE PRINCIPLE OF SMALL CHURCHES

✝

Small is something more than a numerical description.
—Carl Dudley

Mobilizing small churches is a principle for worldwide revival in the twenty-first century.

In 1999 I attended a conference in one of the largest and most dynamic churches in Europe. Over the course of the week, I realized that the conference reflected the worldwide makeup of the church. Some of the leaders were part of large churches like the host church, but most belonged to smaller churches. That experience reinforced my belief that revival and harvest in the twenty-first century is dependent upon ordinary leaders and small churches.

Praise God for the dynamic large churches across the world. God has set the cell church movement into motion through the transition of some of these strong, creative churches.

However, large churches cannot carry the burden of exponential multiplication in the twenty-first century. These churches represent a small fraction of the churches and the Christians in the world. Eighty to ninety percent of all churches in the world have fewer than 100 adult members. God cannot reach the billions being born just by mobilizing large churches to reach more people. These large churches are doing as much as they can.

Therefore, God will use new and smaller churches to complete the exponential expansion that accompanies twenty-first century revival. To reach the masses, God must mobilize churches of 50, 75 and 100 adult members. These churches don't have to grow to thousands. By increasing from under 100 members to 300 to 400 members, smaller churches will bring a significant number of new believers into the church. They will also be strong enough to begin new churches.

Of course, numbers are not magical. A larger church is not necessarily a better church and a church under 100 members is not necessarily a weaker church. However, 100 is the point of growth momentum that is the optimum size for optimum performance. That is the point when spiritual synergism takes over and God can use the church in exponential expansion. This point of breakthrough is known as "critical mass."

In nuclear physics, critical mass is the minimum amount of fissionable material necessary to produce a chain reaction. Critical mass can be understood as momentum and synergy. (Critical mass and how it fits into the process of becoming a cell church will be discussed in chapter 19.) In a cell church, critical mass indicates the size when the implementing unit and the coordinating unit fuse together in an integrated whole that can result in dynamic holiness and explosive harvest. Small stagnant churches never reach that point.

The Sigmoid Curve that is introduced in this chapter addresses the problem of stagnation and the critical factors for breaking through it.

Lessons from the Sigmoid Curve

Laurence Singlehurst, Director of YWAM in England, often uses a statement that he learned from his grandmother. "Left to itself everything tends to swerve to rot." This is one way of stating the Second Law of Thermodynamics defined as "a tendency in nature to proceed toward a state of greater molecular disorder." This basic premise that everything, if not energized from the outside, runs out of steam is explained in the Sigmoid Curve pictured at the top of the next page.

The Sigmoid Curve suggests that a strategy must be developed to overcome the tendency toward disorder and entropy. A concerted effort must be made to continue a process or it runs out of steam and growth flattens out. Charles Handy describes this concept in his book *The*

The Sigmoid Curve

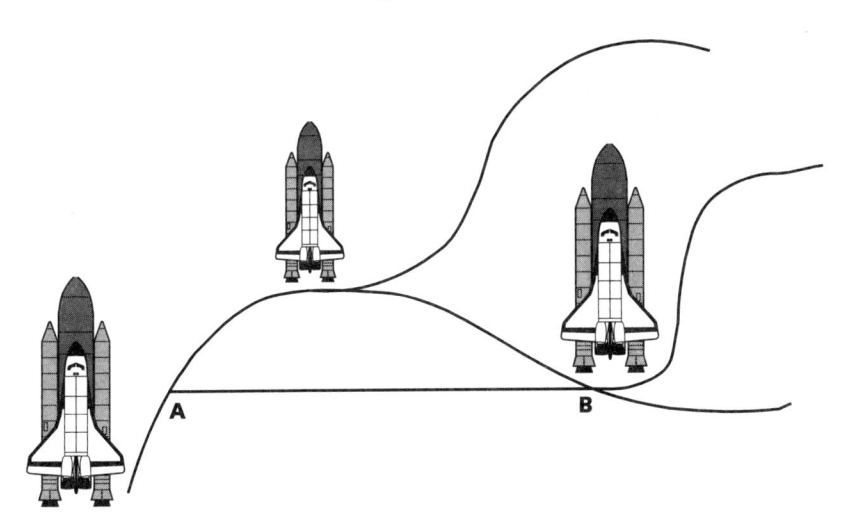

Empty Raincoat. "It is one of the paradoxes of success that the thing and the ways which got you where you are, are seldom the things to keep you there."[1]

BARRIERS

The Sigmoid Curve exposes the danger of stagnation and explains the importance of momentum. Therefore, it has implications for a new church start, for a church under 100 members and for larger churches transitioning into cell churches.

Satan neutralizes churches by moving them endlessly between point A and point B as seen in the Sigmoid Curve. Like the children of Israel, a church will "circle the mountain" over and over, never crossing the Jordan into the Promised Land.

Peter Wagner states a basic truth of the Sigmoid Curve. "It is much more preferable to sustain growth momentum than to lose it and then attempt to regain it."[2] It is easier to have a new thrust at point A while there is still momentum than to try something new to regain momentum at point B. An inert object is more difficult to move than an object already in motion. Smaller churches that have been stuck at point B for years present a special problem because momentum has been lost and stagnation has set in. A church can break out of stagnation by developing a strategy for the six factors listed in the chart below.

Breakthrough Factors

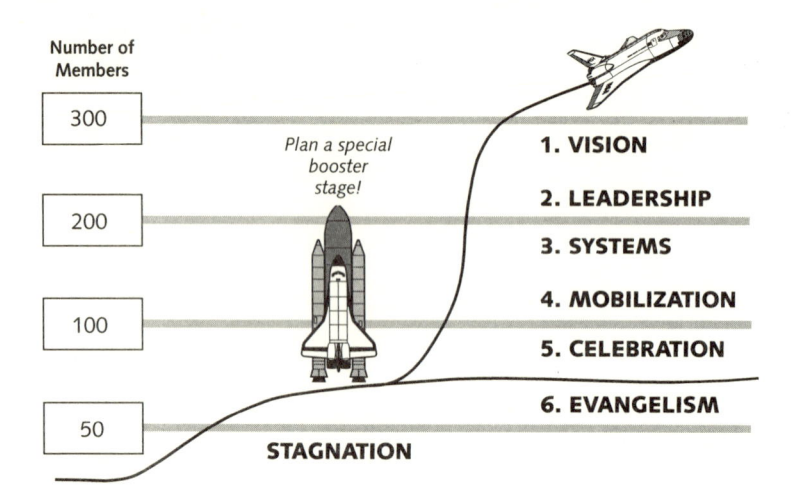

Number of Members		
300		1. VISION
	Plan a special booster stage!	2. LEADERSHIP
200		3. SYSTEMS
		4. MOBILIZATION
100		5. CELEBRATION
		6. EVANGELISM
50	**STAGNATION**	

Churches with less than 100 members, whether stagnant or new, face the same six barriers to growth. Both new church starts and small stagnant churches must develop strategies to break through the following six barriers:

1. The fragmented vision barrier
2. The ineffective leadership barrier
3. The unpredictable systems barrier
4. The unproductive members barrier
5. The dead celebration barrier
6. The ordinary evangelism barrier

THE FRAGMENTED VISION BARRIER

Many small churches are small because they either have no vision, a small vision or multiple visions. Any one of these will paralyze a church, but the problem of multiple visions is probably the most frequent and dangerous.

Churches remain the same year after year, not because they have no vision but because they have too many visions. A single church might have visions for: Bible study, women's work, worship, discipleship, children's work, youth work, prison ministry, marriage ministry, particular gifts, and political or social causes. These many good visions keep small churches small and ineffective churches ineffective by standing in the way of a unified vision.

Each vision establishes its own kingdom and each kingdom has a king or queen. To encroach upon another kingdom means war. Or the church allows all kingdoms to stake out territory and for the sake of peace to control that particular part of the church. This is the "balkanization" of the church. This multiple kingdom, multiple vision approach keeps the church fragmented and weak.

Jesus said that a true kingdom could not be divided against itself. Yet that is exactly what the twentieth century church has done. The local church with multiple visions is the Kingdom of God divided against itself.

Successful churches have one vision. "Vision plus vision equals division." This statement by Dion Robert from the Ivory Coast is a powerfully prophetic word to the twenty-first century church, especially for stagnant and struggling small churches.

Is there a way out of this multiple kingdom nightmare? There is! All leaders must die to their personal kingdoms. There is only one Kingdom and that is God's Kingdom. If a small church is to grow it must sacrifice all visions and kingdoms but God's. Then all the individual visions are united in one powerful vision.

How do you build one big vision? By combining all of the small visions into one vision. God can use a church that is small in numbers to implement a large vision. And God can help a small church grow toward the size of one vision.

THE INEFFECTIVE LEADERSHIP BARRIER

Many churches hit a wall at 70 to 80 members and are unable to break through to critical mass. These churches may have one of the following leadership styles:

1. *One-man-show leadership.* Typically in a small church, several or all of the primary roles of leadership are concentrated in one person.

Consequently, the church cannot grow beyond the time, ability and energy of that one leader. The answer is to mobilize more members for leadership.

A church must develop an effective leadership structure that functions in the four essential principles of leadership: coordinating, supporting, supervising and implementing. Smaller churches often stagnate because one or several of these principles of leadership is either lacking or ineffective.

2. *Ballot-box leadership.* The church has leadership by committee or by congregation. There are so many people giving their opinions and directing the vision of the church that the church is paralyzed. To break through this, a church needs to unify its leadership into one voice. That one voice may be a team of leaders but the team must speak with one voice and one vision.

Peter Wagner suggests three essentials for a leadership team in a new start that are true of a small church as well. First, there should be prior agreement with the philosophy of ministry. It is risky to have people on a leadership team with the idea that you will later indoctrinate them into your ministry philosophy. Second, the leadership team should have spiritual gifts that will contribute to the implementation of the ministry philosophy. Third, they must have loyalty. Total loyalty of every leader to the senior pastor is a must for healthy growth.[3]

3. *Medicine-man leadership.* Lyle Schaller uses the terms "medicine men" and "tribal chiefs" to explain this prevalent leadership problem. Leadership in a church is separated into religious activities and business activities. The "medicine men" carry out religious duties but the "tribal chiefs" actually control the church. The "tribal chiefs" are often the governing board of a church. The board has veto control over the vision and actions of the church; consequently, the pastor or staff operates as a "medicine man," carrying out religious duties. These "medicine men" shake holy water over activities and chant impressive rituals but have little to do with the real implementing vision of the church.[4]

4. *Shepherd leadership.* Leaders need the heart of a shepherd. However, a church doesn't need a shepherd leadership system if it wishes to grow. The team of leaders should function as a rancher rather than a shepherd. The shepherd model knows all the people by name and does everything for them. A rancher model means that the sheep are cared for within a system of leadership. The difference is who takes care of the sheep. The

shepherd must do it personally. The rancher empowers others to share in the care.

The Jethro system of leadership is a "rancher" model of leadership that is ideally suited for growth above the 100 member level. Therefore, smaller churches must implement the Jethro structure as quickly as possible. This means organizing the cells under leaders of two to five cells and even early in the process designating a leader over 100 in order to release the senior leader to coordinate the church.

THE UNPREDICTABLE SYSTEMS BARRIER

A predictable system is required for a small church to break through the smallness barrier (See chapter 11). An unpredictable system is often found in smaller churches with a fragmented vision. Multiple visions result in multiple methods, and multiple methods destroy predictability.

A system is a wineskin for containing the wine: the spirit and life. Wineskins by themselves are just empty containers, and life without wineskins is wasted. Christ's wineskin system works when God's people are joined in a predictable design of small groups and large groups.

Predictability is not the opposite of freedom. In fact, predictable components enhance the possibility of freedom of action. The person unwilling to submit to a predictable plan is demanding the right of anarchy. This never results in true freedom.

Therefore, in a cell church the most basic unit, the cell, must be predictable. Without a predictable cell pattern, leaders cannot be trained, materials cannot be developed and methodology cannot be standardized. Materials help unify visions and systems.

The cell unit is predictable because all the cells use one agenda that the church's leadership team received from God. The theme of each cell meeting is predictable because it is tied to the teaching in the large group worship. Predictability is possible because leaders meet together for coordination and ministry to each other and everyone uses the same equipping track.

A small church cannot afford the luxury of randomness. It must concentrate its energy and efforts toward reaching the optimum size for growth and therefore must operate with a predictable system.

THE UNPRODUCTIVE MEMBERS BARRIER

The Strachan Principle reveals an important truth: "The successful expansion of any movement is in direct proportion to its success in mobilizing and occupying its total membership in constant propagation of its beliefs."[5]

This means that every person in an endeavor must be mobilized in order to maximize efficiency. The New Testament church is a classic example of this principle at work. Jesus was able to mobilize every member to do the basic tasks. In Jesus' system there are no spectators because He created a producer system, not a consumer system.

A successful organization involves every person in the task, from the highest executive to the newest employee. This eliminates dead wood. For a volunteer organization like the church this may be a dream, but it is a dream worth pursuing. A special system is necessary so that every person can participate.

The Strachan Principle was one of the key teachings of Elton Trueblood for almost half a century. In fact, the title and theme of *The Company of the Committed* reflects this principle and is summed up by Trueblood:

> Perhaps the greatest single weakness of the contemporary Christian church is that millions of supposed members are not really involved at all and, what is worse, do not think it strange that they are not. As soon as we recognize Christ's intention to make His church a militant company we understand at once that the conventional arrangement cannot suffice. There is no real chance of victory in a campaign if ninety percent of the soldiers are untrained and uninvolved, but that is exactly where we stand now.[6]

A new church must mobilize every member in the following eight areas to maintain momentum. A stagnant church must mobilize in these areas to regain lost momentum and growth.

- Mobilize at the point of community. Every member lives out the Christian life of holiness and harvest in a dynamic small group community.
- Mobilize at the point of equipping. Every member is prepared for Christian life and ministry through intensive and extensive training.

- Mobilize in contacting the lost. Every member is encouraged to contact lost people in their geographical and/or social context.
- Mobilize leaders. Every member is prepared for spiritual leadership within a simple and transferable system of ministry.
- Mobilize the large group as support of the cell system. Every member is supported with an effective training, administrative and celebration system.
- Mobilize at the point of spiritual power. Every member is taught to pray and depend upon God's presence and power, not human effort.
- Mobilize for expansion. Every member expects to participate in multiplication of the gospel in Jerusalem, Judea, Samaria and the world.
- Mobilize at the point of time commitment. Members are able to manage time in such a way as to be an effective leader of a cell.

THE DEAD CELEBRATION BARRIER

Some small churches remain small because they fail to tap into the growth potential of the large group wing. Christian Schwarz identified eight quality characteristics that are necessary for growth. Quality characteristic number five is "inspiring worship." Schwarz concludes: "There is a strong correlation between an 'inspiring worship experience' and a church's quality and quantity."[7]

Properly used, the large group meeting contributes to the stability and growth of a new cell church or to the transition of an existing church into an operational cell church. However, two extreme attitudes toward the large group meeting can harm a cell church in its early stages of development.

Over-dependence on the large meeting can be harmful. Producing "inspiring worship" can consume so much of the time, energy and resources of leaders that little time remains for developing effective cell life. New members that are attracted by high maintenance celebration and quality children's programs may never catch the small group values of the church. Therefore, the best leaders are required to keep the large group activities running and to service the expectations of the members attracted through the large group meeting. Leaders must learn to balance celebration and cell life in order to establish both.

On the other hand, the absence of an effective large group celebration can be equally harmful. Leaders beginning a new church often fall into this trap. These leaders are convinced that community cell life is essential for the church. Therefore, they focus totally on developing the small group system and neglect the large group meeting. Often the new start refuses to begin any kind of large group expression until 100 or 200 members are living in cell life. In trying to correct the problem of over-emphasis on the large group, this approach neglects celebration and consequently loses an important tool for developing momentum.

Jesus solved the problem of the large group and small group with His public and private ministry. Jesus' ministry ran along two parallel tracks. He taught and prepared the crowds in a public ministry and he taught and prepared His leaders in His private ministry. Jesus recognized the importance of a large group public ministry that could support and coordinate the private ministry.

Jesus' Public & Private Ministry

Public Ministry
- The Masses
- Low Maintenance Meetings
- Assimilate Followers
- Width of Ministry
- Use Large Groups
- Quantity

Private Ministry
- The Core
- High Impact Encounters
- Train Leaders
- Depth of Ministry
- Use Small Groups
- Quality

The proper kind of celebration offers the following benefits to a new start:

- Large group celebration can be used to assimilate crowds and support cell life. It can be a fishing pond and holding tank for seekers. Involving new members in celebration activities gives a way to prepare members for meaningful activities.

- The large group can be used to teach the vision and to change the values of members who are not part of the initial core of leaders.
- Future leaders can be kept busy in meaningful ministry while the core leaders develop the model. This solves a major problem in the initial stage of a new start or a transition. What do you do with members who want to get into cells before the model is ready? These members can be prepared in the large group to eventually enter a cell.
- Celebration in the large group helps build momentum and supports the cell system through which growth will happen.
- Effective celebration promotes unity and casts the vision.
- Inspiring worship models the large group wing.
- Celebration serves as a farm system for developing future leaders. A new start is very vulnerable in the beginning. If one or two people bail out of the core team the project is severely damaged. However, leaders that are being developed through the celebration can be brought into the early leadership core to replace leaders that may leave.
- The celebration part of the church provides an opportunity to continue to contact and assimilate new members while developing a working model.

THE ORDINARY EVANGELISM BARRIER

In order to complete the cell church systems and give credibility to the strategy, a significant number of new members must be brought in by the process. In the case of Jesus' church, the 120 or even the 500 could not have maintained the momentum of the movement. The 3000 and 5000 that came into the movement after Pentecost guaranteed the movement's success.

In the development of a cell church, a significant number of new members must be brought into the church at two key points. The church must bring enough new people into the process to test out and model the initial systems. Jesus did this with the 70. After developing the initial systems, the church must bring in enough new members to reach critical mass growth. Jesus did this with the 120 that probably represented a group that was two or three times that size.

In order to reach the number of members required to model the system and establish critical mass, a church must intensify and multiply evangelism. Ordinary types of evangelism done with ordinary enthusiasm and intensity will not move a small church into critical mass. In order to achieve optimum size for growth, a church must do super evangelism that will gather a significant number of followers.

A strategy for "super evangelism" will be characterized by the following:

1. A broader range of evangelism methods will be used
2. Greater priority will be given to evangelism in the calendar
3. A larger number of members will be mobilized for evangelism
4. More intense passion will be applied to evangelism

Super evangelism differs from ordinary evangelism in degree and focus more than in substance. The same methods of evangelism are used in "super evangelism" but with greater intensity. Every method of evangelism must be used: relationship evangelism, group evangelism and mass evangelism.

Super evangelism means that every member must be involved in contacting and cultivating the lost. Relationship evangelism is not enough to break through by itself. A church must continue to contact friends, relatives and acquaintances. Multiplication of contacts is required to break through. This means that some kind of group and mass evangelism strategy must be developed in order to reach viability as a cell church. The formula introduced in chapter 4 helps us understand this.

Formula for Revival

Prayer X Enthusiasm X **CONTACTS** + Assimilation X Cells = REVIVAL

The objective is to gather enough members to reach critical mass of at least 120 committed adults. Realistically that means that a larger number than 120 must be connected to the effort. In order to break through stagnation and build up to critical mass, a church must embrace a purposeful strategy to multiply contacts.

14

THE PRINCIPLE OF ASSIMILATION

✝

Wesley knew how to pen his sheep!
—George Whitefield

Assimilating every new believer into productive ministry is a principle for worldwide revival in the twenty-first century.

George Whitefield was a contemporary and friend of John Wesley. It was Whitefield who introduced Wesley to "field preaching," where an evangelist preached to crowds in open fields. Both Wesley and Whitefield preached to thousands during the eighteenth century. Many consider Whitefield a better preacher and evangelist than Wesley. In appeal and popularity, George Whitefield was the Billy Graham of the eighteenth century.

In his memoirs, Benjamin Franklin speaks of Whitefield with great admiration. "Every accent, every emphasis, every modulation of voice was so perfectly well-turned and well-placed, that, without being interested in the subject, one could not help being pleased with the discourse." Franklin described the experience of listening to Whitefield preach as "a pleasure of much the same kind with that received from an excellent piece of music." Franklin was more interested in scientific experiments than spiritual truth and even devised an experiment to test Whitefield's speaking voice. Franklin concluded that Whitefield could easily address 30,000 people "standing in an open place."[1]

WESLEY, NOT WHITEFIELD MOVEMENT

Michael Henderson raises an interesting question about Whitefield in his book *John Wesley's Class Meeting*. "Why then is it known as the Wesleyan Revival rather than the Whitefield Revival?"[2]

Whitefield himself reveals the answer in comments he made toward the end of his life. He concluded that Wesley had been successful in evangelism and *assimilation* while he, (Whitefield) although successful in evangelism, had been a failure in assimilation. Whitefield said that Wesley had put his converts into "classes" (cells), "something that I neglected to do." Whitefield confessed to John Pool, a former follower who became a disciple of Wesley, that Wesley's fruit remained because Wesley "knew how to pen his sheep." About his own ministry he lamented, "My people are a rope of sand."[3] Whitefield knew that nothing had been put into place to hold his converts together during or after his ministry.

After personally interviewing Whitefield on this issue, Adam Clark, an early Methodist historian wrote, "Did Mr. Whitefield see his error (in not using classes)? He did, but not till it was too late. His people, long unused to it, would not come under this discipline."[4]

Finding the answer to assimilation is essential for church planters, pastors of existing churches, leaders of mission sending organizations and para-church ministries. Church planters must find answers about response and assimilation because new churches can only be built by successfully forming the response into groups and congregations.

Pastors of existing churches need to solve their assimilation problem because new members enter through the front door and exit through a big back door. Mission organizations need an answer to effective assimilation in order to participate in response when it explodes all around them. Para-church ministries need to solve the assimilation problem because they are often successful in harvesting through special media events but have a history of losing the response before it can be conserved within a local church.

It is sad but true: revival in the twentieth century church was more like Whitefield than like Wesley.

A Reaping and Keeping Question

Most church leaders probably believe that the church had a reaping and harvesting problem in the twentieth century. An honest evaluation of what has happened may reveal that harvest was not the only problem, or even the most serious problem of the church.

What if we could count all of the people who made a decision to become a Christian during the last half of the twentieth century? Suppose all of those who responded to the Gospel were now active in a church somewhere. Most pastors would be thrilled! In fact, additional services or larger meeting places would be required.

This view of the past growth of the church might move us to ask "keeping" questions instead of "reaping" questions. Why has the church been unable to keep these people? How does the church assimilate those who respond to the Gospel? If this is indeed a century of harvest, how will the church assimilate that harvest?

Without an effective assimilation system, the church will realize no more from the harvest in the twenty-first century than it has in the twentieth; no more from the pagan 10/40 world than it has realized from the Christian West. To be able to assimilate large numbers of new converts into a local church and prepare them to be part of the harvest seems impossible today. But if the church could do it, it would fundamentally change how the church reaches the world.

Assimilation is one of the essential elements in the formula for revival introduced in chapter 4. It is so important and so often neglected that I will cover it in detail as an expansion principle in this chapter.

Formula for Revival

Prayer X Enthusiasm X Contacts + **ASSIMILATION** X Cells = REVIVAL

Russia

The recent record of the church in Russia points out weaknesses in the old approach of good harvest and poor assimilation. After the fall of the "iron curtain" in August of 1991, the former Soviet Union broke into 15 fragments. This was not only an incredible political event but an amazing spiritual event. Citizens of the old Soviet Union who had been indoctrinated as atheists for 70 years opened up to the Gospel in ways never imagined.

When the door to the former Soviet Union opened, evangelizing ministries descended upon these new countries with great zeal. A large number of mission agencies responded to the unprecedented opportunity by committing significant amounts of personnel and resources to harvest the response. A few of these also focused on the long-range development of local churches.

In spite of the uncoordinated effort made by the churches in the West, unusual response occurred. Over the next several years, evangelists reported on the great numbers who were turning to Christ. When I heard stories about thousands believing, I wanted to cry out: "What are you doing here telling me about this? Why aren't you there, preparing the church to nurture the ones you won?"

The Russian harvest was more about reaping than conserving. Missionaries preached, prophesied and promoted but never got around to planting enough churches to assimilate the harvest.

Evidently they expected the existing churches that had survived communism to fill the gap between harvest and conservation. But the old church wineskins were just as ineffective in Russia as in the West at gathering and containing the harvest.

> Most of the evangelistic efforts of the church begin with the multitudes under the assumption that the church is qualified to conserve what good is done. The result is our spectacular emphasis upon numbers of converts, candidates for baptism, and more members for the church, with little or no genuine concern manifested toward the establishment of these souls in the love and power of God, let alone the preservation and continuation of the work.[5]

The assumption was that the church in the communist world could use the same church design as the church in the West and have greater results. Why would we think that churches that lived under the oppression and paranoia of communism for 70 years could use the same traditional design as churches in a free society and yet have better results?

"Fugitive Preachers"

John Wesley had little patience with what he called "fugitive preachers" who "presented a message and called for commitment but did not form the people into groups for follow-up."[6] Eventually Wesley refused to preach in an area unless classes (cells) were first formed to care for the new believers. His comment: "How dare you beget children for the Murderer!"

Ministries working in responsive countries may be tempted to detach from the church at both ends of the mission process. They have little or no local church accountability and no effective strategy for planting or using the churches that exist. Others have church roots back home but only seed-sowing methods or social ministries in the target country. The end result is the same: response without responsibility.

In far too many cases, harvest has come in the midst of a mentality that preaches and evangelizes without adequately planting and assimilating. At best this results in spiritual abandonment; at the worst, spiritual abortion. "What good would it have been for His ultimate objective to arouse the masses to follow Him if these people had no subsequent supervision nor instruction in the Way?"[7]

This harvesting approach is shortsighted and irresponsible. When the window of opportunity closes or response slows down, much of the fruit of preaching and evangelizing is lost because the church that remains is not prepared to contain and continue the harvest. Preaching and evangelizing cannot be separated from planting new churches and strengthening existing ones.

The only way for a church to stop this bleeding is to use an effective assimilation and equipping system. Harvest (reaping) and holiness (keeping) are two sides of the same revival coin and must never be separated. If an assimilation process is not in place, no matter how effective the harvest may be, the harvest will be lost.

The New Testament Church Harvested and Assimilated

Assimilation is one of the major differences between Jesus' church and the twentieth century church. The first century church was able to win, assimilate and mobilize large numbers of converts. Jesus' system that kicked into operation after Pentecost was quite impressive because it was able to:

- Operate in spiritual power and life
- Get the attention of unbelievers and bring them to conversion
- Assimilate new believers into a reproducing community
- Quickly transform new believers through community edification
- Involve new believers in the expansion process
- Develop necessary leaders through its community system
- Transplant the church in "Jerusalem, Judea, Samaria and the world"

And all of this was accomplished with ordinary believers, without seminaries, denominations, special programs, para-church organizations or mass communications.

Assimilating thousands of new believers into the church in a brief period of time is one of the miracles of Pentecost. The Pentecost converts were gathered out of raw response and transformed during a brief preparation period in Jerusalem in such a way that they were able to return home and transplant the nature and design of church.

I am not suggesting that we will ever find a quick fix or easy formula for church harvest. But I believe we can rediscover the dynamic connection between initial response and church expansion we see in the first century church. With the media possibilities of today, if the church could duplicate only a fraction of what happened immediately after Pentecost, the harvesting potential would increase exponentially.

> It is ironic when one stops to think about it. In an age when facilities for rapid communication of the Gospel are available to the church as never before, we are actually accomplishing less in winning the world for God than before the invention of the horseless carriage.[8]

THE METHOD OF ASSIMILATION

Assimilation was the major challenge of the church during its first weeks of existence. 8000 new converts were added to the church in the first week. This type of increase continued in the early days of the church. How could a movement of 500 assimilate 8000 new members? These new members had been recruited in a large group meeting when Peter preached and the other disciples worked the large crowd. The new church would continue to come together for these special large group meetings. Some kind of supplement meeting would be required because the large group at the Temple could not assimilate the harvest into the practical life of the movement. The large group could not adequately prepare the new believers to establish the movement in their own cultures.

Let us consider the practical logistics of this situation. 500 Christians had to care for 8000 new converts. This is a ratio of one Christian for every 16 new believers! A reproducible method, an effective care system, an on-the-job training center, a practical demonstration and an inexpensive place were all required for this.

Jesus had prepared for the situation that arose at Pentecost. He had assimilated and taught His leaders in a small group. This small group approach was reproducible and could be managed and expanded. Jesus also used homes as a venue for His small group. The homes gave a degree of privacy and allowed Jesus to disciple in a more relaxed and personal way than possible in large crowds.

JERUSALEM MEETING PLACES

Some of the 500 Christians and the 8000 new converts were from Jerusalem. Early in Jesus' ministry it is recorded "and a great multitude from Galilee followed; also from Judea and Jerusalem . . ."(Mark 3:7).

We can speculate that a significant number of the 8000 early believers were from Jerusalem or had relatives there It is logical then that the first century church organized in small groups in the homes of the Christians and new believers who lived in Jerusalem and the surrounding area.

Some of these Jerusalem citizens are mentioned in the Gospels. The home of John Mark and his Mother served as a center for Jesus and would be used to assimilate large numbers of new believers during the first days of the church. The upper room undoubtedly was used for group meetings.

Joseph of Arimathea, as a wealthy man, would have had a large home that could accommodate several groups. The same is true of Nicodemus.

The home where Jesus healed the lame man who was lowered down through the roof was surely a meeting place. Blind Bartimaeus had a family and a house that could be used for a meeting. The same is true of the lame man that was healed by the Pool of Saloam. Barnabus had property in Jerusalem that he later sold to help with the needs of the new believers. This property could be used to provide a meeting place.

Groups could have met in the suburbs as well. Jesus was often in the home of Lazarus, Mary and Martha in Bethany, six miles from Jerusalem. The home at Emmaus where Jesus walked with Cleopas and another disciple after the resurrection was only four miles from Jerusalem.

It makes sense that the home of every Christian in Jerusalem and the surrounding areas was used for the purpose of assimilation.

Were There Enough Homes in Jerusalem?

How many homes were needed to accommodate these new converts? Lets look at the numbers. Eight thousand new believers would equal 700 group meetings with eleven to twelve adults in each group. Seven hundred homes in Jerusalem would be required if one group met in one home every day of the week. It is within reason that 700 of the 8500 believers had homes or relatives with homes in Jerusalem. Of course, we can divide that by seven if each group met on only one day of the week. I believe, however, that the Scripture indicates each group met every day in the beginning.

But this is not a problem because home groups give several other options. Let us suppose that one group met in the morning, another in the afternoon and yet another in the evening. Meeting three groups per day means that only 234 homes would be required to provide a home for each of the 700 groups.

If only 234 homes were opened in Jerusalem, the Pentecost church could experience exactly what is recorded in Acts. All 8000 met daily in a large group and small group expression. "And day by day continuing with one mind in the temple, and breaking bread from house to house, they were taking their meals together with gladness and sincerity of heart, praising God, and having favor with all the people. And the Lord was adding to their number day by day those who were being saved" (Acts 2:46-47).

This practical small group and home strategy gave a way to assimilate a large number of new believers. Jesus' church, Wesley's church and cell churches today are all successful in assimilation because of the community design. These models are organized around a basic family unit that is able logistically and doctrinally to assimilate new members. This kind of assimilation is essential for twenty-first century revival.

15
THE PRINCIPLE OF BALANCE

✝

The small group, then, must be both supplemental and normative...
supplemental in that it does not replace corporate worship;
normative in the sense of being basic church structure,
equally important with corporate worship.
—Howard Snyder

Balancing the church in large group and small group life is a principle for worldwide revival in the twenty-first century.

For years John Stokes dreamed of getting Osce, his one winged eagle, back into the sky. The eagle had been shot and left with a four-inch stump on one side. John used Osce in educational programs for zoos and foundations dedicated to the protection of America's eagles.

Besides eagles, John's other passion was hang-gliding. These two passions led him to design an eagle-size gliding harness, a sling-like pouch so that Osce could once again fly. To practice, John first suspended Osce in the harness from a beam in a barn to make sure that the eagle would not harm itself.

On the big day, Stokes took his glider to Lookout Mountain Flight Park near Trenton, GA. At 7 A.M. he got into his harness and then an assistant put Osce into the special harness above John. The pilot of an ultra-light airplane took off with the glider behind. At 2000 feet, Stokes released the towline. He and Osce were alone, gliding on the wind like eagles. After 13 years of watching other birds from the ground, the one-winged eagle was back where he belonged.[1]

This *Reader's Digest* story includes a picture of John and Osce in flight. John is suspended from his glider and the eagle is hanging in its harness below the glider's wings just over John. The magnificent head of the eagle looks out from the harness, eyes bright with the thrill of flight.

But the picture is tragic in many ways. For the eagle it is an illusion of flight. It is artificial and mechanical. It is better than nothing, but so much less than intended.

The story shows the difficulty of getting a one-winged bird airborne. Machines, special harnesses, airplanes and an expert in hang-gliding were necessary to duplicate the natural flight of an eagle with two wings. This picture reminded me of the one-winged church and all of the extras necessary to get it back in the sky as God intended.

THE TWO-WINGED CHURCH

The story of the two-winged church has helped me understand the importance of a balanced large group and small group paradigm. I can vividly remember the details of the Saturday afternoon when the concepts of the large group and small group came together for me. That moment of epiphany grew into the following parable.

Once upon a time God created a church with two wings. One was a large-group wing and the other was a small-group wing. With these two wings the church could soar high into the heavens, come into the presence of Creator and do His bidding over all the earth.

One day the wicked serpent who had no wings, came to the two-winged church and said, "Do you know you can fly with just one wing?" "Yes! You can fly with just a large group wing." And so the church that had been created with two wings began to try to fly with just the large-group wing. And sure enough, if it beat that large-group wing long enough and hard enough it could get air borne. But it never flew very high, never went very far from its original take-off point, and as one-winged things are prone to do, many times it went in circles. But it could fly.

This happened sometime in the fourth century.

From that time forward the church, created as a two-winged church, used only the large-group wing. Finally the small-group wing died at the side of the two-winged church.

From time to time the church remembered those days in the past when it had been able to soar high into the heavens, come into the presence of the Creator and do His bidding over all the earth. But now it was too late. The two-winged church had become a one-winged, earth bound institution.

One day the Creator returned and recreated another two-winged church: with a large-group wing and a small-group wing. Once again the church could soar high into the heavens, come into the presence of the Creator and do His bidding over all the earth.

Flying with One Wing

It does not matter which one of an eagle's wings is shot off. The absence of either wing dooms the bird to a flightless existence unless an incredible amount of artificial assistance makes up for the absent wing.

For long periods of its history, the church has attempted to fly with only one wing. The traditional church has tried to do God's will by using only the large-group, one-day a week wing. The house church has tried to fly with only the small-group wing.

Ten years ago pastors often asked the question, "Where is the evidence for small groups in the New Testament?" During the past decade a large body of biblical scholarship and numerous working models have answered that question to the satisfaction of many pastors. More recently, I have been surprised that another question has been asked. "Where is the evidence for the large group in the New Testament?"

These two questions reveal the power of paradigms. Paradigms are those perceptions and perspectives that color how we interpret life, receive information and apply the facts around us. If our paradigm is church as a large group then we see the large group in the New Testament and may be blinded to the small group. If our paradigm is church as small groups, then we see small groups and may be blinded to the large group expression in the New Testament. The twenty-first century church needs a balanced perspective.

House Church Definition

The term "house church" has been used over the years in at least three definitions. First, the term has been used in a practical sense. Many churches start in a home and then move into a traditional expression with a church building. This practical startup group is often referred to as a house church. Second, some traditional churches have also used the term "house church" in a program sense. Small groups that meet in homes as an appendage to traditional programs are called house churches.

Third, the term house church has also been used in a doctrinal sense. Independent groups of Christians meet in a house for both the public and private expression of church. The number of members may vary but generally begins with eight to ten people and can grow to the number of people who can crowd into a house. To these house church proponents, a house church is not just a practical way to begin a church or a program to help minister in an existing church. They have a core doctrinal belief that the church must meet in a house and must be small.

I am using the term in this chapter in the last sense: an independent group of Christians who meet in a house (or some similar facility) for both the public and private expression of church for doctrinal reasons.

The Absence of a Large Group

This definition of house church has periodically surfaced in church history for two reasons. One, outside political powers have prohibited a large group expression of the church and forced the church into a small group expression. The church in China today is an example of this. Two, from time to time radical or revival elements in the church have reacted to large group abuses or weaknesses and have reshaped the church into a small group configuration. The house church movement in the West during the twentieth century is an example of this.

At times, the church must survive without a highly visible local large group. As we move into the twenty-first century, several factors may inhibit the full expression of the large group wing of the church in some areas of the world:

1. Places of persecution where the church must reduce its large group visibility. In these cases, the large group is expressed only at a size that is able to escape the persecution of the government. But invariably, even in these situations, the church finds some way to experience church in both a small-group and large-group expression.

2. Scattered village areas like those parts of Africa where the large group cannot easily express itself geographically.
3. Countries dominated by a state church. Christians in the beginning of a movement may join together across church lines in houses. Wesley's movement began in this way.
4. Members in the Catholic Church may participate in small-group community as a separate way of life. This would follow the historical precedent of Catholics operating in semi-independent "orders" in addition to the traditional Catholic expression of church. The cell-church movement could become a twenty-first century Catholic "order" in the same sense that an unofficial charismatic "order" operated in the twentieth century Catholic Church.

In all of the above situations, the local large group expression of the church is hindered by outside social, political, religious, geographical, institutional or cultural forces. I believe the situations listed above are the circumstantial and not the preferred form of the church. In most places in the world, the church can and should express itself in both a large and small-group setting.

In the remaining pages of this chapter, I want to do two things. First, I want to give supporting evidence for the place of the local large-group wing in the twenty-first century church. Second, I want to give a word of caution and clarity about a new approach to the old house church way of being church.

EVIDENCE FROM SCRIPTURE

The following large-group meetings are mentioned in the book of Acts and support the large-group expression of the church. Some of these expressions are meetings and others are events or special occasions. They differ in size from scores of people to thousands but they are large in nature.

Acts 1	The whole church waiting in one accord in the upper room to receive God's promise
Acts 2	The whole church in evangelism and witness
Acts 3	The whole church preaching after the healing of the lame beggar

Acts 5	The whole church in great fear because of Ananias and Sapphira
Acts 7	The whole church ministering to the needs of a segment of the church
Acts 7	The whole church solving a problem
Acts 7	The whole church chooses the Seven
Acts 11	Peter explains about the conversion of Gentiles
Acts 11	Barnabas and Saul teach the church at Antioch
Acts 12	The whole church in prayer for Peter in prison
Acts 13	The whole church at Antioch selects and sends Barnabas and Saul
Acts 14	The whole Antioch church hears the missionary report of Paul and Barnabas

EVIDENCE FROM THE NATURE OF NEW TESTAMENT MEETINGS

The claim is made that no church buildings used for large group meetings during the first three centuries have been discovered. According to this argument, the church could have only met in a small house church meeting for the first 300 years of the church. This conclusion is highly suspect for several reasons.

First of all, church buildings do not define the early church and its meetings. The church didn't need Roman cathedrals or twentieth century church facilities in the first three centuries. The absence of special church buildings does not disprove the presence of large meetings. Large crowds can meet without large buildings. In fact, Jesus taught large groups in public places without a church building. A long line of evangelists, such as Billy Graham, have conducted large meetings outside of church buildings during the twentieth century.

The church at Pentecost expressed itself in several different types and sizes of meetings without special buildings. They met (possibly all within the course of one day) in the Upper Room as a congregation local expression, in the Temple courtyard as a universal public expression and in the homes of Christians as a small group expression.

Another practical factor sheds further light upon the early church and it's meeting places. Benches, chairs and pews were not used in the early centuries. Therefore, much larger groups could assemble in smaller rooms. Hence, 120 followers of Jesus could be in the upper room of a house in Jerusalem on the day of Pentecost. A large crowd was in a house when the lame man was lowered down through the roof. The church was in an upper room when the young man fell out the window while Paul was preaching.

When the first century church came together in any one of these three ways, it used whatever building or place necessary for that particular expression. The early church met in large groups in the Temple courtyard, in the catacombs, in public buildings, on mountains, in gardens, in upper rooms and in ordinary homes.

Theology, not a building, defines the New Testament church. The point is that Christians in the first century gathered for large meetings, not that Christians met in buildings. A balanced cell church is not dependent upon a building because buildings are functional, not sacred. A balanced cell church will find some way to get together in both a small-group and large-group venue. The place, architecture and frequency of that meeting are incidental and flexible.

Evidence from Archeology

An argument from archeological silence has been offered to support the premise that the church did not meet in larger congregation expressions during the first three centuries. The claim is that archeology has failed to verify the existence of large group sites.

However, it is very possible that some local large group meeting places have been verified. In December of 1998, I visited the Sea of Galilee and Capernaum, the hometown of Peter, Andrew, James and John. Capernaum was the center of Jesus' early ministry. The site of Capernaum was discovered relatively late in archeological history and is untainted by historical revisions that plague some sites in the Holy Land. It has produced some exciting discoveries.

I stood at the site of what is supposed to be Peter's house. If it isn't Peter's house it is the house of a prominent first century Christian. The house was enlarged several times during the first three centuries in order to accommodate larger and larger crowds. Part of this remodeling was done during the first century. Eventually the house could support a congregation at least as large as the 120 adults that gathered in the Upper Room, and probably much larger.

Why was Peter's house remodeled? A restricted house church paradigm cannot explain the need for this remodeling. I believe this, as well as other historical evidence, verifies that the church during the first three centuries was indeed meeting in three expressions:

1. A universal city expression when appropriate
2. A local congregation expression unless persecuted
3. A small group expression in every situation

EVIDENCE FROM BIOLOGY

Cells and organs are only complete when they fit properly into a larger functioning body. For example, an organ such as a liver needs to fit into a body in order to complete its purpose and live without artificial support.

In a cell church, the cell is the basic unit of the life of Christ. But a cell is also part of a larger unit, just as a cell in the body is a unit but part of the whole body. The church is a multi-cellular body made up of many cells. Because Christ's body is a multi-cellular body, it can grow to any size that is appropriate for His purpose. As a multi-cellular organism the church can be a church of 100 or a church of thousands.

I question whether any house church is complete until it functions with both a cell context and a larger local church context. The house church without cells is an independent organ that functions outside of an integrated body, or it is a single large cell. This kind of single cell body is like an amoeba. It is a body, but it is limited in the functions and tasks it can perform.

Independent and self-sufficient organs are not possible in God's biological world without artificial help from outside machines. A heart or liver will continue to function outside of the body only with a great deal of medical help. I do not believe it is possible in the New Testament world either. Without a larger local body expression, the house church is only a solitary cell or a disconnected organ.

EVIDENCE FROM PERSECUTION

Most house churches in areas of persecution such as China find a way to function in both a large group and small group expression. In times of persecution, the church raises the public large-group expression just as high as it will go before the government chops its head off. The church then operates in a large-group expression up to that level until the government relaxes or increases pressure.

Billy Graham recounts several visits to house churches in China during his 1988 visit. His description reveals a house church meeting in a facility that could accommodate a large group. "We arrived unannounced but not unexpected, at a three-story building that held an independent house church. People were crammed everywhere, including on the stairways; three-quarters of them appeared to be young. On the first two floors, they were watching color television sets that were monitoring the service on the third floor."[2]

Why does the persecuted church risk more persecution by testing the limits of oppressive governments in order to meet in larger groups? If these churches believe in the small group expression of church alone they will be satisfied to remain in only small groups.

During a recent decade of persecution in Ethiopia (1982-1992) the church was driven underground into cells. For ten years these Christians whispered their songs of worship so that their neighbors would not turn them in to the communist government. During this time, this Mennonite Church of Ethiopia grew from 5000 to 50,000 members. After the oppression was lifted, a Christian woman commented, "When we were whispering our songs in the small groups we longed for the time that we would be able to sing out loud together in worship."

This is an interesting contrast. Persecuted Christians who are forced to meet in small groups long to participate in large-group worship with other Christians. God puts the large group in their hearts, even if persecution restricts a large group application. On the other hand, some Christians who have the freedom to worship in a large group see the large group as unimportant or unnecessary because of historical abuses or doctrinal interpretations.

Evidence from New Testament Leadership

A popular term used to describe house church leadership is "flat leadership." This means that leaders are connected in an equal relationship rather than at authority levels and leadership for a larger church is unnecessary. This flat-leadership paradigm seems to ignore what is actually happening in the New Testament. I do not see flat leadership in the ministry of Jesus or Paul. No matter how much I dislike the abuses of leadership, I must not allow historical abuses to distort the nature of leadership in the New Testament. To read flat leadership back into the New Testament to me is historical revisionism.

Leadership in the New Testament operates beyond a strictly small group or house church level. In Paul's system the leader roles of elder and deacon functioned beyond the single-cell house church level. Aquila and Priscilla function as house church leaders but no titles are ever used for them. Therefore, some church situation other than a classic house church must have required the elder and deacon roles. These roles as described in the New Testament are required when cells of the church fit together in a large body configuration.

A balanced two-wing approach gives a way for these different types of New Testament leadership to work. The solution is not to remove or water down authority in the New Testament leadership structure; the solution is to go back to New Testament servant leadership. The twenty-first century church needs servant leadership, not flat leadership.

A distortion of the nature of the church invariably results in the distortion of the leadership of the church. The large-group-wing paradigm distorts leadership by overemphasizing authority. The small-group-wing paradigm distorts leadership by overemphasizing independence, individualism and personal freedom.

A New Hybrid House Church

A new hybrid house church approach suggests a different sort of large-group expression. This new model is explained in a book by Wolfgang Simson, *Houses that Change the World*.[3]

In this hybrid approach, the small-group expression of the church continues to be small independent groups of Christians meeting in houses in the classic house church expression. The new twist is that the independent groups are encouraged to meet together from time to time in a "city church" expression as an "interdependent" expression of large group worship. This city church expression is supposed to take the place of the local large-group expression of the church. Local churches with a large-group expression such as a traditional church or a cell church are unnecessary in this hybrid house church model.

This approach seems to express the church from a para-church perspective. Such a church is strong in small-group ministry and open to broad universal cooperation but weak in the area of local church expression.

The problem in the hybrid house church model is that the large-group and small-group expressions of the church are not allowed to come together as one integrated local body that is larger than a house church. The only option for being church in Simson's hybrid house teaching is for a church to operate as a single cell in a house-church expression and from time to time to operate in a large group expression as a city church. A multi-cellular local church seems to be at best discouraged, and at worst denounced.

I believe this approach distorts the New Testament picture of the church. The local church is the place where both the large-group and small-group wings of the church are integrated into one body. It is at the local church level that the church flies with both wings. The hybrid house church has created a bird with a strong small-group wing but with a large-group wing that only flaps when it gathers as a flock. In its city expression, the large group is so far removed in distance, authority and common purpose that it severely weakens the life of the church at the implementing local church level.

Of course, a local cell church can and should gather together in area city celebrations with other churches when possible. This is beginning to happen in different cities around the world. A city celebration is an appropriate venue for the church to experience a "universal" aspect of the church. But cell churches gather for these kinds of universal, city expressions as functioning two-winged churches. They do not gather together as one-winged house groups that are looking for a large-group expression so they can flap a vague large-group wing.

INDEPENDENCE IS A DANGER

In 1991 I met with a group of leaders from several house churches. These house churches had all grown out of the same para-church ministry. They met separately each week in small groups in homes, but without a large-group expression.

The leaders of these house churches were exploring the possibility of forming into one church. The first time we met together, I shared some of the basic values and concepts of cell church life. These values fit their theology of ministry. I met with them several other times in an attempt to develop a strategy for coordinating their work as one church.

As we moved along, I began to notice a strange dynamic. They could not agree on a leader or a common strategy. They were all so independent that they could not bring themselves to function as one coordinated unit. Here were leaders with the same theology, the same approach to ministry, the same training and even the same covering ministry, yet they could not cooperate with each other in a local church expression.

What was their problem? Their church paradigm was unbalanced. Their incomplete paradigm had developed an independent approach to ministry that made it difficult to submit to one another and to spiritual authority.

If independent house churches find it difficult to cooperate at a local church level, why do we think they will be effective in cooperating at a city church level? House churches need to practice large group life at the local level before expecting large group life to work at the universal city level.

I praise God that the cell church can take many different forms. However, I believe that the New Testament design of the church will express itself someway at the local church level in both large-group and small-group life. It is my prayer that the wonderful leaders who love the house church will receive a revelation from God about the balanced nature of the church.

A Rum and Song Ee

Over the last several decades God has revealed a balanced church to others around the world in many different ways. Recently a Korean pastor shared his beautiful story of God's revelation to him.

Rev. Tai Soo Han pastors Don Am Dong Evangelical Church in Seoul, Korea. Tai Soo began his ministry in a traditional church as an intern responsible for the young people. He became concerned about the life of the church and was convinced that sermon-centered ministry was limited in changing the life style of believers.

In 1976 he heard Rev. Lee Dong Won preach about small groups. Tai Soo met him, learned more about small groups and accepted the word as a revelation from God. In his spirit came the conviction that "this is it!"

Soon after, Tai Soo planted a new church and also served as youth minister in a 50-year-old traditional church. He began with 20 to 30 young people and put them into small groups. This grew to 35 cells and 200 members.

His first daughter was born during this time and he named her A Rum. A Rum means "flower bouquet" and in Korean can also mean "the biggest." He chose this name because of the revelation from God that the church is balanced with a large-group and small-group design. "My first daughter represents my large group ministry."

Over the next few years Tai Soo moved his church four different times to different locations in Seoul. His members stayed with him through all of the moves and began to bear fruit in evangelism through small groups. His second daughter was born during this time. He named her Song Ee which means "one flower" to represent the small group.

God's church is a lovely bouquet of flowers made up of beautiful single flowers.

PART 4
REVIVAL STRATEGY

*God is working out in time a plan which he conceived in a past eternity
and will consummate in a future eternity.*
—John Stott

16
CULTURAL STRATEGY

✝

*Our goal is not to tear down and destroy the structure of culture
but to seek an incarnation of Christ in each and every particular culture,
to see the character and beauty of Jesus manifested
in each distinct cultural world.*
—Charles L. Chaney

Bridging culture with the Gospel is a strategic paradigm for worldwide revival in the twenty-first century.

The disciples followed Jesus through Samaria on one of His detours. His route was unusual because first century Jews walked around Samaria to avoid what they considered to be a race inferior in culture and religion.

John said that Jesus, "*Had* to pass through Samaria" (John 4:4). This was a spiritual necessity. Jesus had an appointment to share the Gospel with a woman at Jacob's Well. I believe that another part of the necessity to go through Samaria was cultural. Jesus bridged a wide cultural gulf concerning Samaritans and women. The geographical shortcut through Samaria was a straight path to cultural truths that His followers needed to learn.

The Gospel always has a cultural context. However, adapting to culture is never easy because culture sets the boundaries of who we are and what we do. Culture defines our language, dress, traditions, food, customs, smells, perceptions, history and architecture. Culture is about familiarity, safety, comfort and "the way we do things." Other cultures shock our inner sense of appropriate social behavior and values.

Jesus' disciples experienced culture shock as they marveled at the events in Samaria.

Culture shock

Following Jesus to Thailand resulted in several memorable experiences of culture shock for me as well.

My culture shock began after the first full week in Thailand. The heat, the smells, and the traffic astounded me as I drove my family on the wrong side of the road across Bangkok to Thonburi Christian Church. During worship the sounds of the strange tonal language overwhelmed me. After worship, sitting on the floor of the Pastor's home around a bamboo mat, our family was honored with a Thai meal. When I began to eat, my taste buds were shocked because the food was so hot and spicy that it literally hurt.

I found the greatest shock in the church itself. It was a carbon copy of the church I had left in Texas only a few days before. The order of service, the Western hymns, the pulpit, rows of seats and even the two boards at the front of the auditorium with the amount of the morning offering and attendance were there. It shocked me that the church in one of the least Christian countries in the world was not different in nature or design.

Dr. Francis DuBose, while professor at Golden Gate Baptist Seminary in San Francisco, visited Thailand in the early 1980s. His visit followed an extensive missions research trip in Africa. Dr. DuBose talked about the "psyche of the African Christian." The African Christians might begin their worship with the pomp and trappings they had learned from missionaries. The first songs would be the obligatory Western hymns. Then they would beat the drums and sing their own songs. Dr. DuBose said, "That is the moment they really started to worship." To an African their musical instrument of choice, the drum, was a door to their psyche. Culture can be a door to the hearts of a people.

Food and Culture

I eventually learned to drive on the left side of the road and to communicate in the Thai language. I adapted to the hot peppers, and even came to crave the spicy dishes. From time to time though I experienced culture shock because of the food underneath the pepper.

A young woman and her mother who lived two hours north of Bangkok prepared a meal for Mary and me. She ran a small restaurant and served some specialty dishes. Our party included an older couple and a pretty, prim Thai missionary. She had grown up in a city in southern Thailand.

Conversation before dinner revealed that the main dish was fruitbat, a delicacy in that part of Thailand.

I fervently prayed the missionary prayer. "Lord I will get it down if you will keep it down." However, I also devised a plan. My plan was to have the three Thais eat the major portion of the meat and for me to move the absolute maximum amount of fruitbat around on my plate underneath the rice and vegetables and to put the absolute minimum in my mouth.

My plan began to fall apart when I realized that the Thai couple only had one or two good teeth and the fruitbat was being fried very crisp. But I still had the young Thai woman who had a good set of teeth and I hoped a healthy appetite.

A platter of fruitbat was placed in the center of our table, and I relaxed a little because eating that platter seemed doable. However, to my alarm the woman began frying more fruitbat. I quickly noticed that the young Thai woman was not attacking the fruitbat with any more vigor than Mary and me. I wanted to shout to her, "You are Thai." "What is your problem?" "Stop being a prima donna!" "Eat fruitbat!"

The fruitbat platter seemed to be growing instead of disappearing. I had to pick up my pace in eating the fruitbat because I had hidden as much as I could under the rice and vegetables.

So, I fell back on plan B. Thais will help each other's plate like an indulgent grandmother. I assumed the Thai grandmother role and started helping everyone's plate with portions of fruitbat. Each time I would take a piece of fruitbat for myself, I would put one or two pieces on the plates of everyone else. The first time I did that, the young Thai missionary looked up at me with a little displeased look. The second time I gave her some fruitbat she gave me a hard look. Finally after the third or fourth time she decided that I was teasing her.

We did get through the meal without insulting our host. However, I wanted to gag Mary at the end of the meal when our host asked us how we liked the fruitbat. Trying to be nice she said, "Oh, it was very good!" The response of our host made my stomach turn. "Next time I will get some really big fruitbat for you."

Culture does have humorous moments, but it is deadly serious when living it out.

Jesus and Culture

The incarnation had a cultural context and was a cultural event. Jesus "emptied" Himself of the surroundings of heavenly culture and became part of human culture in a small country on the backside of the Roman Empire.

He used the language, the customs, the traditions, the manners and the dress of His culture. He did not go out in the desert as a hermit to escape society. Jesus lived in a Jewish sub-culture, but put a world face to it. In the broader culture the languages were Greek, Latin, Hebrew and Aramaic. The government was Roman, the worldview was Greek, and the spirit world had multiple expressions with scores of pagan religions.

Prayer to Jesus was a cultural language. The model prayer Jesus taught is about His Kingdom culture coming and being done "on earth as it is in heaven." Jesus' great commission is a cultural commission. To "go" guarantees a cross-cultural experience because the farther we go from our Jerusalem into Judea, Samaria and the world, the greater the cultural challenge.

A church that will reach the billions in the twenty-first century world must apply Jesus' first century incarnation model. Using that model, Christianity was able to bridge the diverse cultures of the first century world while maintaining the integrity of the culture of God's Kingdom.

> Our goal is not to tear down and destroy the structure of culture but to seek an incarnation of Christ in each and every particular culture, to see the character and beauty of Jesus manifested in each distinct cultural world.[1]

Filters

The Gospel is never compromised and never changes because "Jesus Christ is the same: yesterday, today and forever." However, through the method and the messenger, the Gospel is presented in a way that people of a different culture can hear, understand and receive. Paul's statement,

"I become all things to all people," is not about the Gospel but about culture.

People in other cultures should not be seen as totally different. Similarities outweigh differences in spite of appearances. "People differ widely but people don't differ wildly."

The church best accomplishes God's mission to witness to all people when it allows similarities to bridge cultural differences. Some principles and values are universal and apply to every culture. Common theology and functions work themselves through contextual filters: cultural, political, religious and social filters. Out of this process an indigenous strategy can be developed. This is the reason that Christians in cross-cultural mission situations can learn from each other.

Contextual Filters

COMMON THEOLOGY
God's Love	Man's Sin
Scripture	Salvation
Trinity	Faith

COMMON FUNCTIONS
Evangelism	Prayer
Bible Study	Missions
Leadership	Worship
Discipleship	Groups

CULTURAL FILTER
POLITICAL FILTER
RELIGIOUS FILTER
SOCIAL FILTER

INDIGENOUS STRATEGY

Becoming a Christian is a cultural decision. The Gospel must be filtered through belief systems in order for its truth to be accepted. A person who is not a Christian must understand the Gospel out of the context of his or her own earthly culture. "Jesus died for these people around the world. He did not die to preserve our Western way of life. He did not die to make Muslims stop praying five times a day. He did not die to make Brahmins eat meat."[2]

A Buddhist and the Death of Christ

Using a western approach to explain the death of Christ to a Buddhist means that person will probably never "hear" the Gospel. The typical western explanation of the death of Christ goes something like this: "Christ died on the cross for you. He suffered a terrible death. He was humiliated. He was abused and brutally whipped. He was nailed to a cross between two criminals."

For those who believe in innocent vicarious suffering this explanation may bring about a great appreciation and gratitude for the suffering of Christ. But to share that with a Buddhist almost certainly means that the Gospel will not be "heard" with understanding. Buddhism knows nothing of innocent, sacrificial or vicarious suffering. Buddhism stands upon one basic principle of impersonal logic. "Do good and you receive good, do evil and you receive evil."

The reverse application of this kharma principle results in the dangerous and damaging conclusion that the more suffering in a person's life, the more evil that person must have done. The Buddhist thinks, "Look how much Jesus is suffering. This must mean that he is a terrible person or a powerless god."

A new Gospel filter is required. Christ must be introduced to a Buddhist at the point of creation and incarnation before explaining the meaning of the cross. This does not compromise the doctrine of the sacrificial death of Christ; it just begins the Gospel presentation in a way that a Buddhist can hear within the context of their cultural framework. Paul used this cultural approach with the Atheneans at Mars Hill. Ralph Winter argues:

> I see the world church as the gathering together of a great symphony orchestra where we don't make every new person coming in play a violin in order to fit in with the rest. We invite the people to come in to play the same score . . . the Word of God . . . but to play their own instruments, and in this way there will issue forth a heavenly sound that will grow in the splendor and glory of God as each new instrument is added.[3]

Culture is Dangerous

The church is a historical paradox. On the one hand the Bible and the church have been the greatest instruments for justice and freedom in the world. The gradual movement from absolute dictatorship to personal freedom cannot be imagined apart from the influence of Christians and the principles in the Bible.

However, earthly culture can also threaten the integrity of the church. Governments use earthly culture to control political agendas and earthly cultures use governments to promote their social agendas. When the church is bound to any earthly culture, it is blinded to Kingdom values and truths. In that case, the church can be used by government or can use government for political and personal purposes.

Many tragedies in the history of mankind resulted from the church confusing Kingdom culture with social, political, economic and religious culture. The Crusades grew out of a cultural interpretation of the Gospel that became political. Thousands were either killed or forced to convert to the political and religious will of the West.

The Roman Catholic Church experienced the darkest days of its history when church culture and political culture became one and the same. For more than 1000 years, political culture drove the Catholic Church to terrible acts such as the Spanish Inquisition and the persecution of other church expressions. Millions of innocent people died because of this unholy marriage of politics and religion. This same unholy alliance between politics and religion drove Reformation churches to persecute and kill Catholics and other Christian groups that were seen as a threat. The marriage of politics and religion caused the Church of England to perpetuate the same kind of horrible persecution and oppression in the name of the church.

Germany, while under the rule of the Nazi Party, is a terrifying example of Christian values silenced by and sacrificed to political culture. Germany was a land of churches when Hitler came to power. Some church leaders such as Martin Neimueler opposed Hitler's policies. However, many German church leaders looked the other way as the Nazi Party restored economic and political stability to Germany at the expense of groups like the Jews. In far too many cases, the German political and social culture spoke for and through the church rather than the church speaking to the culture and the society. The cross was bent into the shape of a political swastika that silenced the church.

A Personal Word about Earthly Culture

Another example of confusing Kingdom and earthly culture is the history of the church in the southern United States. Most, but not all, churches in the south lived out a southern rather than a biblical culture regarding human relationships. These churches and their pastors supported the social, political, economic and religious culture that doomed a group of people to slavery because of their skin color. Pastors, elders and deacons interpreted the Bible and the church from the surrounding culture of slavery.

As a child of the south with Baptist roots, I am haunted by a historical possibility. Suppose that all of the churches in the southern states had lived out a Kingdom culture instead of mirroring the culture of the day. (Some churches, such as the Quakers, did just that.)

I believe that just the Baptist churches in the United States could have changed history. Millions of men, women and children could have enjoyed freedom for the first "four score and seven years" of the life of the nation. Six hundred thousand men would not have died in the Civil War. The United States of America would have escaped debasing the dream of living out the truth that "all men are created equal."

In the years that followed the Civil War, suppose that these same churches had repented and spoken out against the segregation that continued. I believe that the freedom bought by blood and decreed by law would have become a reality. Dr. Martin Luther King Jr. and other civil rights martyrs would not have died. Sunday mornings would be the most racially integrated time in America. The United States of America would value and protect every child equally as a beautiful creation of God no matter what the color of their skin.

Culture Can Blind us to Biblical Truth

Some may claim that I am imposing twenty-first century values upon the nineteenth and twentieth century world. No, I am imposing first century church values upon every century. Some churches and leaders lived out New Testament values in the nineteenth century. John Wesley preached against slavery in the eighteenth century. In the nineteenth century many churches in the north and even some in the south preached against slavery.

During the debate about slavery, the Mason Dixon Line was drawn in between the states of Pennsylvania and Maryland. It became a boundary separating slave-holding states from free states. Churches on both sides of the line were reading the same Bible. How could their conclusions be so different? The answer is culture. Earthly culture is driven by economics, sanctioned by society, and protected and controlled by political systems. When the church is controlled by earthly culture, the truth of the Bible is easily distorted and compromised. And leaders are intimidated and silent.

The church leaders in the south did not perpetuate prejudice by putting on Ku Klux Klan hoods and burning crosses. Their fear to speak out against popular culture perpetuated injustice. The silence of the church allowed bad economic, social and political systems to survive.

Confusing Kingdom culture with a particular earthly culture continues to effect the ministry of the church across the world. This confusion in the twenty-first century may not be as dramatic or as obvious as the illustrations above, but it is just as dangerous to the church. Future Christians may see our cultural silence in the same light as we now see the silence of our forefathers.

"The bible shows the church in the midst of culture, struggling to be faithful but sometimes adulterated by unnatural alliances with paganism and Jewish legalism."[4]

LOVE IS THE BRIDGE TO CULTURE

Jesus was able to bridge great cultural differences because of love. "God so loved the world" is a cultural declaration. Love can cover a multitude of cultural sins and differences. Love is not puffed up with its own personal and cultural rightness; it sees life from the perspective of others. Love values people, protects the dignity of everyone and celebrates differences. Love neutralizes the pride of life and sees inner qualities rather than outer differences. Love looks into the heart.

Around the world mothers love their children in the same way. Parents dream the same dreams for their sons and daughters. Friendship is cherished. Heartache, depression, exhilaration and laughter are experienced universally. People long for freedom and dignity. Around the world the babies that God creates are all the same before culture makes them different.

A song from the Broadway musical *South Pacific* explains the power of culture to teach love or hate:

> You've got to be taught before it's too late;
> Before you are six or seven or eight;
> To hate all the people your relatives hate.
> You've got to be carefully taught.

Jesus knew that if the heart of man changes then culture changes. Change the heart and the culture becomes better. Change the culture and the heart can remain the same.

True revival always penetrates to the roots of earthly cultures and changes the fruits of culture to God's Kingdom values. Revival in the twenty-first century will not happen until the church begins to live out God's kingdom culture on earth.

17
TRANSPLANTING STRATEGY

✝

The fruit of a church . . . is a new church.
—Christian Schwarz

Transplanting strong churches instead of planting seeds is a strategic paradigm for worldwide revival in the twenty-first century.

In Israel the tall palm date trees near the Dead Sea are gradually being replaced with shorter palm date trees. These shorter trees are easier to care for and to harvest. In a desert country that treasures every tree, the taller trees are dug up and transplanted in the cities.

Transplanting trees is also a common practice in Houston, Texas. Almost all of the trees that are less than 30 years old are transplanted. The original trees are removed to develop a housing sub-division. Then new trees are transplanted around the houses.

Special equipment is required for transplanting trees. A huge machine that looks like jaws is attached to a large truck. These jaws are placed around a tree and a large segment of earth is dug out of the ground with the tree and its roots in the middle. Using this method, very large trees can be transplanted if someone is willing to pay the price for instant shade and beauty.

I first learned about transplanting trees while in high school. One of my projects in a vocational agriculture class was to plant 1000 slash pine seedlings. I again experienced transplanting trees firsthand when my father retired and planted a peach orchard with 1000 trees.

Orchards are not planted from seeds but from transplanted trees that are two years old. These trees have been carefully selected and cared for in a nursery. A transplanted tree is larger, stronger and reproduces more quickly than a planted seed. Transplanted fruit trees are also healthier because they are grafted into a special stock that is resistant to root disease.

Seed Planting Strategy

For decades the church has operated with a seed-planting mission paradigm. One person or one family goes out into a new area to plant a new church. The seed-sowing planting strategy has resulted in what I call a "margarine mission strategy:" spread it just as thin and as far as it will go. Churches and mission agencies spread new starts as thin and as evenly as possible all over the world.

In a northern city of the United States, a denomination with the margarine parish paradigm had three churches within a four-mile radius of each other. Two were new church starts. Each church was struggling to build enough momentum to break through to critical mass. The leaders of the three churches wanted to join together as one cell church and establish a strong base so that eventually they could transplant other churches.

The leaders of these churches prayed about the problem and developed an excellent prospectus of how they could join together, reach critical mass more quickly and then begin to reproduce themselves. It looked like an excellent strategy. The plan was presented to the denominational committee responsible for new church starts and helped support the salaries of two of the three pastors.

They turned them down. Why? I have no doubt they were operating in good faith with their paradigm of church planting. They made a decision from a "margarine mission strategy" and their "dots on a map" tracking system. In their annual report three green dots on a map look a lot better than one dot, especially if last year you had three dots. It does not matter if the dots represent small, struggling churches.

I have concluded that this is the most difficult and ineffective of all church starting strategies. Little margin for error is possible in this approach. It is almost impossible to develop momentum, leaving the church plant under attack from all directions. The result is often a church that is stunted and unproductive. This may explain why more than 80 percent of the churches in the world never grow beyond 50 to 100 adult members.

The number of churches is not always the best indicator of the strength of the church in a country or area. Wales has more churches per person than any other country in the world but the average size is less than 15 members per church. The size and quality of the church must be considered when evaluating the strength of the church.

This strategy is so popular because territory is easier to sell back home than quality. Spreading the Gospel everywhere feels good, seems fair because the church is responding to need, looks good on world mission maps and makes for wonderful human interest stories for raising money.

In some cases the church cannot be transplanted but must be planted as a small seed with one missionary. However, the seed planting strategy method has not been just an alternative option to church planting. This approach is the strategy of choice that the church has used for more than a century.

JESUS USED A TRANSPLANT MODEL

The New Testament model of starting churches is transplanting a tree, not planting a seed. Jesus developed a strong strategic church in Jerusalem from which new church starts would be transplanted all over the world. Paul followed this strategy as he transplanted churches from his home base in Antioch. Paul selected target cities and concentrated as much personnel and time into those areas as possible. Even when he was thrown out of a target area he continued to send his support leaders back as often as possible to strengthen his bases.

Think of Jesus' stages of the church as a growing tree as presented in the chart below. The sending church on the left side of the chart represents a strategic church large and strong enough to begin another church. One unit would be a seed (one person or a couple). Two or three innovators would represent a small seedling. A group of twelve would be a small tree with a good root system and the possibility of fruit in a year or so. Jesus' 30 to 70 person support network is a growing tree that is mature enough to produce fruit immediately. A base congregation of 120 is a young full-grown tree that can begin to transplant other trees very quickly.

Church Transplanting

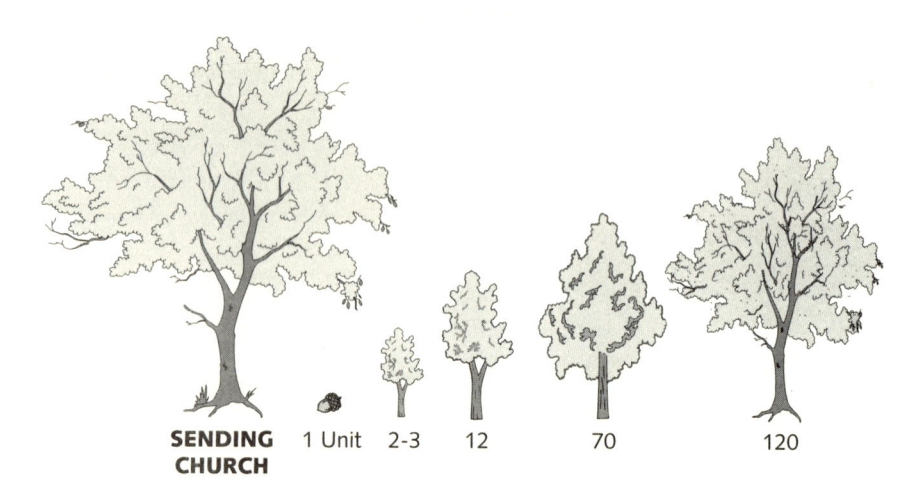

SENDING CHURCH   1 Unit   2-3   12   70   120

The traditional church has used adaptations of the transplant model. In the *hive model* new churches are formed by transplanting a leader and a portion of the original church into a new area. In the *mission model*, a mother church sends out a number of leaders and members to establish a new mission. With the popular *satellite model*, large churches begin a satellite church on a new church campus in a growing area of a city. The senior pastor of the mother church often preaches at both churches until a choice is made about which campus will become the central church. Both sites eventually become strong independent churches.

Unfortunately, these models have not been used as frequently in traditional overseas mission situations, and they have been used to begin traditional staff-based churches instead of community cell-based churches.

Advantages of a Church Transplant

A transplanting strategy has several important advantages over the old seed planting method. Transplanting a church has the advantage in the areas of vision, maturity, experience, momentum, vigor, leadership, evangelism, flexibility, multiplication and options.

First, the new start has a support base with the same vision and values. In fact, the vision, values and culture have formed within a mother church so that a cell culture is in place. Those coming in with hidden agendas are met with an existing community culture that is protected by a strong core.

Second, the larger and more mature a tree is when planted, the stronger it will be and the sooner it will produce fruit. This is true about beginning churches as well. The larger and healthier the church planting team, the stronger the new church will be and the sooner it will produce fruit. In a transplant, the "tree" is large enough to quickly take root and to grow.

Third, because an experienced and trained team is beginning the new work, they are strong enough to model the basic life of the church. A transplant provides tested cell structures and an understanding of the infrastructure of a cell church.

Fourth, momentum can be developed and maintained in a transplant. Essential operating systems can be put into place because cell church infrastructure already exists. Therefore, cells can be set up that can immediately model for new members what it means to live in this kind of church life.

Fifth, a transplant has growth vigor that helps it resist disease and adversity. Peach growers complain that every disease known to man will attack a peach tree. Fruit trees need as much health and vigor as possible to survive and be fruitful. This is also true of a new cell church. A transplanted church has a better ability to overcome adversities than a seed planted with a few Christians.

Sixth, a transplant has enough experienced leaders to model ministry through the life of the cell. Leaders on the team can operate at the four essential leadership levels: coordination, support, supervision and implementation.

Seventh, evangelism contacts are accelerated. Every team member can lead a special contact group. This gives the team the potential for rapidly increasing the number of people connected to the new start. This potential for accelerated contacts also provides the structure for assimilating the new converts into meaningful and productive community life.

Eighth, a transplant gives flexibility in relation to political and religious opposition. A cell church can begin with high or low visibility and exposure depending upon the strength of the opposition. A cell church can even be transplanted into a hostile situation.

Ninth, a transplant can begin to multiply much more quickly. Transplanting a cell church greatly accelerates the growth of a new start. The principle of multiplication applies to all areas of church life. "Just as the true fruit of an apple tree is not an apple, but another tree; the true fruit of a small group is not a new Christian, but another group. The true fruit of a church is not a new group, but a new church. The true fruit of a leader is not a follower, but a new leader. The true fruit of an evangelist is not a convert, but new evangelists."[1]

The life of a tree is in a new tree, not in the tree's fruit. The purpose of a tree is not to produce fruit. The fruit is a secondary benefit for trees. The purpose of a tree is to produce another tree from the fruit. In the bigger picture, the fruit of a tree is an orchard of trees.

Ten, a transplanting model gives a church the option of supporting congregations as part of the mother church or of transplanting a new church. I began to understand this several years ago when the pastor of a strong growing church presented the case study of his church to me.

The pastor explained that his church had operated for years as one church with several integrated congregations. The congregations were all serviced from the same administrative and logistical structure. The church leaders decided to form the congregations into independent churches (missions) in order to promote more growth. Therefore, leaders were assigned, facilities were developed, ministries were duplicated and administrative structures were set up in each new church.

The pastor showed me a chart of growth. It revealed a steady increase for several years, but after implementing the independent-congregations strategy the overall growth immediately leveled off. The pastor commented that they killed their growth "as dead as cold meat."

Why? The support system of administration, logistics and facilities in the mother church had originally served all of the congregations. When these congregations became separate churches, the support system had to be duplicated for each new church. The energy and effort of the new churches was directed toward support systems rather than toward evangelism and growth.

The support system of administration and coordination in a cell church is like an umbrella that stretches over the church. Internal growth can take place by developing new congregations that are supported and protected by the administrative umbrella of the church. A cell church can also grow externally by beginning a new church that has its own administrative and logistical umbrella. Instead of stretching new church starts as thin as possible, the cell church has the option of stretching the support umbrella over dynamic congregations that focus on evangelism and edification. Then, at the proper time and place, a cell church can transplant another separate church from its own support umbrella.

In the twenty-first century, after the first wave of cell church models, I believe cell churches will be transplanted. Imagine what will happen when cell churches begin to transplant dynamic churches. This is why there can be such optimism in the face of the population explosion. At a certain point cell churches will begin to transplant churches exponentially.

A Transplanting Church Model

Antioch Church in Waco, Texas is a classic example of a church transplant. This church was birthed out of the vision of its pastor, Jimmy Seibert. As a young Christian he made a request of God. "Lord, if you have a special dream in your heart, dream it through me. And if there is something no one else is willing to do, do it through me."

The vision was birthed in the womb of Highland Baptist Church in Waco, Texas as a college congregation. For a decade, Highland provided a safe environment in which the dream could grow. Jimmy Seibert and this student-centered congregation have been driven by six passions: a passion for prayer, a passion for worship, a passion for cell community, a passion for holiness, a passion for ministry and a passion for evangelism and missions.

First, prayer has been the driving force that has moved the congregation. Second, the congregation has moved into the presence and glory of God in worship and praise. Third, the congregation was organized into a pure cell structure. Fourth, the congregation used a one-year training course called *Master's Commission* to develop a committed core of leaders who were "willing to live and die" for Christ. Fifth, the congregation targeted students who are one of the groups most responsive to the Gospel. Sixth, the congregation created a dynamic sending arm called Antioch Ministry International.

Effective integrated systems were developed through which these passions could be lived out. Members of the congregation worshiped and prayed passionately. University students and young singles were won and nurtured through the cells. Potential leaders were prepared through short-term mission projects and an intensive discipleship program. Members learned sacrificial ministry in cell life. Finally, these committed Christians were sent around the world to begin new cell churches. This has proved to be a powerful combination.

Highland Baptist Church and the college congregation (including a significant number of older adults) decided to send the college congregation out as a separate church. Antioch Church was transplanted June 6, 1999. Before its first service the leaders and core members raised $150,000 to purchase an abandoned super market near the low-income neighborhoods where the congregation would focus its local ministry. More than 500 people attended the first service at its temporary location at the Heart of Texas coliseum.

On the first Sunday, the new church sent out a team of 20 members on a mission trip to India. The church begins with missionaries in 15 different countries. By the end of 1999, more than 1000 were participating in worship and cell life. This is a transplant of a church tree of huge proportions that will quickly be able to transplant other churches. I believe the mother church, Highland Baptist Church, will quickly return to its previous size.

Antioch is now applying the transplant principle to its mission strategy. For instance, the church formed a strong team of 14 leaders who went to Turkey. The strategy of the team is to establish a strong base congregation in one of the population centers of Turkey. This is an example of a transplanted church that is now transplanting other churches. I believe that God has prepared this church to transplant trees . . . and orchards.

18
INDIGENOUS STRATEGY

✝

*Our paternalism is not only a paternalism toward other peoples;
it is also a paternalism towards God.*
—William A. Smalley

Establishing indigenous urban churches is a strategic paradigm for worldwide revival in the twenty-first century.

Standing by a small graveyard near Lake Victoria in Kenya, I was deeply moved by the sacrifice of the early missionaries who were buried there. Those graves caused me to think about thousands of missionaries who left the comfort and safety of home to take the Gospel to the remotest corners of the world during the past two centuries. Their lives are a testimony of dedication, courage and sacrifice.

To expand in the twenty-first century, the church needs the courage and commitment of these early missionaries. However, a different mission paradigm must be used today. It is not enough to change only the practices of missionaries because churches, denominations and mission agencies are responsible for missionary strategies. These sending groups must develop new strategies for indigenous missions.

William A. Smalley, a former professor of linguistics, defines an indigenous church as one in which "the changes that take place under the guidance of the Holy Spirit meet the needs and fulfill the meanings of that society and not of any outside group."[1] Smalley believes that anything less than a totally indigenous church is a form of paternalism "because we do not trust the Holy Spirit to adapt the church to culture." He maintains that "we are treating the Holy Spirit as a small child with a new toy too complicated and dangerous to handle. Our paternalism is not only a paternalism toward other peoples; it is also a paternalism toward God."[2]

THE WATER OF LIFE IN FOREIGN CUPS

A story from Indian evangelist Sadhu Sunder Singh illustrates the importance of presenting the Gospel in an indigenous and cultural way. A high caste Hindu fainted from the summer heat while sitting on a train in a railway station. A train employee ran to a water faucet, filled a cup with water and brought it to the man. In spite of his condition, the Hindu refused to drink. He would rather die than accept water in the cup of someone from another caste.

Another person noticed that the high-caste passenger had left his own cup on the seat beside him. He grabbed it, filed it with water and returned to offer it to the panting victim. Immediately he accepted the water with gratitude.

Singh's comments about the story go to the very heart of indigenous missions. "This is what I have been trying to say to missionaries from abroad. You have been offering the water of life to the people of India in a foreign cup, and we have been slow to receive it. If you will offer it in our own cup . . . in an indigenous form . . . then we are much more likely to accept it."[3]

The following four interrelated principles are essential in order for the church to offer the water of life in indigenous rather than foreign cups. We will look at each principle in detail in this chapter and will use them as foundational principles for developing mission strategy.

- An indigenous sequence is essential
- Nationals are the best indigenous missionaries
- Cities are the proper place to begin indigenous missions
- Strategic churches are the greatest hope for indigenous expansion

AN INDIGENOUS SEQUENCE IS ESSENTIAL

In Acts 1:8, Jesus gives the direction and the sequence of the Gospel. Jesus' followers and the Gospel are to go to "Jerusalem, Judea, Samaria and the world." This phrase has both a geographical and cultural connotation. However, the presence of the word "Samaria" suggests that culture is important to how Jesus used the phrase. His Gospel is to penetrate every geographical area, people group and culture.

The grid below helps us visualize the indigenous sequence of the church. The left circle suggests that the *most* culturally forgiving mission context is to share the Gospel in a major city, a Jerusalem. The right circle suggests that the *least* culturally forgiving mission context is a village out in the world because witnessing must cross major barriers of language, culture, prejudice, finance and distance.

Jesus strung the sequence of Jerusalem, Judea, Samaria and the world together for a reason. Each point becomes more culturally distant from the preceding one. To go directly from "Jerusalem" to the "world" is too great a distance both geographically and culturally. In the chart below I have added the bottom sequence of a major city, a city, a town and a village. This sequence also reflects distance between each place that is too great to ignore. A great distance separates a major city from a village and that distance is important in developing an indigenous strategy.

Indigenous Expansion

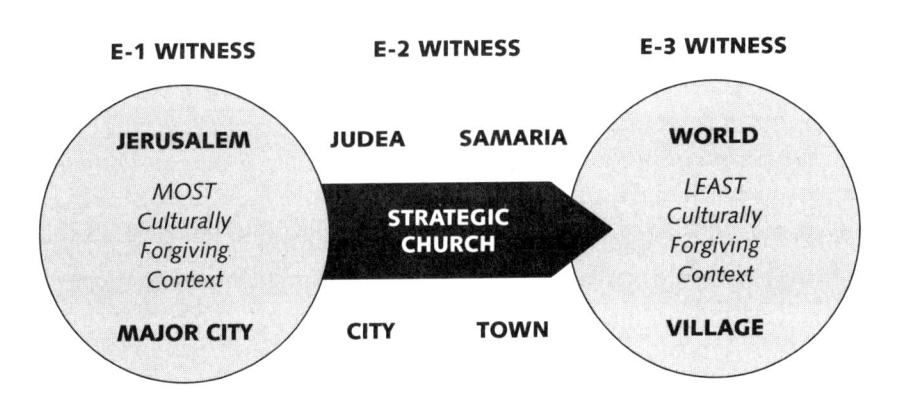

E-1 WITNESS	E-2 WITNESS	E-3 WITNESS
JERUSALEM	JUDEA SAMARIA	WORLD
MOST Culturally Forgiving Context	STRATEGIC CHURCH	LEAST Culturally Forgiving Context
MAJOR CITY	CITY TOWN	VILLAGE

The chart also includes Ralph Winter's wonderful insights on three types of witness that he identifies in Acts 1:8: E-1 Witness, E-2 Witness and E-3 Witness.[4] Winter's teaching supports the importance of sequence in missions and provides a way to chart a mission journey.

1. Penetration into Jerusalem and Judea is E-1 witness. E-1 is "near neighbor" witness and only needs to penetrate one level: the level of communication. E-1 is "near" witness.
2. Penetration into Samaria is E-2 witness. E-2 is "bridge" witness that must cross over the level of communicating the gospel plus the level of prejudice and culture. E-2 is "close" witness.
3. Penetration into the "world" is E-3 witness. E-3 is "cross-cultural" witness and is utterly different in language and culture and is the most extreme of all witness. E-3 is "far" and foreign witness.

Winter believes that "the easiest, most obvious surge forward in evangelism in the world today will come if Christian believers in every part of the world are moved to reach outside their churches and win their cultural near neighbors to Christ. They are better able to do this than any foreign missionary."[5] The New Testament church "turned the world upside down" with E-1 evangelism when the first converts returned home and witnessed to their friends, families and fellow countrymen.

The old foreign missionary strategy has had a measure of success until it is measured against the New Testament church. The New Testament church was able to maximize E-1 witness and E-2 witness. Many different people groups were in Jerusalem on the day of Pentecost. However, they received an E-1 and E-2-witness from Jews of the same religion, language and in many cases culture. Maybe in the beginning this was not an intentional strategy on the part of the Apostles. It was certainly God's strategy for the expansion of the church.

Winter suggests that four out of five of the lost people in the world cannot be reached with E-1 "neighbor" witness or E-2 "bridge" witness. Given the old foreign mission paradigm and strategies, this may be true. It is very difficult for the traditional large group church to participate in New Testament E-1 expansion. The church is restricted to use E-3 witness where foreign missionaries are sent to witness to people in culturally distant areas. These strategies for sending foreign (E-3) missionaries have been more popular than strategies for preparing and sending national churches to nearby areas. To send nationals out from indigenous churches is E-1 and E-2 witness.

However, a cell-based transplant model can maximize E-1 and E-2 encounters and minimize the dependence upon E-3 encounters for church growth. The goal of the church in every mission opportunity must be to give the water of life in indigenous (E-1 and E-2) cups.

NATIONALS ARE THE BEST INDIGENOUS MISSIONARIES

The church must develop strategies to use nationals in close-cultural missions that complement its cross-cultural mission strategy. Let me state this national "close-cultural" principle. The greater the distance from Jerusalem, the more indigenous leaders are needed to help establish strategic bases. This indicates that E-3 witness is the most difficult of all the witness types.

Winter concludes that "E-1 evangelism . . . where a person communicates to his own people . . . is obviously the most potent kind of evangelism."[6] The challenge is to find strategies that multiply quality E-1 encounters.

In 1997 Cesar A. Buitrago, pastor of a growing Spanish speaking cell church in San Jose, California, traveled to Spain on a missions trip. On the first part of the trip Cesar trained cell group leaders. Toward the end of the trip, he visited Morocco.

During the four-hour ferry ride from the Spanish coast to Tanger, Morocco, Cesar noticed hundreds of Moroccans travelling to Tanger with large briefcases and electrical appliances. These Moroccans lived in Europe and returned to Morocco once a year.

After returning to Spain, Cesar met a pastor who had been trying to begin a church in Morocco for seven years. During those years this pastor had only three converts. He was betrayed by one of these "disciples," jailed and finally expelled from the country for witnessing to Muslims. He now lives in Spain, but his burden is still to reach the Muslims in Morocco.

Cesar was deeply touched by the story of this pastor. He wondered, "In light of this kind of resistance to the Gospel by the people and government of Morocco, how can God possibly reach that Muslim country?" Then, he remembered the hundreds of Moroccans he had seen on the ferry travelling from Europe to Tanger. He made the strategy connection. "The most natural and easy thing to do would be to plant a Moroccan church in Spain where we have total religious freedom among these Moroccans who already speak Spanish. And later, send national Moroccan missionaries to their own country."

Cesar concluded, "We need a paradigm shift in missions. Very sadly, many outside groups are still trying to reach the Muslims in Morocco while thousands of Muslims in Spain have no Christian witness." In other words, Cesar realized that E-3 witness was ineffective in Morocco. But, he also realized that E-1 and E-2 witness was possible with the Moroccans who lived in Europe. The European Moroccans who become Christians could become E-1 witnesses to family, friends and fellow countrymen in Morocco.

Cesar left his mission ferry ride with a new mission revelation. Unfortunately, most Christian leaders get off of their mission ferry rides with the same old mission paradigm. Consequently, foreign missionaries continue to be sent to countries and people groups that are difficult to penetrate by outsiders.

CITIES ARE THE PLACE TO BEGIN INDIGENOUS MISSIONS

In the nineteenth century, most of the first Christian missionaries to Thailand traveled north by boat from Bangkok as far as they could go. Then they rode elephants into the jungles. Then they walked or took canoes into the tribal areas of the country.

These animistic tribes tended to be more responsive to the Gospel than the thousands of Thai Buddhists these missionaries passed on their journey to the jungles. However, these tribes were also the most culturally extreme segment of Thai society. Because of cultural differences, it was impossible for the early missionaries to use the Christians in the tribes to evangelize the other native Thais. In fact, Christianity was stereotyped as a simple religion that could fool the uneducated tribal people but could not compete with the sophisticated philosophy of Buddhism. Consequently, for more than 100 years an indigenous Thai face was not given to the Gospel. As a result, Thailand remains one of the least Christian nations in the world.

What would have happened if the first missionaries in Thailand had established indigenous urban bases in Bangkok and other principle cities? We can only speculate about the results, but I believe there can be no speculation about what the New Testament strategy would have been. Jesus or Paul would have penetrated the major people group in an urban center.

Jesus understood the importance of cities and established the flow of missions out from them. A major portion of His ministry was committed to Jerusalem. His sequence of mission expansion took the gospel from major cities to smaller cities, to towns and finally to villages.

Paul also made the city the geographical and cultural epicenter for the expansion of the church. According to Roger Greenway in *Apostle to the City*, Paul's strategy was to reach the cities. The early church built base churches in the major cities of Ephesus, Antioch, Damascus, Corinth and Rome.

The city must be the staging point for indigenous missions in the twenty-first century. Of the six billion people who presently live in the world, nearly three billion are urban dwellers. Over 200,000 new urban dwellers are added daily and 78 million annually. This is the equivalent of adding a new Dallas every five days, or a new Thailand each year. Migration is producing up to 60% of the urban growth with the rest coming from natural increase.

During the life of William Carey, the father of "modern" missions, five percent of the world lived in cities. By the year 1900 approximately nine percent of the population was urban dwellers. Today 50% live in cities. In 1995 70% of the people in the USA and Europe lived in urban areas. In 50 years it is estimated that 80% of the people in the world will live in a city. This is why the strategy for church expansion in the New Testament is so significant. In a primarily rural world (at least 90% in rural situations) the first century church had an urban to rural strategy and not a rural to urban strategy. Why? The city offers the best opportunity for neighbor and bridge witness.

I am not advocating the neglect of rural areas in the world. I am calling for an emphasis upon New Testament urban missions to birth a movement that can eventually penetrate the towns and villages with E-1 and E-2 witness.

STRATEGIC CHURCHES ARE THE GREATEST HOPE FOR INDIGENOUS EXPANSION

In order to expand the church in the twenty-first century, strategic churches must be developed in population centers where people who are culturally different work and live. Notice the strategic church arrow between the two circles in the Indigenous Expansion Grid. A strategic church is the connecting link in the expansion of the church from Jerusalem to the world and from cities to villages.

```
JERUSALEM    JUDEA   SAMARIA      WORLD
   MOST                           LEAST
Culturally    STRATEGIC        Culturally
Forgiving      CHURCH  ───▶    Forgiving
 Context                         Context
MAJOR CITY    CITY    TOWN      VILLAGE
```

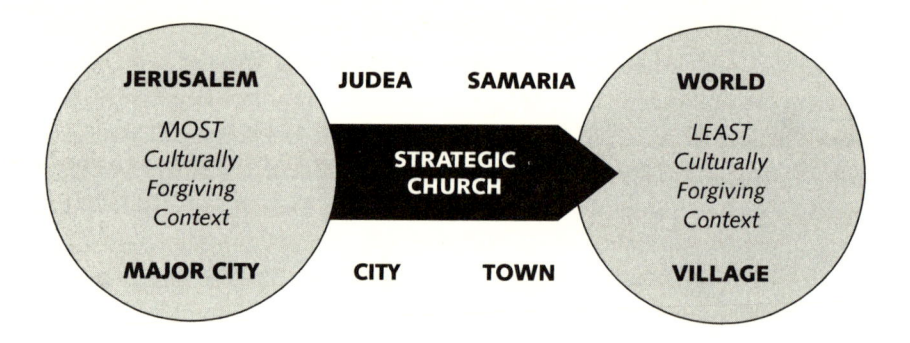

I call these "strategic churches" because of where they are located and because of the kind of church they are. They are located in population centers where people who need to be reached by the Gospel live and work. These strategic churches are reproducible cell-based churches that have the capacity to train every member for holiness and harvest.

The following steps are involved in developing strategic churches:

- Begin with a church in a major population center
- Target and win converts from groups that have not received the Gospel
- Train these "bridge" Christians
- Send those nationals back to their own smaller cities to establish other indigenous strategic churches
- Then the strategic churches in the smaller cities send nationals to towns where strategic churches are built
- Then from the town base the surrounding villages are evangelized by villagers won in the town

This strategy process gives the church a way to maximize its E-1 witness encounters and to escape missions at the cultural extreme of E-3 far and foreign missions. In other words, it maximizes quality E-1 and E-2 encounters by building indigenous churches in strategic mission areas.

A strategic church strategy is practically indigenous because it uses a mother church to coordinate the extension of the gospel to the most distant people groups. It is culturally indigenous because it sends indigenous teams to witness to those who are most like them. Establishing strategic churches is financially indigenous because each strategic church is able to support the startup of other strategic churches in smaller cities and towns. It is strategically indigenous because it can gradually adapt the cell church strategy to all types of cultures.

Of course, there are always exceptions where E-3 foreign missionaries are the only way. However, our goal in the twenty-first century must be a "near and close" missionary strategy.

An exception to the strategic church approach may be more isolated tribes that are small in numbers, cut off from the culture around them and have no written language. Special mission groups such as New Tribes have been called to this unique mission role. However, even in these situations, national Christians who are connected to these tribes in trade, marriage or proximity may be a better alternative than sending foreign missionaries. A more indigenous approach would be for an outside expert in linguistic skills to train a local national "bridge" Christian from a nearby strategic church. Then send that "bridge" Christian to live with a tribe, translate the Bible into the language of the tribe and begin a strategic church that can penetrate the rest of the tribe.

PAZ: INDIGENOUS MODEL IN THE AMAZON

A ministry in Brazil that works in the Amazon River Basin is a good example of this strategy. Paz International is a ministry founded in 1976 by Luke and Christine Huber. It is headquartered in the city of Santarem in northern Brazil. Over a period of 20 years, Paz has started more than 250 churches in the Amazon Basin as well as Japan, Portugal and Mozambique.

Paz International represents all of the exciting and good things that are associated with frontline missions. First of all, Paz is centered in the Amazon Basin. This river system has ten separate basins, each as large as the Mississippi River Basin in the United States. The Amazon Basin consists of 17 million people who live in an unexplored frontier covering 2.3 million square miles of rainforest, lakes and tributaries.

Paz builds boats, outfits them and sends them up and down the tributaries of the Amazon. In addition to their boats, they fly into inaccessible areas. Paz is involved in educational ministry. Under local church supervision, Christian elementary schools are functioning in many of the cities and towns along the rivers. Paz's medical boats help river people with health care, food, clothing and other forms of social assistance. Paz also helps construct wells up and down the rivers.

I first came into contact with this ministry in 1997. Paz's vision has not changed over the years. Their vision is to plant 100,000 churches focusing on the Amazon Basin and to fuel a nationally led movement to establish God's Kingdom in a great harvest field across the world. Luke Huber, the mission's late founder, wanted to see at least one church in each of the Amazon's estimated 80,000 villages.

God has changed and adjusted the method for the vision to be implemented. The ministry now thinks in terms of strong strategic churches in the population centers of the Amazon Basin. The vision begins in cities and moves to villages instead beginning and ending with villages. Paz envisions strong base cell churches that will be centers for training, supporting, financing and sending teams into towns and from the towns into the villages. Paz has divided the Basin into 15 strategic areas, each with an existing or proposed base of operation.

In the past, Paz worked more from the traditional mission base paradigm. A mission base consisted of a team of missionaries in an area who train, plan and send missionaries into towns and villages to plant churches. Now, they have begun to think more in terms of church bases. The strategy is to develop strong Antioch-type cell church bases in strategic areas. These base churches will then be responsible for implementing the church planting/transplanting strategy into surrounding cities, towns, and villages.

Jeff Hrubrik, Director of Paz International, expressed the strategy of this ministry in a paragraph in a recent update. "We want to strategically move into each municipality beginning with the key cities. Although our ultimate goal is the river villages, we have learned that we need a strong base to raise up local leaders, prayer covering and financial support to then spread out to the 'uttermost parts' or the hidden river villages."[7]

HOPE OF BANGKOK:
INDIGENOUS URBAN MODEL

Over the past two decades, Hope of Bangkok Church has grown to be one of the largest churches in Thailand. It has the most aggressive and successful expansion strategy of all church groups in that Buddhist nation.

This cell church began as a "vacuum cleaner" model and sucked up many members and leaders from other churches in Bangkok and the surrounding regions. To be completely fair, most of the earlier successful churches in Bangkok also used this same approach. However, Hope of Bangkok was more successful at it and continued to count leaders and members from other churches for a longer period of time. Hope of Bangkok went another step beyond the other "vacuum cleaner" churches. Not only were members and leaders from other churches recruited to be part of the early core, but entire churches were allowed, if not encouraged, to change the name on their church sign and join Hope of Bangkok. This aggressive proselytizing led to an ugly schism between Hope of Bangkok and other churches in Thailand. In one of the least Christian nations in the world, the church polarized. Today a large percentage of the members of this church and its daughter churches are new converts, but old suspicions and feelings still remain.

The traditional churches in Thailand compounded the mistakes made by Hope of Bangkok by overreacting to the perceived threat of the new church. It is difficult to see how revival can break out in Thailand until this wound is healed. (Please join with me in prayer for the reconciliation of the church in Thailand.)

However, these mistakes should not negate the lessons that can be learned from this model. In one of the most difficult countries of the world for Christianity to grow, this church has grown significantly. It has grown for several reasons:

- It has a dynamic cell-based ministry.
- It is indigenous (founded by a Thai leader who became a Christian while studying in Australia).
- The movement has an urban strategy of beginning churches in regional cities.
- From the beginning it has had an intentional and aggressive growth strategy.

We learn from this flawed but powerful model that urban, indigenous cell churches with a strategy will grow just like they did in the first century.

19
CRITICAL MASS STRATEGY

✝

*How long will it take? The rest of your life, but here's the good news —
you should start to see results in three to five years.*
—Lloyd Dobyns

Developing critical mass momentum is a strategic paradigm for worldwide revival in the twenty-first century.

Pentecost is an illustration of the explosive power and energy released by God through the church. "And there were added that day about three thousand souls. And they were continually devoting themselves to the apostles' teaching and to fellowship, to the breaking of bread and to prayer. And everyone kept feeling a sense of awe; and many wonders and signs were taking place through the Apostles. And day by day continuing with one mind, in the temple, and breaking bread from house to house, they were taking their meals together with gladness and sincerity of heart, praising God, and having favor with all the people. And the Lord was adding to their number day by day those who were being saved" (Acts 2:41-47).

Christ has not called us to visualize the church at the size of thousands. He uses one critical number to model the church we see in Acts. He wants to use us to develop a base congregation of 120 as a new start or as a prototype within an existing church. This first hurdle is the biggest one. When the base congregation comes together, everything that is necessary to be the Body of Christ is in place.

Why is 120 Important?

The first reason for the importance of 120 people is that Jesus modeled the church at this size. Jesus had promised that He would "build His church." And, the first church that He built was one base congregation of 120 members in the upper room in Jerusalem. The life and dynamics of Jesus' base congregation of 120 assured the success of the church when it grew to thousands. We know from the biblical accounts that the broader group in the first church was probably 500 followers including men, women and children. Around this 500 were the crowds that attached themselves to the movement during His three-year ministry. But the foundational core of His first church was 120 followers.

Second, the 120 unit is the point of critical mass. As defined in an earlier chapter, critical mass is the minimum amount of fissionable material necessary to produce a chain reaction. In building a cell church, critical mass indicates the size when the working unit and the coordinating unit fuse together in an integrated whole that can reproduce itself. Divine synergism kicks in at the point of 120 when the total operates in a more powerful way than the sum of the individual parts.

Third, the number is not magical; rather, it is the number when the essential qualities and tasks of the church can begin to operate as one unit. Previous chapters in this book explain elements of spiritual life that are necessary for a group to reach critical mass and become a base congregation. A group of 70 to 120 adults must be living out these spiritual elements before a healthy base congregation will function properly:

- Listening to God in prayer
- Worshiping in spirit and truth
- Hearing and doing the Word
- Operating in the power of gifts
- Submitting to Kingdom authority
- Living together in community
- Caring for new believers
- Nurturing accountability for each other
- Raising up spiritual leaders
- Reaching out to a lost and hurting world

When these qualities come together within the context of the basic working unit and the coordinating unit of the church of 120 members, critical mass is experienced.

Fourth, building a church at the size of 120 attainable. One base congregation is doable in a new church start. I can make plans to grow to 120 in the upper room, and I can also get a handle on a remnant of 120 within a large existing church. I can conceptualize the infrastructure necessary to support one base congregation, while the structure of a church of thousands is beyond my grasp.

Fifth, the church at this number is able to withstand the attacks of Satan. Jesus promised that "the gates of hell will not prevail against my church." Jesus' church was established with 120 followers. Satan knows the importance of a church operating at the optimum size of Jesus' model. Therefore, he draws the battle line some point before the church reaches optimum size. Satan then marshals his energy and effort so leaders and methods will not result in enough momentum to break through the single congregation barrier.

Sixth, a church of this size can birth other churches. This is the reproductive size and maturity of the church. With an initial group of 120 a church prototype can be established. The basic ministry unit (cell) of the church can be modeled and the basic coordinating unit (congregation) can be modeled. When the ministry and coordinating units of the church are operating, the church is able to expand.

Seventh, the dynamics of 120 allows the church to grow much larger. Inherent within one base congregation is the infrastructure to be a church of thousands or tens of thousands. No other structure is required and no new strategy is necessary to grow to a larger size. One base congregation has everything in place for a church to be 1000 members or 5000 members or 50,000 members. Just keep multiplying the same kind of congregational unit. Carl George observed that a church that organizes into congregations and groups of approximately ten people as its "spiritual and emotional center," never has to be reorganized. "It can accommodate every church size from 50 to 500,000. Churches can maintain quality and meaningful care giving no matter how many of these spiritual kinship groups comprise the whole church."[1]

CRITICAL MASS DEVELOPS FROM A PROTOTYPE

Critical mass does not happen automatically but is the result of a process that leads to a working prototype. A prototype is a small model of a larger project. In a prototype, the viability of a total concept or system can be tested out. The Gospels reveal how Jesus developed critical-mass momentum by carefully forming a prototype. With 120 committed followers, Jesus modeled the smallest implementing unit of cell and the larger coordinating unit of a congregation.

At the turn of the century in Glasgow, Scotland two men formed a partnership and began a furniture company. In the early years the company did very well in a market characterized by easy-to-please customers who wanted large basic furniture.

The next generation formed two associated family companies out of the original business. Business was much more difficult during the second generation and customers were harder to please. However, both companies survived to pass the two companies on to the third generation. Today the grandchildren of the original founders own two separate furniture companies in Glasgow.

One of the third generation companies invested heavily in new equipment, brought in top-level management and hired skilled designers from various successful companies. This company reorganized their system around a prototype shop where every piece of furniture was developed and assigned detailed specifications. The company called these specifications and drawings "the bible." No one started an assembly line without reading all of the memos and drawings related to their section of "the bible." Problems could be identified and quickly corrected because of the prototype procedures. This company has shown significant growth since its reorganization and is now one of the largest furniture manufacturing companies in Scotland.

The other company poured its money into large and impressive looking buildings but never developed a prototype shop. Consequently this company has no standard system for controlling the quality of each piece of furniture. Without prototype drawings, responsibility for and correction of a problem has been next to impossible. When a problem comes up on an assembly line, the foreman typically blames other departments.

On more than one occasion, the owner of the struggling company brought in experts for consultation. Always the same suggestion was made. "You must prototype the furniture you are selling." The company without the prototype shop has up to this point been unwilling to stop long enough to develop a system for prototyping. It continues to fall farther behind the growth of its sister company.

We learn from this story that a prototype is important. We also learn that some leaders resist going back and completing a prototype. This is true in the business world as well as in the church.

Two Types of Prototypes

The prototype concept is used in two ways in the development of a cell church. Prototype can mean a base congregation of 120 members that is operating with all essential systems. This is the model of the support and coordinating unit of a cell church. Prototype can also refer to the pattern cell from which all other cells will grow. A prototype cell is the building block of the prototype base congregation. The prototype cell is the model of the ministry and implementing unit of a cell church.

Jesus developed His prototype congregation incrementally around several leadership stages. These different leadership stages can be understood by studying the numbers that are associated with them. The numbers — two to three, twelve, 70, and 120 represent leadership stages in Jesus' strategy. The "two to three" number was Jesus and John the Baptist and then Peter, James and John. Then the three became twelve and the twelve became 70. This prototype was completed with the 120 leaders in the upper room. Each stage became part of the next size of the prototype. The twelve were part of the 70 and the 70 were part of the 120. The 120 was the completed model for the thousands that followed.

The chart at the top of the following page shows these two essential units as they relate to each other. A cell church organizes and operates around them. It is imperative for a church to develop a healthy prototype model of both units. These two units are essential for reaching critical mass and establishing a church that lives in continual revival.

Breakthrough Factors

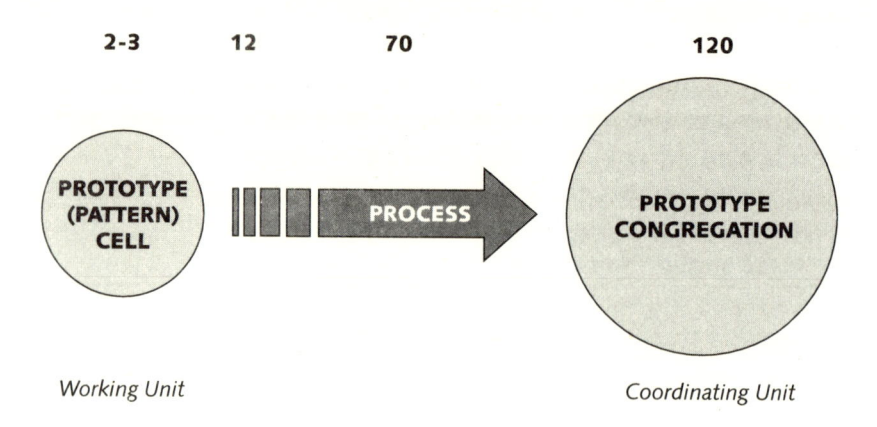

| 2-3 | 12 | 70 | 120 |

PROTOTYPE (PATTERN) CELL → PROCESS → **PROTOTYPE CONGREGATION**

Working Unit — *Coordinating Unit*

BANGKOK URBAN STRATEGY

I learned the lesson of the base congregation and critical mass the hard way. Between 1976 and 1984, I was part of a church planting team in Bangkok, Thailand. The team was built around veteran missionary Judson Lennon and eventually grew to five as new missionaries were assigned to the project.

The vision was conceived in my heart in Texas but born on top of the 26-story Chokchai Building in Bangkok in 1975. Judson Lennon, Bill Smith and I stood on the tallest point in Bangkok with our Area Director, his assistant and our Mission Administrator. Looking out over the city of millions, we dreamed of developing a comprehensive church planting strategy for Bangkok. The effort was named Bangkok Urban Strategy and later shortened to BUS.

Every week we met for prayer and planning. A 52-week neighborhood strategy began to take shape. The plan was for a neighborhood team made up of a missionary and national Christians to witness to Thais, bring them to conversion, form them into groups and use the groups to begin a church. The team would follow the same steps each week:

- Learn essential concepts of neighborhood cell ministry
- Implement those concepts in a target neighborhood

- Evaluate what had happened
- Go through the process again

During the first three years the strategy was tested, indigenous materials were developed and methodology was put in place. The initial three member team became four with the addition of Bill Hitt. In another year Floyd Kendall joined the team. We continued to refine the strategy and to develop indigenous materials.

OPPOSITION TO CHANGE

Eventually, the natural process of change produced opposition. I now know we should have anticipated opposition and planned for it. However, we were consumed with the vision and believed that eventually the vision would prove itself. Opposition centered in the missionary community and then surfaced as doubts among the nationals.

The Bangkok Urban Strategy team believed that "comprehensive" meant that all of the missionaries and institutions in Bangkok in our organization would eventually operate within the context of the strategy. This definition of comprehensive touched the lives and ministries of every missionary in Bangkok and every institution associated with us. This ultimately doomed the vision because criticism toward the project increased in direct proportion to how comprehensive the strategy was expected to be.

I am sure that the team could have done a better job in preparing for the change. We did not realize the extent of the radical nature of the vision, the level of commitment to the old way and the depth of the resistance to change. For whatever reason, the effort began to polarize at several points. Urban and rural missions became an issue as more and more church planting missionaries were assigned to Bangkok. The question of church planting and institutional missions became a problem because the mission had several large and well-staffed institutions in Bangkok that had their own separate visions. The strategy even began to touch on personal missionary issues such as housing because BUS wanted to get missionaries off missionary compounds and into Thai neighborhoods.

Because BUS was initiating the change, it was increasingly seen as the problem. BUS was charged with the ultimate missionary sin of being "uncooperative." Because of this polarization, the BUS team felt that after the initial testing it was essential to broaden the strategy as much as possible to silence the opposition and convince the doubters that it would work.

A FATAL MISTAKE

We decided to begin five different church plants in five different areas of Bangkok through five different existing mother churches. We fell right into the Devil's trap of dividing and conquering. We had fragmented our strength and split our forces.

With five separate projects we could never build up enough momentum to prove the system to the satisfaction of the silent majority and to those in authority. In hindsight, we should have focused all of our personnel and resources toward developing one strong and viable base congregation. Then we could have transplanted other base congregations into target areas of the city.

Some good things happened in the project. For the first time in two decades our organization began several new churches in Bangkok. Relationship evangelism was introduced and shown to be a viable method. Small groups were established as an essential element in the church. The importance of penetrating neighborhoods was accepted. A new boldness in evangelism emerged. Today some of these principles are still evident in Bangkok.

However, almost a decade after our rooftop experience at the Chokchai Building, the painful decision was made to let BUS die a natural death. During one of our weekly meetings the team pronounced the obituary over BUS and buried it as a structure with the hope that it would continue to live as a movement. Unfortunately, it continued in Thailand only as a blip in the yearly statistics and as some isolated methods and concepts.

LESSONS FROM FAILURE

The experience in Bangkok was like death to me. For eight years I had dreamed of developing an urban church model. My greatest regret has been that the strategy came very close to working in spite of our mistakes and the opposition to change.

Though painful, the experience taught me several important lessons about change, the base congregation and myself. The situation in Thailand forced me back to the basics. Response to the Gospel was so slow in Thailand that a strategy had to go back to the essentials and the power of God. Nothing could be taken for granted and all bases had to be covered. In the process, I returned to the New Testament to understand how Jesus developed the first church. My theology was clarified in the trenches. My concept of the presence, power and purpose of Christ was learned in the neighborhoods of Bangkok. I was tested in the fire of failure. Out of the failure I learned that God could still use me in His Kingdom. In hindsight, I can not imagine my ministry today apart from my painful experience in BUS.

Let me simply state the lesson I learned in Bangkok about the base congregation: concentrate your strategy, don't fragment your forces and transplant from strength.

How Long Will It Take?

Human nature is the same in every new endeavor. The standard American corporate questions about change are: "What do we do? (But keep it simple)," and "How long will it take? (But keep it short)"

These are the same two underlying attitudes I have sensed from church leaders interested in changing to the cell church way. Always there is a desire for immediate results and simple (and painless) strategies.

Change does not happen that way! When business consultants address the second question: "How long will it take?" they say, "The rest of your life, but — here's the good news — you should start to see results in three to five years."

This is the way I see the development of a cell church. One year of preparation is necessary to internalize the vision, values and commitment in a core of selected leaders. In addition to the first year, becoming an operating cell church stretches into a two-year, five-year and seven-year process. One year is required for preparation. Then it takes at least two years to learn how to do it and to put the basic systems in place. Another two years are required to assimilate the rest of the church body into the cell culture. And then, another two years are required before unusual growth associated with many operating cell churches is experienced.

20
STEP-BY-STEP STRATEGY

✝

*If a series of related tasks can be called a process,
a group of related processes can then be seen as a system.*

Following Jesus' New Testament process is a strategic paradigm for worldwide revival in the twenty-first century.

God created the world in seven days, not just one. The creative processes of each day were dependent upon the previous creative acts as God celebrated after each day and declared that each day was "good." This means that He celebrated the continuing process of creation and not just the finished product. The church must learn to celebrate and use process rather than fearing it.

The unfolding story of the Bible is a process. God patiently moved the children of Israel through hundreds of years of process. The statement that Jesus came in the "fullness of time" implies a process moving toward a moment of completeness. Therefore, we should not be surprised that Jesus used a step-by-step process to build the first church. However, the secret is to properly identify and apply the process.

THE "BIG BANG" THEORY OF CELL CHURCH

One method of beginning a cell church is the popular but flawed "big bang" theory. In the "big bang" theory a cell church develops out of a cataclysmic event by which the church appears complete and fully formed. The theory is the opposite of the process principle Jesus used to build the first church, and it contradicts the factual evidence about how successful cell churches have been developed in the twentieth century. Every successful cell church that I know anything about went through a process, sometimes for several years, and through several stages.

Church leaders, especially pastors of large churches, are attracted to the "big bang" theory because it seems to eliminate much of the pain and the patience required in a step-by-step process. It promises to give instant gratification to vision. However, the "big bang" theory is a fatal attraction. It weakens the learning process of leaders and compromises the developing process necessary to strengthen the infrastructure.

Large cell churches may contaminate leaders with the "big bang" theory by teaching about the finished product of cell church rather than the process that brought them to the finished product. In conferences, these cell churches share exciting statistics and stories about current and projected growth. Leaders attending these conferences receive a revelation vision from God and an anointing to become a cell church. However, when they go back home, frustration sets in because the leader can't ignite the "big bang." They are left with a "dud" because they do not understand the process that leads to the type of growth observed in these large cell churches.

These successful cell churches teach an incomplete process by leaving out the early stages of their growth. They teach a "big bang" Pentecost experience and skip over the years of process that Jesus carefully, patiently and painfully took them through. Their success actually covers up the process and dooms churches that try to "big bang" their finished product to frustration and failure.

A teaching cell church must go back to the beginning and document the step-by-step process that brought them to the place of transition and growth. The beginning process is what a new cell church needs to understand and what an existing cell church needs to teach.

A Leadership Process

For years I searched the Gospels for the process that Jesus used to build the first church. I know now why the process always eluded me. The Gospels were written from different perspectives, with different objectives, and with different chronological orders. Finally, during an extensive parallel study of the Gospels the numbers jumped out at me: 2 or 3, 12, 70, 120, and 3000. I realized that the same numbers are present in each of the Gospels and reveal Jesus' process for building His church and establishing the New Testament movement.

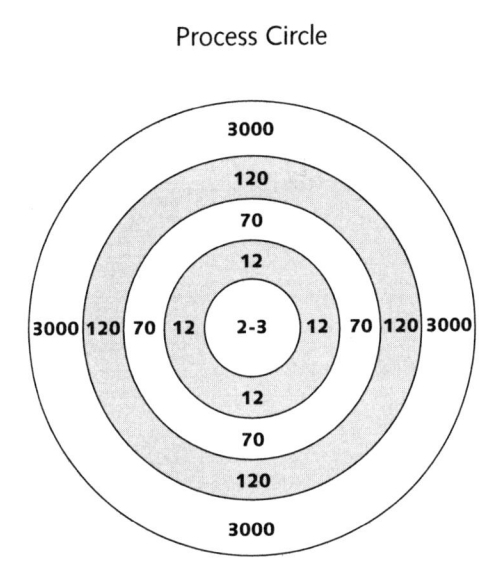

Process Circle

Jesus' process developed incrementally around leaders. In the Process Circle above, Jesus first gathered a pool of potential followers and leaders from which He would choose His initial core of twelve. This core of leaders was called to commitment and obedience. Jesus then tested His system with a group of committed leaders that grew from twelve to 70. He organized His church while the 70 grew to the coordinating unit of 120. Jesus consolidated and completed His model with the 120 in the upper room. At this point the church reached critical mass and expanded to 3000 and beyond!

The upper end of the numbers shows the potential size, not the required size or even the preferred size of the church. A local church can be any size that God desires, but it will operate with at least one base congregation like Jesus' 120.

A Step-by-Step Process

Let us consider the process Jesus used to build the first church within a ministry period of three to four years. That is the amount of time Jesus devoted to the process before "big bang" evangelism happened at Pentecost. (Most churches today find that Jesus' timeline must be extended to at least seven years before experiencing exponential growth.)

The following chart shows the leadership process, the structural process and the tools process. In this chapter I will focus on the processes necessary to develop the first pattern cell and the steps in developing the leadership structure. The tools and support systems of the cell church process will be covered in the following chapter.

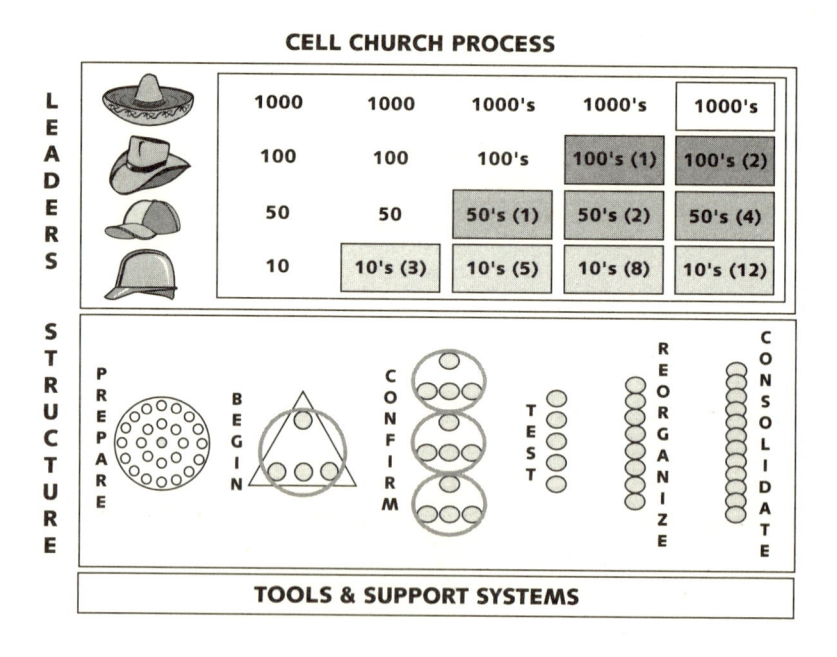

CELL CHURCH PROCESS

LEADERS						
	🎩	1000	1000	1000's	1000's	1000's
	🤠	100	100	100's	100's (1)	100's (2)
	🧢	50	50	50's (1)	50's (2)	50's (4)
	⛑	10	10's (3)	10's (5)	10's (8)	10's (12)

| STRUCTURE | PREPARE | BEGIN | CONFIRM | TEST | REORGANIZE | CONSOLIDATE |

TOOLS & SUPPORT SYSTEMS

Some form of this process will be used in every attempt to become a cell church. The process applies to a new start, a small church that desires to break through stagnation or a large church that needs to develop its first cell church coordinating congregation. "A journey of a thousand miles begins with one step."

Jesus' Leadership Circle

What did Jesus do first in His process? Imagine a large circle surrounding Jesus as He began His ministry at the Jordan River.

This large circle was empty in the beginning. However, Jesus filled the circle with enough potential leaders to build the first stages of His movement. That leadership circle may have consisted of as many as 70 potential leaders who would be brought into His stages of development at the proper time. Out of this initial pool of followers He identified, prepared and called the twelve and designated the three.

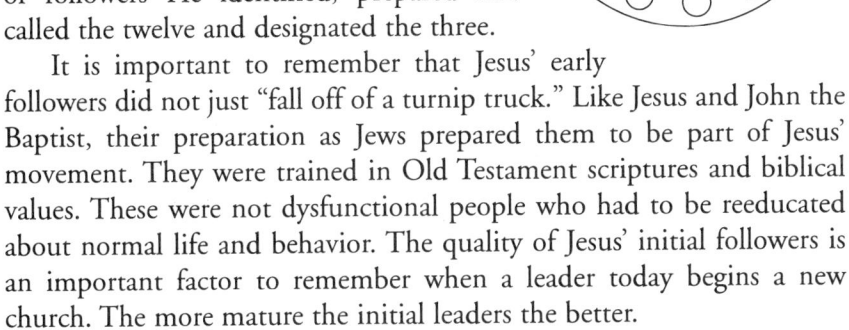

It is important to remember that Jesus' early followers did not just "fall off of a turnip truck." Like Jesus and John the Baptist, their preparation as Jews prepared them to be part of Jesus' movement. They were trained in Old Testament scriptures and biblical values. These were not dysfunctional people who had to be reeducated about normal life and behavior. The quality of Jesus' initial followers is an important factor to remember when a leader today begins a new church. The more mature the initial leaders the better.

The leadership circle in the cell church process chart below is located between the first two process steps of "Prepare" and "Begin." The first step in the process is to follow Jesus' example. Choose key leaders to be part of a leadership circle.

In the transition of an existing church, this leadership circle should have representatives from the church staff, the governing body of the church, key influence leaders and productive members (70 is a good number to begin with in a large church). In a new start, the catalytic leader must gather followers to be part of the leadership circle before beginning the process. This is best done within the structure of a sending mother church.

If a new church is started by a small number of leaders without a team or a mother church, the early months must be used to contact and win potentially productive believers and prepare them in the leadership circle. Additional time and much patience must be allowed for this kind of solo start. In this scenario, initial followers must first be prepared and grow in maturity before they can be used to develop a healthy pattern cell and establish a working prototype.

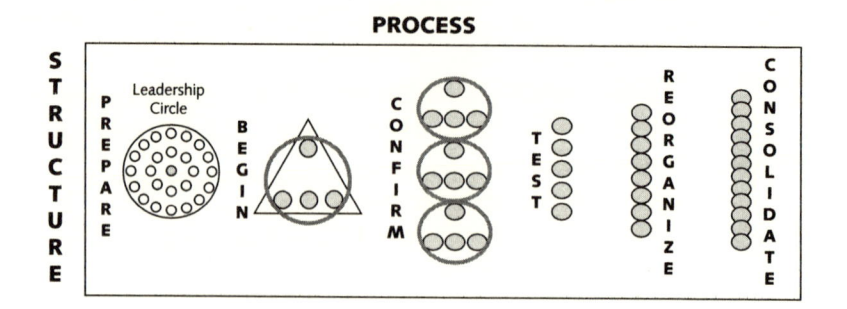

PROCESS

STRUCTURE | PREPARE | Leadership Circle | BEGIN | CONFIRM | TEST | REORGANIZE | CONSOLIDATE

The purpose of the leadership circle is to introduce the concepts, values and vision to a key group of leaders. This can be done in one-on-one meetings, in special vision retreats, in conferences and in the sharing of books and materials. The *Natural Church Development* evaluation of Christian Schwartz is an excellent exercise during the time of preparation. *Experiencing God* by Henry Blackaby helps Christians understand that Bible study is an experience with God and not just study. Paul Weaver of England has a kit designed to help prepare a church to move into a cell church transition called *'Celling' the Church*. TOUCH Outreach Ministries has developed a *Bootcamp* to help prepare a church for transition. *Bootcamp* has been successfully used in countries like Brazil to prepare churches for transition.

Developing a commitment to evangelism should be a primary focus during the leadership circle stage. This initial stage is an excellent time for leaders to experience evangelism personally which will lead to cells committed to new conversion growth. Share groups and interest groups of all kinds provide a venue to develop this evangelism commitment within the leadership circle. Leaders should also experience a witness encounter in which one method of personal witness will be eventually learned by all members. *Alpha*, an investigative study of the life of Jesus, was developed in England for contacting and cultivating seekers. It is an excellent way to establish the value of evangelism among leaders during this initial stage.

Information is not the most important focus for the leadership circle. The issue is commitment: commitment to the vision, commitment to the values, commitment to evangelism and commitment to the project leaders.

BEGINNING A CELL PATTERN

Jesus carefully modeled this basic ministry unit with His twelve because each stage of His process and all of His activities were dependent upon basic Christian community.

The pattern cell must be started early in the process and then tested and adapted as the project moves toward critical mass. A pattern cell will have a way to live out the five elements presented in the illustration of the hand in chapter three: community, equipping, accountability, leadership and evangelism.

The pattern cell unifies the vision, sets up quality control, establishes spiritual authority and integrates all systems. Core leaders must receive the cell DNA from God while living together in cell life. The leaders of the pattern cell must die to all personal agendas, discover necessary tools for implementation, commit to the vision and have a reproducible pattern for the cell meeting.

In the Process Chart the initial pattern cell is represented by a triangle with four circles. The circle at the top is Jesus and the three circles at the bottom are Peter, James and John. Spouses should be included in this first cell experience.

Leaders responsible for developing a cell agenda do not have to reinvent the wheel. A general cell agenda has emerged over the past several decades and is explained in the materials of Ralph Neighbour and is used by cell churches around the world.

For most churches the cell meeting agenda flows through four relationship experiences:

- *You to me and me to you* as the members bond in community
- *Us to God* in worship as the group focuses on Christ in their midst
- *God to us* in edification as application of the Word takes place
- *God through us* in ministry to reaching the lost and hurting in the world

This is the normal order of the agenda. The order may, however, be adjusted from time to time in order to help the cell in its growth process. For instance, the focus on the vision for reaching out (God through us) can be moved up if it is necessary or the bonding element (you to me and me to you) can be extended when a new group is starting up.

The cell is too important to copy someone else's way of doing it. The pattern will be reproduced over and over. If the pattern is flawed then all cells that are birthed out from the pattern will be distorted. Without a pattern cell, no quality control is possible.

After completing the first "Peter, James and John" cycle of approximately three months, leaders should enter into another cycle of three months with three more pattern cells. A new cell is formed around Peter, another around James, and another around John. Each cell should have three additional leaders plus their spouses. In the case of an unmarried leader, add another single or let the cell have an odd number of members.

The leader of the original cell then steps back and supervises the three new cells. This second phase of developing the pattern cell uses what has been learned in the first cell. The goal is to listen to God about the DNA of the cell and to agree upon one cell agenda that will be used by all cells in the future.

CELL EVANGELISM AND THE PATTERN CELL

The initial pattern cell is different from the cells that will come after it in at least two ways. Not all of the ministry tasks (community, equipping, accountability, leadership and evangelism) will be operating at one hundred percent efficiency during the early phases of the prototype. It takes time to learn how to do these tasks and how to integrate them.

Also, the initial pattern cell is the only cell "closed" to unbelievers and new and immature believers. A healthy prototype cannot be developed with disruptive, rebellious or functionally immature people. Therefore, the lost and new believers will not be brought directly into the initial pattern cell. This follows Jesus' model; He carefully chose those who would be part of His initial prototype and took care of others in different venues. Jesus' leaders were not perfect. Thomas was filled with doubts, Peter denied Jesus, James and John fought for position and Judas betrayed Jesus. However, these leaders, in spite of their weaknesses, were not severely disruptive, rebellious or functionally immature people. They were mature enough to consider the claims of Jesus upon them. Jesus saw their weaknesses but also their potential to lead His movement.

During the development of the pattern cell, the leaders must not ignore evangelism. Key leaders who are not yet in the pattern cell should continue evangelism in the leadership circle. During the first few months of the process, the lost and new believers should be cared for in other types of groups rather than in the pattern cell.

The purpose of the pattern cell is to receive confirmation from God. This will probably be the only opportunity for the leaders to listen to God in a special way about the mechanics and dynamics of cell life.

The Importance of a Pattern Cell

The leaders of a cell church establish a cell church culture through a pattern cell. This begins by deciding on a basic cell pattern that all groups and cells will follow and then by providing essential systems through which the culture can be lived out.

The pattern cell is affirmation of God's blessing upon the way the church will live in cell life. Leaders will not live and die for a method from a book or another person, but they will sacrifice for what they receive from God. The pattern cell must be revealed and confirmed by God.

Having one cell pattern establishes spiritual authority and neutralizes the seeds of leadership rebellion that plague many small group systems. The authority of God must surround the pattern cell so that the leaders can assure their members that God is the source. Suppose a leader on your team has always led groups by teaching a Bible study. You ask this leader to follow a certain cell agenda. The Bible teacher might very well respond with the question "Why?" How will you respond?

You can respond by asserting your authority as leader: "You should do this because I say so, and I am the leader!" Or you can assert the authority of a group of leaders: "You should do this because the leadership team wants it done that way." Or you can appeal to the experts: "You should do this because the cell church experts tell us that this is the way to do it." Some leaders who have their own agenda for a cell meeting will defer to these arguments, but not many. Many leaders believe that they have a special word from God for their preference in cell life and will claim that leaders that expect conformity are "quenching the Spirit."

But suppose you respond in another way to the question, "Why should I use this pattern?" "You should do this because the leaders of the church have listened to God and this is the way we believe God wants to operate in our groups." Now you operate out of spiritual authority. In the first instance *you* have a problem. That problem is how to convince this group leader to submit to your authority or the authority of a group of leaders. In the second example, that group leader has a problem. Will the group leader believe that God has spoken to the church leaders?

The commitment of the core leaders strengthens the pattern cell because God has affirmed it to the leaders so that the pattern is not just a method learned from a conference or a book. The leaders become so committed to the pattern cell that they expect both existing groups and new cells to use this one pattern. Every cell leader and every member will live out the DNA of the cell pattern that God has revealed to the leaders. The leaders will then use the systems in the pattern cell as the quality control standard for all cells.

THE LEADERSHIP PROCESS

In a cell church, four principles of leadership must function through four types of leaders before a church reaches critical mass. These leadership roles wear different leadership hats. In a fully functioning cell church leaders will wear one of these hats and fulfill the principles of leadership associated with it.

In the leadership process chart shown at the top of the following page, there are five columns of leadership that correspond with the step-by-step structural development.

In the beginning, the senior leader of the church will wear all four hats: coordinating, supporting, supervising and implementing. The senior leader will lead the first cell and continue to coordinate, support and supervise other areas of the church. The goal is for the senior to gradually put a hat on another leader.

LEADERSHIP PROCESS

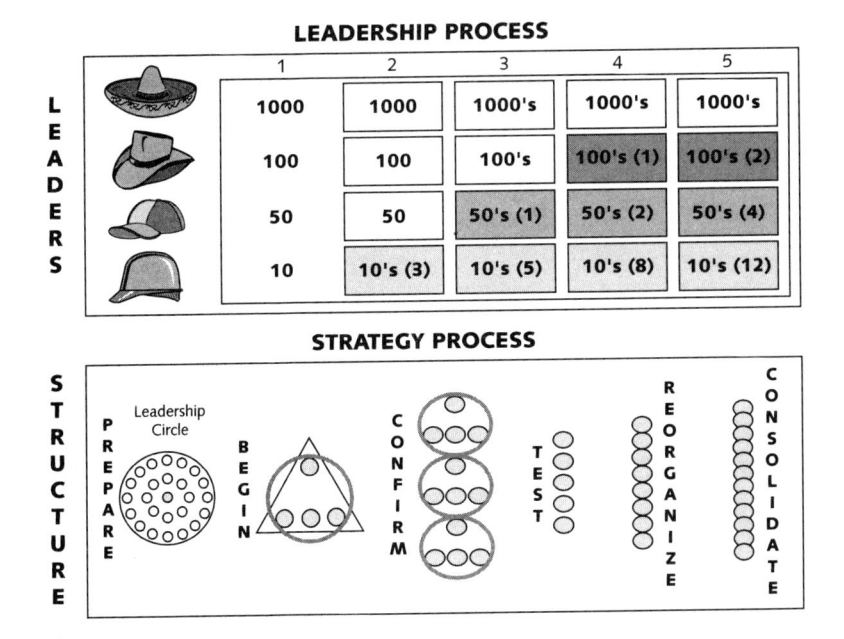

LEADERS	1	2	3	4	5
🎩	1000	1000	1000's	1000's	1000's
🤠	100	100	100's	100's (1)	100's (2)
🧢	50	50	50's (1)	50's (2)	50's (4)
⛑	10	10's (3)	10's (5)	10's (8)	10's (12)

STRATEGY PROCESS

STRUCTURE: PREPARE (Leadership Circle) → BEGIN → CONFIRM → TEST → REORGANIZE → CONSOLIDATE

During the second step, three leaders are leading pattern cells. This means that the senior leader has now taken off the hat of implementing leader, but continues to wear the hat of coordinating leader, supporting leader and supervising leader.

The third step of testing provides an opportunity to establish another leadership role. The senior leader now has five leaders operating as implementing cell leaders (tens). The senior leader now installs one of the previous leaders as a supervising leader (fifties) over the five cells. Let us suppose that Peter, who led one of the original cells, is now the supervising leader over the five test cells (fifties). The senior leader now operates as the coordinating leader (thousands) and as the supporting leader (hundreds).

The fourth step of reorganizing moves the leadership development to another stage. More leaders are now operating as implementing cell leaders and two supporting leaders (fifties), who were previously leaders over one of the cells, oversee the cells. The senior leader now installs a supporting leader over hundreds. This could be Peter who has already served as a supervising leader of fifties. The senior pastor has now installed all of the leadership roles.

Step five consolidates this leadership structure as the operating system of the church. The four principles of leadership are functioning through a coordinating leader (thousands), a supporting leader (hundreds), a supervising leader (fifties) and an implementing leader (tens). The process is complete and the church operates as a fully functioning cell church.

WE MUST TAKE THE FIRST STEP

Jeff attended one of my conferences several years ago. He was pastor of a creative church that operated with small groups. On the first day of the conference, the cell church vision captured his heart. On the second day I taught about the necessity to prototype a pattern cell. Jeff was having trouble with the idea. During a break he explained, "I have several groups that are already meeting. Do you think I should go back and prototype with a special leadership group?"

"Yes!" I replied. "That is what I would do!"

Jeff didn't like this advice. I knew he would return home excited about God's vision but would proceed without a pattern cell.

Later at the first of four modules of advanced training, I once again taught Jeff about the need to use a group of key leaders to prototype the basic cell. Jeff showed me the strategy he had developed in this first module. He confessed that he had not gone back after the first conference and developed a prototype. This second time he had chosen once again not to prototype. Jeff hoped that his existing groups would eventually become his working pattern.

This same sequence of events took place four months later during the second module. Jeff just could not bring himself to go back and prototype the pattern cell. Somehow in his thinking forming a prototype meant retreat or wasting time.

Four months later at the close of the third module I asked the group, "What are you going to do when you go back home this time?" Jeff stood up and said, "The first thing I am going to do is repent and go back and develop a pattern cell."

Jeff did eventually learn his lesson about the importance of the first step. Some leaders never learn!

21
CURRICULUM STRATEGY

✝

There is no further excuse for delaying the militant equipping of every saint for the work of his or her ministry.
—Ralph W. Neighbour, Jr.

Providing tools and support curriculum is a strategic paradigm for worldwide revival in the twenty-first century.

Leaders of a cell church should promise their cell leaders the following: "We will support you with systems and tools that will allow you to work 50 hours a week, be a good husband or wife, be a good parent and be a good cell leader." Anything less means that the most important leader in a cell church will burn out or fail in doing the "work of ministry."

If the cell leader is successful, then all other leaders will be successful. Therefore, it is the responsibility of the coordinating leader, supporting leader and supervising leader to keep that promise to support the cell leader.

Leaders cannot keep this promise without an effective curriculum that is the third part of the cell church process *Tools and Support Systems*.

Materials become a system when combined with methods and mentors. A system has a way to do an objective (method) and someone to see that the method is done (a mentor) and materials. Good materials are essential for implementing an effective system and providing a trigger mechanism for monitoring a task.

CELL CHURCH PROCESS

LEADERS

	1000	1000	1000's	1000's	1000's
	100	100	100's	100's (1)	100's (2)
	50	50	50's (1)	50's (2)	50's (4)
	10	10's (3)	10's (5)	10's (8)	10's (12)

STRUCTURE: PREPARE — BEGIN — CONFIRM — TEST — REORGANIZE — CONSOLIDATE

TOOLS & SUPPORT SYSTEMS

Leaders that choose a curriculum early in the process will be more effective in integrating necessary systems and internalizing cell church culture. The curriculum provides tools and support systems for the process.

THE CURRICULUM GAP

A huge gap exists in the traditional church between materials that can be used for leading unbelievers to conversion and materials for training productive believers.

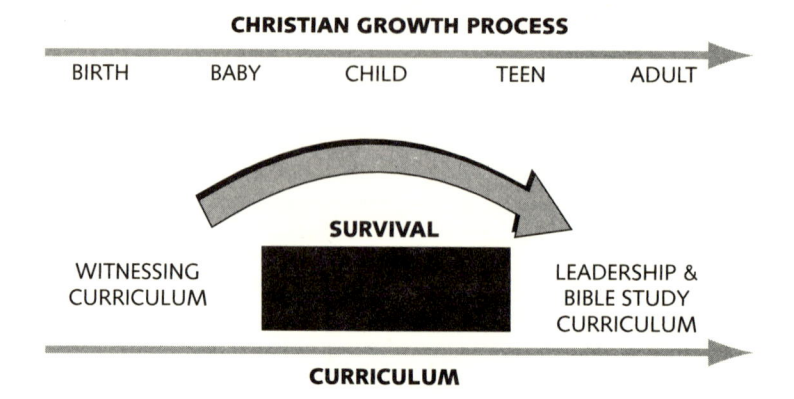

CHRISTIAN GROWTH PROCESS

BIRTH — BABY — CHILD — TEEN — ADULT

SURVIVAL

WITNESSING CURRICULUM — LEADERSHIP & BIBLE STUDY CURRICULUM

CURRICULUM

Many good tools and methods have been developed for witnessing to unbelievers and bringing them to a point of commitment. Other excellent materials and methods have been produced for the advanced phase of the Christian life that moves highly motivated Christians into ministry training or special Bible study. Tragically, after conversion most new believers fall through the curriculum gap. Some show up for Sunday morning worship or special occasions. Others fall into the attending-meetings-routine and contribute to church programs but never grow spiritually. Far too many return to the world, unproductive and unhappy.

What causes this black hole? Without a small-group context, the church has no effective way to care for new believers during the early months of their Christian lives. Consequently, few effective survival materials and methods have been provided for them.

A cell-based church can develop and monitor comprehensive and systematic equipping steps for new believers. Such equipping steps promote health, holiness and harvest in the church and must be installed as a practical system as early as possible.

RALPH NEIGHBOUR AND EQUIPPING

Dr. Ralph Neighbour has made many contributions to the cell church movement. None is more important than his identification of materials necessary to effectively equip a new believer.

For more than three decades, Dr. Neighbour has identified and tested the key growth steps that move a new believer from profession of faith to productive ministry. Dr. Neighbour uses the following curriculum principles: self-study, mentoring, cell life and special life changing encounters. His programmed-learning format involves the new believer in creative and transformational learning.

These Equipping Growth Steps are adapted from Dr. Neighbour's equipping materials. They provide the initial ministry equipping in a cell church. Dr. Neighbour provides a guide for the types of material necessary for moving a new believer from conversion to ministry. If you don't use his materials, you should at least fill his growth slots and use his philosophy of equipping.

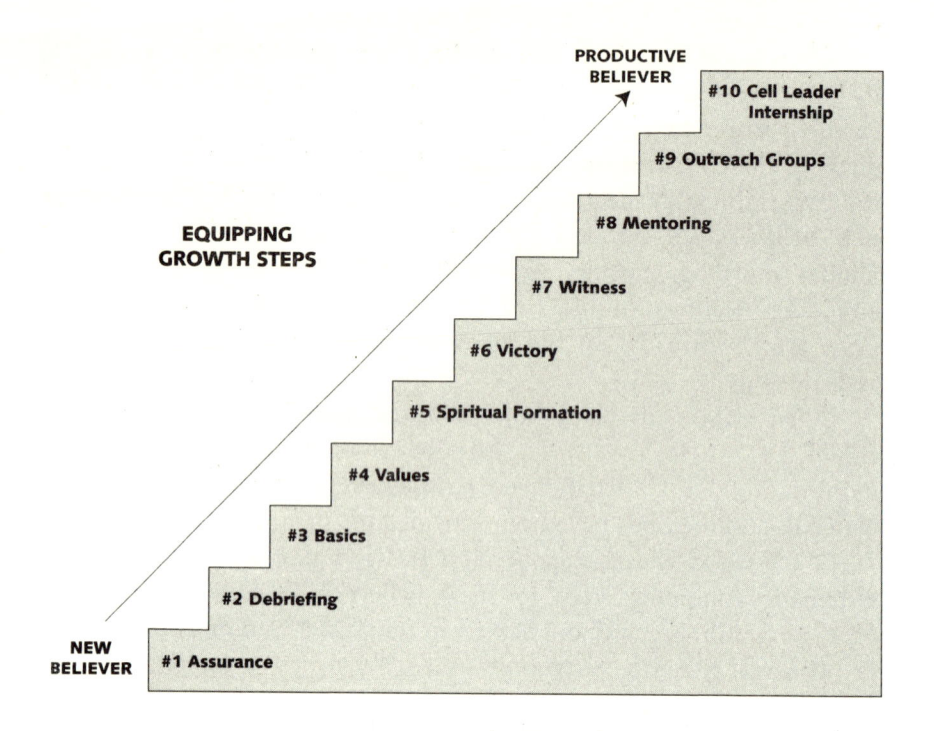

```
                                          PRODUCTIVE
                                           BELIEVER
                                         ↗        #10 Cell Leader
                                                      Internship
                                              #9 Outreach Groups
                                      #8 Mentoring
          EQUIPPING
         GROWTH STEPS            #7 Witness
                              #6 Victory
                        #5 Spiritual Formation
                     #4 Values
                 #3 Basics
             #2 Debriefing
   NEW
 BELIEVER  #1 Assurance
```

A Walk through the Growth Steps

The cell family is responsible for caring for the spiritual baby. The new Christian will be assigned a mentor to walk through the important first year of his new spiritual life and will journey through the following growth steps.

Growth Step #1: The new believer needs assurance of salvation and affirmation in the decision to follow Christ. The goal is for the Christian who helped in the decision process to use a brief and simple piece of material to affirm assurance of salvation. The first time the new believer attends a cell meeting, the cell leader should ask the new believer if the Christian who first shared a witness also shared about assurance. If not, the cell leader should sit down with the new believer and the Christian who helped in the decision process, and with the brochure explain the assurance of salvation. This should take no more than one hour.

Growth Step #2: The new believer must be debriefed and connected to the cell and to the cell leader. He needs to understand the difference between life before becoming a Christian and life after becoming a Christian. The new believer should be aware of the work of Satan in deceiving him about his new life in Christ. The devil tempts the new believer at two extremes. "You will never sin and everything is wonderful forever." That is a lie. "You can never live a Christian life and everything is the same as in the past." That is also a lie. The new believer must understand that the past has been forgiven and he does not have to continue to walk in the guilt and habits of the past. The new believer should see the possibility of walking out the Christian life in freedom, grace and ministry. The cell leader is responsible for using a personal evaluation brochure to help the new believer move out of the old life and into the new.

The piece of material used for this second growth step should be short enough for the new believer to complete in one week. The cell leader should make an appointment to go to the new believer's home for the conclusion of this second growth step. At this time, the cell leader should also take the cell member who will mentor the new believer. If possible, the mentor should be the person who led the new believer through the initial decision process. (The mentor should have completed the equipping steps and should have been trained in the new believer growth step number eight.)

Growth Step #3: The new believer needs to understand basic Christian survival concepts. This step includes going through a simple set of materials that helps the new believer survive as a baby Christian. The materials should be self-study with the mentor. The goal is to help the new believer learn to study with the Holy Spirit as teacher. The mentor should not teach this material, but should be available to answer questions about how to cover the materials as well as about the meaning of the lessons. This experience should last for five or six weeks.

Growth Step #4: The new believer needs to internalize essential Christian values. This step can be one 11-week study or two six-week studies. The goal is to help the new believer establish a pattern of study and living that moves the new believer into a productive Christian life. The objective of this study is not to transfer information but to cause a transformation of life and attitudes.

While the new believer is moving through these first four growth experiences, the support leader over hundreds will provide several key growth encounters. These encounters should be twelve to 15 hours of intensive life changing and attitude rearranging experiences. The content and purpose of an encounter is explained later in this chapter.

Growth Step #5: The new believer will be formed up into the life of the church in a special formation encounter. This encounter covers much of the same materials that pastors often use in a new member class. The difference is in the intensity of the experience and the objective. The objective is to create an encounter through which the new member experiences the importance and commitment of church life.

Growth Step #6: The new believer will participate in a process to be set free from strongholds in a victory encounter. The purpose of this encounter is to move the new believer out of Romans 7 with a life of guilt, self-centeredness and failure into the life of Romans 8 with grace, joy and victory.

Growth Step #7: The new believer will learn how to witness in a witness encounter. Dr. Neighbour uses John 3:16 to present the Gospel to an unbeliever. Other options may be *The Four Spiritual Laws* from Campus Crusade, *The Bridge* from the Navigators and *Steps to Peace with God* from Billy Graham.

After completing the first seven growth steps, the new believer will begin a lifetime of preparation for leadership and/or ministry. The following three growth steps set leadership and ministry into motion.

Growth Step #8: The believer learns to mentor a new believer in the seven growth steps just completed. Mentoring a new believer reinforces the lessons learned in personal study and establishes the believer on the path of leadership and ministry. The believer should be trained to be a mentor in a retreat setting if possible. The potential mentor must understand the importance of mentoring and must receive the skills for being an effective mentor. The leader over hundreds will train mentors and the cell leader will oversee the actual mentoring experience.

Growth Step #9: The believer learns to use a sub-group to contact and cultivate unbelievers. Chapter 4, *The Mathematics of Revival*, shows us that the more contacts with the lost the more conversions. Every new believer should be trained to multiply contacts with the lost through sub groups.

Growth Step #10: The believer has the opportunity to become a cell leader through a leadership training process. The leadership training process should consist of a weekend encounter, an intensive study with a support leader and on-the-job training in the cell.

SPECIAL GROWTH ENCOUNTERS

Six of the steps outlined in the illustration on page 230 are encounters. These encounters should be twelve to 15 intensive hours that are designed to rearrange the attitudes, values, priorities and habits of new believers. Support leaders are responsible for leading this supplemental equipping and are therefore able to help monitor the development of all new members.

The way Jesus planned the Last Supper is a good example of the dynamics of an encounter.

The venue is important. Jesus made preparation in a special place to provide an atmosphere of privacy and community. If possible, get away to a special place. Make proper preparation and set aside enough time to wind down from daily activities. A meal adds to the impact and intimacy of the encounter.

Plan for interaction within the group. Jesus gave opportunity for His disciples to have a lot of personal interaction. John recorded the dynamics within the group as they approached Jerusalem as well as the conversations at the dinner table.

Confront attitudes, roots, and strongholds. "Is it I?" What strongholds are evident in the Last Supper room? Anger, pride, jealousy, envy, pettiness, party spirit, fear, betrayal, deceit and manipulation are boiling below the surface. Jesus was interested in confronting the roots of their attitudes, not just rehashing the fruits of their behavior.

Use old symbols in new ways to get attention. Jesus gave new meaning to the ordinary task of washing dirty feet. Then Jesus gave new meaning to the extraordinary symbol of Passover. At the close of their retreat each person took their own private "Emmaus walk" with Jesus to the garden.

Break the encounter up into specific events and experiences. How did Jesus arrange their time together?

- Ice Breaker: This is towel and basin time where the air is cleared, the world is washed off, the focus is shifted upon Jesus and people struggle to serve others.
- Community: During this time, people share fellowship and it is symbolized by the meal.

- Dialogue: When the disciples asked "Is it I?" they entered into person-to-person interaction as a group. They began to embrace honesty.
- Teaching: This is a time to provide important concepts that explain what the experiences mean.
- Prayer: Jesus led them to the garden. The key question during this time is, Will I pray with Christ?
- Commitment: This encounter happened for Peter at the fire in the courtyard. The encounter must cause people to ask: Will I be identified with Christ?
- Death: Every encounter leads people to the cross. Will I die with Christ?

Gently push toward the limit of commitment. Build an atmosphere of freedom, not coercion. There should be no manipulation. Deal gently with those unwilling to come into God's will. Jesus did not expose Judas.

Plan to continue overnight if possible. Jesus continued the encounter in the Garden of Gethsemane during the night. Undoubtedly on other occasions the group stayed together overnight. On this occasion the soldiers and trial cut short their time together.

Follow up and reinforce the experience. Jesus met this same group later at the Sea of Galilee. The meeting by the seaside has many of the same characteristics as the Last Supper encounter. The Sea of Galilee was a special place. Jesus made preparation by cooking breakfast. Jesus used the symbol of the catch and the shepherd to teach great but practical theological truths. He confronted and ministered to Peter in great gentleness. He followed this meeting up at Pentecost in the upper room.

ONE EQUIPPING SYSTEM

The coordinating leaders of a cell church should choose and commit to one equipping system that every member of the church will complete. The ten growth steps in this chapter are an example of such an equipping system. This basic equipping track is the most fundamental type of training and moves a new believer from conversion to basic leadership.

Churches that fill these curriculum slots early in the cell church process are the most successful. The initial members of the pattern cell and all of the others who are brought into the process must complete the equipping growth-steps to establish an equipping culture. This will show people how things are done. When a new believer enters a cell, he or she will ask cell members about the equipping process. If there is an equipping culture, the mature members will be able to speak from their experience with the process. If they have not been through the materials, the new believer will conclude that equipping is not necessary. More than likely the new believer will not feel a sense of commitment to complete the equipping process either.

Now lets look at this situation with a church that has a cell church culture. The same new believer is encouraged to begin the equipping track by the same cell leader. The new believer talks to the person who has introduced them to Christ and the cell and that person has completed or is in the process of completing the equipping track. The new believer realizes that everyone in the cell has also completed or is completing the process. The new believer responds in a completely different way. The culture encourages the new believer to complete the same equipping track.

A church culture has been established that says, "This is just the way we do it. And it works this way. This is the way you must do it as well."

CONCLUSION
REVIVAL AND DEATH

†

The blood of the martyrs is the seed of the church.

Visual symbols are often developed to express religious beliefs. The symbol of Buddhism is a lotus flower in the shape of a wheel that depicts the cycles of birth and death. Islam is identified with a crescent moon that is a symbol of sovereignty. The star of David is a hexagram formed by combining two equilateral triangles. It symbolizes God's covenant with David that his throne would be established forever and that the Messiah would descend from him.

The cross is the symbol most often associated with Christianity. It is the most radical religious symbol in the world. It represents death and the paradox at the center of the Christian faith which promises that death leads to life. The more I die to my own life the more I live the life of Christ.

The cross sets Christianity apart from all other religions. An article in *Newsweek Magazine* considered how Jews, Muslims and Buddhists view Jesus. At the conclusion of the article the author used the cross to show how the four major religions view Jesus in history.

> Clearly, the cross is what separates the Christ of Christianity from every other Jesus. In Judaism there is no precedent for a

Messiah who dies, much less as a criminal as Jesus did. In Islam, the story of Jesus' death is rejected as an affront to Allah himself. Hindus can accept only a Jesus who passes into peaceful samadhi, a yogi who escapes the degradation of death. The figure of the crucified Christ, says Buddhist Thich Nhat Hanh, "is a very painful image to me. It does not contain joy or peace, and this does not do justice to Jesus." . . . There is, in short, no room in other religions for a Christ who experiences the full burden of mortal existence.[1]

The first apostle, Andrew, is reported to have said the following when threatened with crucifixion: "If I were afraid of the death of the cross, I would not have preached about the majesty, honor and glory of the cross." As Andrew was taken closer to the cross he said, "The nearer I come to the cross, the nearer I come to God; and the farther I am from the cross, the farther I remain from God."[2]

Death is Necessary for Revival

Paul understood the contradiction of the cross. "For the word of the cross is to those who are perishing foolishness, but to us who are being saved it is the power of God."

Christianity has always expanded to the extent of its faith and its death. How far into His death are His followers willing to live? That is how far the Gospel will be extended in the world. How deep will the faith of His followers follow into His death? That validates the truth of the cross to the world.

The twenty-first century world will be convinced of God because of the reality of His death and resurrection in the lives of His followers. His death is the power of God. Our death is the demonstration of the power of God.

The following three scriptures explain how death interacts in the Christian's life.

"Except a corn of wheat fall into the ground and die, it abides alone. But if it dies it brings much fruit" (John 12:24). That is the spiritual experience of salvation by way of death.

"Take up [your] cross daily and follow me" (Luke 9:23). This is the spiritual experience of sanctification through daily death. A life of holiness begins in death.

"When they take you before the [courts] do not worry about what you will say" (Luke 12:11). This is the experience of witness that for some means physical death.

Christians who shirk from daily spiritual death will find it difficult to stand up if physical death is required for faith. Holiness is dying daily to self in order to be prepared to die physically . . . either by natural causes or by persecution.

FEAR OF DEATH IS SATAN'S CONTROL

Fear of death is Satan's ultimate control over Christians and the church. Governments and religions have always used this threat: "If you witness to us, we will kill you!" "If you convert, we will kill you!"

Terrible things happen to and through the church when it either controls or is controlled by the powers of this world. Satan tempted Jesus with the possibility of establishing His Kingdom through the "Kingdoms of this world," but He chose the way of the cross. Jesus' way of changing earthly kingdoms is through love and sacrifice, not political control or coercion.

Christians were martyred by the thousands in the early centuries of the church because of their witness of Christ. In fact, in Greek the word for witness is *martus*. So many Christians died that eventually, the word for witness and martyr became one and the same. Justin Martyr wrote in the mid-second century, "We who once killed one another now do not only not wage war against our enemies, but, in order to avoid lying or deceiving our examiners, we even meet death cheerfully, confessing Christ."

The most tragic time in the life of the church was when it became the persecutor rather than the persecuted. The politically-favored church began to kill martyrs for their interpretation of the Bible rather than becoming martyrs for the faith themselves. In the twenty-first century, Christians must live out a "martyr" spirit, not an accommodation or political spirit. The church must never again be the persecutor. The church must be the witness, the martyr.

Some cultures are so resistant to the gospel and so politically protective of their religion that only the spirit of the martyr will break through. This is happening even today. It may be that the persecution and control of Muslims will be broken by the martyrdom of Christians. If highly publicized, these events might help break the political/religious persecution that is expected within those countries.

DEATH AND GOD'S VISION

God's vision for ministry is always realized by way of death. "God gives us the vision then takes us down into the valley to batter us into the shape of the vision, and, it is in the valley that so many of us faint and give way."[3]

God is sharing His vision with Christians around the world. My problem is that I take God's vision and alter it to my life and desires. I alter God's vision so it is more comfortable to me and to my plans.

I have found that the minute I touch God's vision it is no longer His vision. It is my vision. I then lose the privilege of participating in God's Kingdom vision. I have exchanged His vision with my own.

God must alter me to the shape of His vision. I have learned that God spells "alteration" in a special way, "d-e-a-t-h." Some have suggested that alteration should be spelled "altar-ation."

Every movement of God has demanded the death of some who have been a part it. That death is a death to position, to salary, to prestige, to safety and to convenience. The story of the Bible is the story of alteration. Abraham altered his plans and left the civilization of his birth. Moses altered his plans. Instead of a prince of Egypt, he became a shepherd in the desert of Median. From a shepherd he became a deliverer. Paul was altered from a religious zealot to a missionary.

Recently, I met with a senior pastor to talk about the cell church. As I was leaving, the pastor said, "Before I talked with you I had this vision in my head. Now I have the vision in my heart." I replied, "It is good that you now have the vision in your head and your heart. But, you must have it in one other place. You must have it as a revelation vision in your spirit." Only a revelation vision will sustain us in the face of death.

WATCHMAN NEE

On New Year's Day 1951, Watchman Nee preached one of his last sermons to his church in Shanghai. His text was from the parable of the miracle of the loaves and fishes. His point was that God's blessing upon the loaves and fishes made the difference. He concluded the message with this promise: "There will come a time soon when your abilities will do nothing to save you. There will even come a time when you believe everything is finished. But with His blessing on you that will be the beginning."[4]

Watchman Nee was arrested on April 10, 1952 at the age of 50. He would never know another moment of human freedom. His wife died while he was in prison, and he died in prison on June 1, 1972. He was not allowed to mention the name of God in a final letter to his older sister. However, in the brief letter he revealed his heart to her, "Still, I maintain my own joy."[5] After 20 years of suffering in prison, Watchman Nee still shared in the joy of Christ.

In 1946 Watchman Nee estimated that there were one million Christians in China within a total population of 450 million. According to a published report, a February 1996 internal Communist Party document estimated that more Chinese have joined Christian groups in recent years than the Communist party. While today there are approximately 53 million party members, there are probably twice that number of believers.[6]

One of Watchman Nee's most often quoted Bible verse was 2 Timothy 3:12: "Everyone who wants to live a godly life in Christ Jesus will be persecuted."

A HOLY HISTORY MOMENT

How do we prepare for a holy history moment? By living a holy life daily. By taking up the cross everyday we prepare for that moment of the cross of death. God writes His holy history on earth through ordinary Christians who take up the cross. This is the meaning of Philippians 3:10: "I want to know Christ and the power of his resurrection and the fellowship of sharing in his sufferings, becoming like him in his death." Every moment that I live out Philippians 3:10, I live out a holy history moment.

When Rachael Saint and Elisabeth Elliot returned to the tribe that killed their brother and husband to share Jesus with them, they entered a holy history moment. But holy history moments need not be this dramatic.

They occur when a pastor stakes his position, salary and career upon the revelation vision that God burns in his heart. When key church leaders lay down what they have known church to be in the past and embrace a new thing that they do not fully understand. When church members proclaim, "Yes we want to become what God wants us to be no matter the cost." These are holy history moments that everyday people can embrace.

Radical Praying

In visiting cell churches around the world, I often observe radical New Testament attitudes that I know are holy history moments. I observed such a moment in Belfast, Ireland in 1998. The political reconciliation process in Ireland had reached another critical point between the two sides of this terrible conflict.

I attended a prayer time at Christian Fellowship Church in Belfast, where 120 members assembled at 6:00 A.M. that Thursday morning as they had for months. School children attended and I thought, "This is radical praying when a teenager will get up, dress and go to a prayer meeting at 6:00 in the morning."

Most of the prayers were for the lost friends and relatives of cell members. As we came to the end of the hour the wife of the pastor, Priscilla Reid, who was directing the prayer made a special request. She asked for prayer for the pastors of Belfast who were involved in the peace reconciliation process. Just the day before I had heard on the news that the Loyalist Volunteer Force, a para-military group, threatened to kill any pastor who helped the peace process. This group was taken seriously because they had carried out threats before.

The way that Priscilla made her request reminded me of the radical New Testament spirit that is surfacing in the twenty-first century. She prefaced her request with a brief explanation of the situation. She admitted that she had a personal interest because her husband Paul was one of the pastors that would be singled out. She then said, "Let us pray that God will protect the pastors on both sides who are working for peace and reconciliation."

Then she added, "But let us pray that they will not be silenced. Let us pray that they will not be intimidated."

That was the spirit of the New Testament that overcame every kind of opposition including the threat of death. That is the spirit of courage and boldness that will sweep the persecution and threats before the twenty-first century church.

That radical spirit caused Paul to declare "For to me, to live is Christ and to die is gain" (Philippians 1:21). It is the spirit of the Revelation, "Blessed are the dead who die in the Lord" (Revelation 14:13).

A Day of Wonder

I know of no greater time to be alive and serving God. Voices in the church around the world are speaking about a special day of the Lord in the twenty-first century. This may be the day of the greatest revival that the church has ever known. God is lining up important events around His church. The life of the wine and the structure of the wineskin are working together. Whenever and wherever that has happened in history, radical holiness and harvest have resulted in the expansion of the church.

The history of the twenty-first century church will be part of the holy history recorded in God's history of the ages. It will be the moments of ordinary Christians who believe in the paradigm and paradox of the cross . . . and in its power and glory.

"Look among the nations!"
"Observe!"
"Be astonished!"
"Wonder!"
"Because I am doing something in your days that you would not believe if you were told!" (Habakkuk 1:5)

My prayer is that the church of the twenty-first century will be worthy of these days of wonder and revival.

APPENDIX

The following three-part evaluation will help a church develop a strategy to transition into a cell church. 20 objectives are used to evaluate where a church is and where it is going. The instrument is divided into three major tracks: Begin the Journey, Strengthen the Structure and Complete the Journey.

In the first chart mark from 1 to 7 the place of your church in relation to the objectives. The next chart, Evaluation Explanation, gives a brief explanation of each objective that describes what the church will look like if it is operating at the highest level of "7."

EVALUATION INSTRUMENT FOR TRANSITION TO A CELL CHURCH

Begin the Journey
1. Gather a pool of leaders
2. Clarify the vision & values
3. Mobilize for prayer
4. Retrain church leaders
5. Design the pattern cell
6. Begin youth cells

Strengthen the Structure
7. Install an accountability system
8. Lay the equipping track
9. Establish lifestyle evangelism
10. Develop intern training
11. Provide supplement equipping
12. Form children into community life
13. Organize into leadership units

Complete the Journey
14. Change groups into cells
15. "Cellularize" the calendar & budget
16. Streamline programs
17. Complete the model congregation
18. Form new congregations
19. Develop a training center
20. Prepare for expansion

You can use this evaluation in your church by following these instructions:

1. Teach the vision and values of the cell church to a pool of key leaders.
2. Gather a group of key strategic thinkers and have each of them evaluate where they think the church is in relation to each objective. The evaluation is about where the church is and not where the individual is.
3. Combine all of the scores into one. This will give a good indication of the current progress toward becoming a cell church.
4. Develop action plans by completing the phrase, "We will . . ."
5. Look at the final chart and put the objectives in chronological order.

Appendix

EVALUATION EXPLANATION

PREPARE

1. Gather a pool of leaders	The senior leader has identified, gathered and shared the vision with key leaders who are now ready to do the vision.
2. Clarify the vision & values	The senior pastor and leaders have prepared the whole church body for change by teaching biblical community values.
3. Mobilize for prayer	Leaders and staff spend a significant amount of time during daily work in prayer that encourages the entire church to pray.
4. Retrain church leaders	Staff, leaders and key influencers have been retrained to live in cell life and lead the church according to cell church values.
5. Design the pattern cell	Leaders have received from God the dynamics and mechanics of a pattern cell that is able to be reproduced by all other cells.

STRENGTHEN

6. Begin youth cells	Young people participate in cell life, are equipped, lead cells, edify, sponsor believers and reach their peers for Christ.
7. Install Accountability	Each member of the cell is assigned to a Sponsor/Sponsee relationship or to an accountability partnership.
8. Lay the equipping track	An equipping track is in place by which new members are trained in essential Christian living and prepared for cell life.
9. Begin lifestyle evangelism	Cell members develop an *oikos* list, enter intercessory prayer for the lost and cultivate and witness to lost and prodigals.
10. Develop intern training	Interns at all levels are prepared in personal, classroom & on-the-job training by the leader over 100's and other leaders.
11. Use supplement equipping	Pastors provide special intensive and concentrated equipping in church life, evangelism, spiritual warfare and evangelism.
12. Form children into cell life	Children learn to minister and love God supremely in intergeneration adult cells and in special corporate activities.
13. Organize leadership units	Leaders and interns over units of ten, 50 and 100 have been put in place and equip the saints for ministry.
14. Change groups into cells	All existing groups have been changed into healthy cells that are operating in the five essential components of cell life.
15. "Cellularize" administration	Leaders operate from a yearly cell plan which gives priority to cell activities and needs in the church calendar and budget.

COMPLETE

16. Streamline programs	Activities, programs and ministries which compete with cell life are identified and targeted to be reengineered or replaced.
17. Build a base congregation	A base congregation is built around two to three innovators, twelve core leaders and a support network of 70.
18. Form congregations	Congregations provide leadership and training for cell ministry and are formed around geographical and affinity cells.
19. Develop a training center	The church has begun to train its own members to be pastors and missionaries through intensive in-house training.
20. Prepare for expansion	The church has a plan for responding to exponential growth that is greater than what their human vision can conceive.

The following chart uses the same 20 objectives but places them in a general sequence in relationship to the process taught in chapter 20. The 20 objectives are staggered along the process in the three basic process categories of prepare, strengthen and complete.

CELL CHURCH STRATEGY SEQUENCE

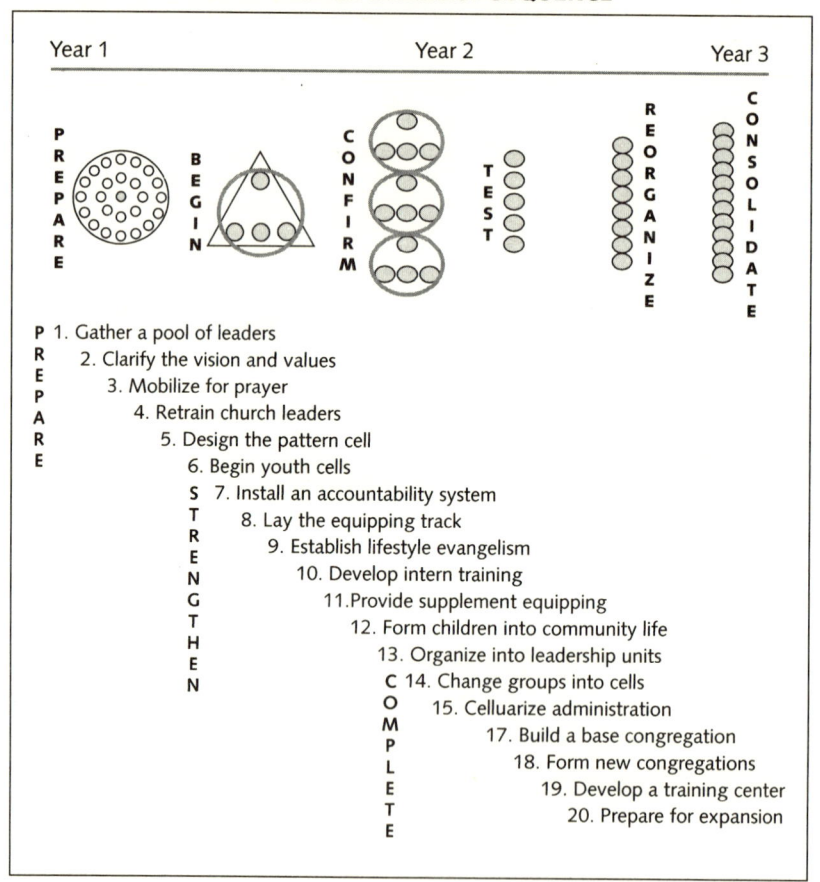

Year 1 — Year 2 — Year 3

PREPARE / BEGIN / CONFIRM / TEST / REORGANIZE / CONSOLIDATE

P 1. Gather a pool of leaders
R 2. Clarify the vision and values
E 3. Mobilize for prayer
P 4. Retrain church leaders
A 5. Design the pattern cell
R 6. Begin youth cells
E
 S 7. Install an accountability system
 T 8. Lay the equipping track
 R 9. Establish lifestyle evangelism
 E 10. Develop intern training
 N 11. Provide supplement equipping
 G 12. Form children into community life
 T 13. Organize into leadership units
 H
 E C 14. Change groups into cells
 N O 15. Celluarize administration
   M 17. Build a base congregation
   P 18. Form new congregations
   L 19. Develop a training center
   E 20. Prepare for expansion
   T
   E

NOTES

To the Reader
"Some day when . . ." George Elton Ladd, "The Gospel of the Kingdom," in *Perspectives on the World Christian Movement*, ed. Ralph D. Winter and Steven C. Hawthorne (Pasadena, CA: William Carey Library, 1999), 74.
[1] Martin Luther, *Luther's Works*, vol. 53, Preface to The German and Order of Service, gen. ed. Helmut T. Lehman, trans. Paul Zeller Strodach (Philadelphia: Fortress Press, 1965), 63-64.
[2] Elton Trueblood, *Your Other Vocation* (New York: Harper Brothers, 1952), 32.

Introduction
"Every generation is . . ." Billy Graham, *Just as I Am* (New York: Harper Collins, 1997), 669.
[1] ibid.
[2] Billy Graham, "The King is Coming," in *Let the Earth Hear His Voice*, Official Reference Volume for the International Congress on World Evangelization, Lausanne, Switzerland, ed. J. D. Douglas (Minneapolis: World Wide Publications,1975), 1466, quoted in Robert E. Coleman, "The Hope of a Coming World Revival," in Perspectives on the World Christian Movement, ed. Ralph D. Winter and Steven C. Hawthorne (Pasadena, CA: William Carey Library, 1999), 74.
[3] ibid.

Chapter One
[1] David Briscoe, "Earth's Six Billionth Inhabitant Expected to Arrive October Twelfth," *Houston Chronicle*, 27 May 1999, 34A.
[2] ibid.
[3] Carl F. George, *The Coming Church Revolution* (Grand Rapids, MI: Baker Books, 1994), 44.
[4] Robert E. Coleman, *The Master Plan of Evangelism* (Old Tappen, NJ: Revell Co., 1963), 18.

Chapter Two
[1] Ralph D. Winter, "The Two Structures of God's Redemptive Mission," in *Perspectives on the World Christian Movement*, ed. Ralph D. Winter and Steven C. Hawthorne (Pasadena, CA: William Carey Library, 1999), 74.

Chapter Three
"Christianity means community . . ." Dietrich Bonhoeffer, *Life Together* (New York: Harper Collins, 1954), 21.
[1] Christian Schwarz, *Natural Church Development* (Carol Stream, IL: Churchsmart Resources, 1996), 32.

Chapter Four
"The epidemic end . . ." John Hayward, "Mathematical Modeling of Church Growth" (pre-published draft, University of Glamorgan, 1998), 11.
[1] ibid.
[2] ibid., 16.
[3] ibid., 18.
[4] ibid.
[5] ibid., 20.
[6] ibid., 12.

Chapter Five
"The early church . . ." John Bright, *The Kingdom of God* (Nashville: Abingdon Press, 1953), 245.

[1] Archibald M. Hunter, *The Work and Words of Jesus* (Philadelphia: The Westminster Press, 1950), 68-80.
[2] Alfred Loisy, *The Gospel and the Church*, trans. Christopher Home (New York: Charles Scribner's Sons, 1912), 166.
[3] Bright, 245.
[4] Howard Snyder, *The Problem of Wineskins* (Downers Grove, IL: Inter-Varsity Press, 1975), 156-157.

Revival Roots
"In scripture the . . ." Howard Snyder, *The Community of the King* (Downers Grove, IL: Inter-Varsity Press, 1977), 56.

Chapter Six
"The Gospels are . . ." Coleman, 16.
[1] John Stott, *The Spirit, the Church, and the World* (Downers Grove, IL: InterVarsity Press, 1990), 32.
[2] Kevin Giles, *What on Earth is the Church?* (North Blackburn, Australia: Dove, 1995), 44-45.
[3] Michael Henderson, *John Wesley's Class Meeting* (Nappanee, IN: Evangel Publishing House, 1997), 133.
[4] John Stott, 32.
[5] Stanley J. Grenz, *Theology for the Community of God* (Carlisle, UK: Paternoster Press, 1994), 626.
[6] Stott, 82.
[7] Roland Allen, *Missionary Methods: St. Paul's or Ours?* (Grand Rapids: Eerdmans, 1962), 4.

Chapter Seven
"As a body . . ." John Stott, 60.
[1] ibid., 34.
[2] Coleman, 69.
[3] Bonhoeffer, 21.
[4] Coleman, 66.
[5] Grenz, 627.

Chapter Eight
"The believers . . ." G. K. Chesterson, *Orthodoxy* (New York: John Lane Co., 1909), 278-279.
[1] Stott, 101.
[2] Ray C. Stedman, *Body Life* (Glendale, CA: Regal Books, 1972), 67.
[3] Elton Trueblood, *A Place to Stand* (New York: Harper and Row, 1969), 94-95.
[4] Francis A. Schaeffer, *True Spirituality* (Wheaton, IL: Tyndale House Publishers, 1973), 171.
[5] Trueblood, *A Place to Stand*, 95.
[6] E.Y. Mullins, *Why is Christianity True?* (Philadelphia: American Baptist Publication Society, 1911), 186.
[7] Trueblood, *A Place to Stand*, 92.

Chapter Nine
"People are looking . . ." Coleman, 80.
[1] Oswald Chambers, *My Utmost for his Highest* (New York: Dodd, Mead, and Company, 1963), 304.
[2] Coleman, 56.
[3] Henderson, 116.
[4] ibid., 104.

Chapter Ten
"The time which . . ." Coleman, 43.
[1] Stephen E. Ambrose, *Citizen Soldiers* (New York: Touchstone, 1997), 332.
[2] Coleman, 21.
[3] ibid.
[4] ibid., 33.
[5] ibid., 34.
[6] ibid., 35.
[7] ibid., 109.

[8] Ambrose, 473.
[9] ibid.

Revival Principles
"Through the purging . . ." Robert Coleman, "The Hope of a Coming World Revival," in *Perspectives on the World Christian Movement*, 190.

Chapter Eleven
"The system . . ." Michael Gerber, *The E-Myth* (New York: Harper Business, 1986), 79.
[1] Fritjof Capra, *The Turning Point* quoted in Gerber, 47.
[2] Henderson, 94.
[3] ibid., 94-95.
[4] ibid., 28.
[5] ibid., 106.
[6] George Barna, *The Power of Vision* (Ventura, CA: Regal Books, 1992), 52.
[7] Gerber, 79.

Chapter Twelve
"All the links . . ." Elton Trueblood, *The Incendiary Fellowship* (New York: Harper and Row, 1967), 33.
[1] Gerber, 61.
[2] ibid.
[3] Elton Trueblood, *The Incendiary Fellowship*, 33.
[4] Elton Trueblood, *The Yoke of Christ* (New York: Harper and Brothers, 1958), 25.
[5] Elizabeth O'Conner, *Call to Commitment*, (New York: Harper and Row, 1963), 46.

Chapter Thirteen
"Small is something . . ." Carl Dudley quoted in C. Peter Wagner, 137.
[1] Charles Handy, *The Empty Raincoat* (London: Hutchinson, 1994), 49.
[2] Wagner, 126.
[3] ibid., 129.
[4] Lyle E. Schaller, *The Change Agent* (Nashville: Abingdon, 1978), 133-134.
[5] Neil Braun, *Laity Mobilized* (Grand Rapids, MI: Eerdmans, 1971), 127.
[6] Elton Trueblood, *The Company of the Committed* (New York: Harper and Brothers, 1961), 38.
[7] Schwarz, 31.

Chapter Fourteen
[1] *Memoirs of the Life and Writing of Benjamin Franklin*, I:87 quoted in Henderson, 23.
[2] Henderson, 29.
[3] ibid., 30.
[4] ibid.
[5] Coleman, *The Master Plan of Evangelism*, 33.
[6] Henderson, 114.
[7] Coleman, 31.
[8] ibid., 36.

Chapter Fifteen
"The small group . . ." Snyder, *The Problem of Wineskins*, 144.
[1] Kristin von Kreisler, "The Bravest Eagle," *Reader's Digest*, December 1997, 78-83.
[2] Graham, 720.
[3] Wolfgang Simson, "Houses that Change the World," (draft copy, 1998).

Revival Strategy
"God is working . . ." John Stott, "The Living God is a Missionary God," in *Perspectives on the World Christian Movement*, 8.

Chapter Sixteen
"Our goal is . . ." Charles L. Chaney, *Church Planting at the End of the Twentieth Century* (Wheaton, IL: Tyndale House, 1987), 28.
[1] ibid.
[2] Ralph D. Winter, "The New Macedonia," in *Perspectives on the World Christian Movement*, 353.
[3] ibid., 350.
[4] Howard Snyder, *The Community of the King*, 56.

Chapter Seventeen
"The fruit of . . ." Schwarz, 68.
[1] ibid.

Chapter Eighteen
"Our paternalism is . . ." William A. Smalley, "Cultural Implications," in *Perspectives on the World Christian Movement*, 479.
[1] ibid., 476.
[2] ibid., 479.
[3] K. P. Yohannan, *The Coming Revolution in World Missions* (Altamonte Springs, FL: Creation House, 1986), 142.
[4] Winter, 339.
[5] ibid., 345.
[6] ibid., 344.
[7] You can find out more about Paz International by contacting them: P.O. Box 913, Morton, IL 61550.

Chapter Nineteen
[1] Carl George, "What is a Meta-Church?" *Cell Church Magazine*, vol. 2 issue 2, 5.

Chapter Twenty
"If a series . . ." Peter Scholtes, et al., *The Team Handbook* (Madison, WI: Joiner, 1990), 2-3.

Chapter Twenty-one
"There is no . . ." Ralph W. Neighbour Jr., *Where Do We Go from Here?* (Houston: TOUCH Publications, 1990), 329.

Conclusion
[1] Kenneth L. Woodward, "The Other Jesus," *Newsweek*, 27 March 2000, 81.
[2] dc Talk and The Voice of the Martyrs, *Jesus Freaks* (Tulsa, OK: Asbury Publishing, 1999), 150.
[3] Chambers, 188.
[4] Bob Laurent, *Watchman Nee* (Uhrichsville, OH: Barbour Publishing, 1998), 164.
[5] ibid., 177-178.
[6] ibid., 184.

INDEX

10/40 Window, 28-29

Abraham, 78, 80, 240
Africa, 28, 33, 95, 163, 176
Alpha, 52, 220
Ambrose, Stephen, 108, 113
Antioch Church, 164, 191-192
Asia, 28, 74
Assimilation, 9, 22, 49, 52, 121, 149-151, 153-157
Australia, 28, 33, 203, 250

Baptist, 52, 108-109, 176, 182, 191-192, 209, 219, 250
Base congregation, 188, 192, 205-207, 209-210, 212-213, 217
Blackaby, Henry, 220
Bonhoeffer, Dietrich, 35, 81, 249-250
Brazil, 33, 37, 108, 201, 220
Bright, John, 55, 57, 160, 249
Buddhism, 29, 180, 198, 237

Canon, 92
Carey, William, 199, 249
Catholic Orders, 31-32
Cell Church Mission Network, 34
Chambers, Oswald, 101, 250, 252
China, 27, 29, 33-34, 36, 99, 162, 166-167, 241
Church of England, 119, 181
Coleman, Robert, 14, 65, 95, 105, 110, 115, 249-251
Critical mass, 10, 138, 141, 147-148, 186, 205-211, 213, 217, 221, 224
Cross, 13, 47, 79-80, 83-84, 178-180, 182, 195-197, 234, 237-239, 241, 243
Crusades, 33, 35, 97, 181

DNA, 36-37, 68-69, 72, 79, 221-222, 224
DuBose, Francis, 176

E-1 Witness, 195-200
E-2 Witness, 195-200
E-3 Witness, 195-198, 200
Elliot, Elisabeth, 242
England, 33, 45, 52, 103, 118-121, 125, 127, 138, 181, 220

Equipping, 37-40, 53, 96, 98, 112, 124-125, 129-130, 133, 143-144, 153, 221-222, 227, 229, 231, 233-235, 245
Equipping Track, 40, 53, 143, 234-235, 245
Ethiopia, 167
Europe, 30-31, 33, 68, 74, 137, 197-199

Faith, 59, 82-85, 89, 97-99, 101, 121, 186, 229, 237-239
Franklin, Benjamin, 72, 149, 251

Genome Project, 36
George, Carl, 207, 249, 251-252
Gerber, Michael, 117, 130, 251
Gifts, 37-39, 59, 85, 89-90, 92-93, 108, 111, 124, 130-132, 136, 141-142, 206
Giles, Kevin, 66, 250
Graham, Billy, 15, 17-18, 149, 164, 167, 232, 249, 251
Great Commission, 31-33, 178

Handy, Charles, 138, 251
Hayward, John, 45, 50, 249
Henderson, Michael, 66, 119, 150, 250-251
Highland Baptist Church, 191-192
Hinduism, 29, 80
Hive model, 188
Homes, 24, 44, 51, 71, 80, 82, 96, 99, 105, 111, 155-156, 162, 164-165, 169
Hong Kong, 34, 46-47, 123
Hope of Bangkok Church, 202
House church, 34, 161-164, 166-170
Hybels, Bill, 52

Immanence, 60-61, 82
India, 29, 33, 192, 194
International Charismatic Mission, 52
Islam, 29, 237-238

Jethro, 9, 42, 105-111, 113-114, 143

Kingdom, 9, 13-17, 23, 25, 55-62, 98, 100, 102, 127, 141, 178, 181-184, 202, 206, 213, 239-240, 249
Kingdom of God, 13-14, 16, 25, 55-58, 141, 249

Leadership, 9, 37-39, 42, 66, 81-82, 105-114, 119, 123-124, 129-133, 136, 140-143, 145, 147, 167-168, 189, 209, 216, 218-226, 232, 234, 245
Luther, Martin, 11, 182, 249

McDonald's, 127
Miracles, 71-72, 87-92, 109, 154
Mission model, 188
Modality, 31-32
Morocco, 197-198
Moses, 23-24, 106-109, 240

Nee, Watchman, 241, 252
Neighbour, Ralph, 7, 52, 221, 227, 229, 232, 252
New believers, 32, 39-40, 42, 44, 52-54, 68, 95-97, 100-104, 138, 153-156, 206, 222-223, 229, 233
New Zealand, 28, 33

O'Connor, Elizabeth, 135, 251

Parachurch, 31
Paul, 17, 32-33, 56, 58, 67-68, 73-74, 102, 107, 109, 118, 132-133, 164-165, 168, 178, 180, 187, 198-199, 220, 238, 240, 242-243, 249-250
Paz International, 201-202, 252
Pentecost, 35, 44, 48-50, 65, 67-74, 79, 82, 96-97, 99, 102, 104, 134, 147, 154-156, 164-165, 196, 205, 216, 218, 234
Prayer, 25, 29, 34, 39, 49-50, 59, 70, 77, 90-91, 93, 97, 124, 164, 170, 177-178, 191, 202-203, 205-206, 210, 234, 242-243, 245
Prototype, 205, 207-209, 220, 222-223, 226

Quakers, 182

Reformation, 9, 11-12, 33, 59, 92, 181
Resurrection, 9, 60, 82-84, 87-89, 91-93, 99, 156, 238, 241
RNA, 37
Robert, Dion, 15, 125, 141
Russia, 151-152

Satellite model, 188
Schaeffer, Francis, 91, 250
Schaller, Lyle, 142, 251
Schwarz, Christian, 35, 145, 185, 249, 251-252
Scotland, 208
Sermon on the Mount, 58, 102
Sigmoid Curve, 138-139
Simson, Wolfgang, 168-169, 251
Singh, Sadhu Sunder, 194

Singlehurst, Laurence, 45, 138
Smalley, William A., 193, 252
Snyder, Howard, 57, 63, 159, 250-252
Sodality, 31-33
South America, 28
Soviet Union, 151-152
Spiritual gifts, 38, 85, 90, 136, 142
Strachan Principle, 144

Tabernacle, 23-24, 60
Thailand, 5, 67, 130, 176-177, 198-199, 202-203, 210, 212-213
TOUCH Brazil, 37
TOUCH Outreach Ministries, 4, 220
Training, 9, 32, 42, 53, 71-72, 82, 95-104, 108-109, 112, 129, 144-145, 155, 170, 192, 202, 226, 228-229, 232, 234, 245
Transcendence, 60-61, 82
Trueblood, Elton, 12, 91, 129, 134, 144, 249-251

Wagner, Peter, 59, 139, 142, 251
Wales, 45, 187
Weaver, Paul, 220
Wesley, John, 17, 66, 103, 118-128, 149-150, 153, 182, 250
West Memorial Baptist Church, 52
Whitefield, George, 149-150
Willow Creek Community Church, 52
Winter, Ralph 195-197, 249, 252
Wong, Ben, 34, 43, 123

ADDITIONAL RESOURCES ON THE CELL CHURCH

THE SECOND REFORMATION, *by William A. Beckham*
Don't jump head-first into a cell church transition or church plant without reading this book! Beckham brilliantly walks you through the logic of a cell/celebration structure from a biblical and historical perspective. He provides you with a step-by-step strategy for launching your first cells. This wonderful companion to Neighbour's material will ground you in the values and vision necessary for a successful transition to cells. 253 pgs.

REAP THE HARVEST, *by Joel Comiskey*
This book casts a vision for cell groups that will work in your church. Based on research of the best cell churches around the world and practical experience by the author, *Reap the Harvest* will reveal the 16 proven principles behind cell-church growth and effectiveness. It will also provide you with a strong biblical and historical foundation that anyone can understand. Great to share with key leaders as you transition to cell groups. 240 pgs.

WHERE DO WE GO FROM HERE?
THE 10TH ANNIVERSARY EDITION, *by Ralph W. Neighbour, Jr.*
With updated data on new cell church models, new information on equipping and harvest events and practical teaching on how to begin a transition, this book will continue to stir hearts to dream about what the church can be. You will find hope for the church in North America and discover the new things that Dr. Neighbour has learned over the last 10 years. Share this vision with a friend. 400 pgs.

LIFE IN HIS BODY, *by David Finnell*
Communicate the vision of the cells to everyone in your church with this simple tool. The short chapters followed by discussion questions clearly define cell life for your leaders and members so that they can catch a lifestyle of prayer, community and evangelism. This book will give your church hope and vision as your members discover the possibilities of the New Testament community. 160 pgs.

GROUPS OF 12, *by Joel Comiskey*
Finally, the definitive work that clears the confusion about the Groups of 12 model. Thousands of pastors have traveled to International Charismatic Mission to see it in operation. In this new title, Joel has dug deeply into ICM and other G-12 churches to learn the simple G-12 principles that can be transferred to your church. This book will contrast this new model from the classic structure and show you exactly what to do with this new model of cell ministry. 182 pgs.

Order Toll-Free from TOUCH Outreach Ministries
1-800-735-5865 • Order Online: www.touchusa.org

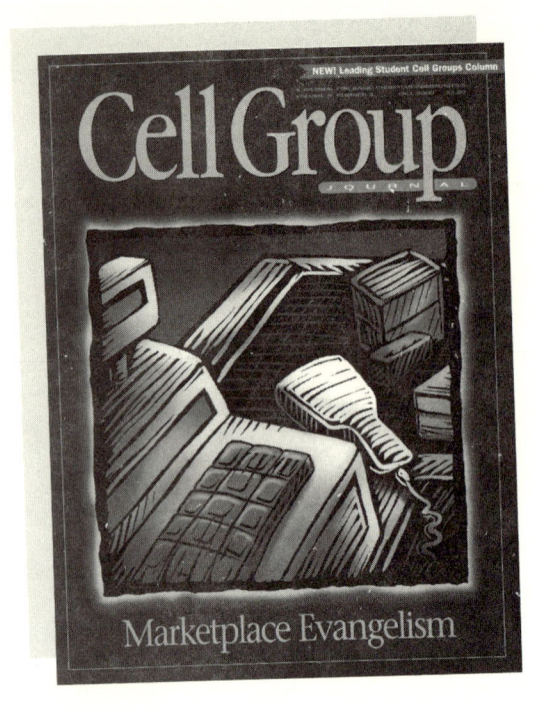

Equip Your Cell Leaders!

CellGroup JOURNAL

CellGroup Journal, unlike any other periodical, is focused on the needs and desires of cell leaders in your church. Every quarterly issue contains practical feature articles and columns from some of the most respected leaders in the US including Ralph W. Neighbour, Jr., Billy Hornsby on leadership, Karen Hurston on evangelism, Gerrit Gustafson on worship, Sam Scaggs on missions, and Larry Kreider with a closing note on a variety of topics. Pastor's get fed too . . . each issue contains an article for pastors by a pastor who has learned a good lesson in cell life and wants to share. Bulk discounts are available for larger subscriptions. Call today to subscribe for all your cell leaders and staff!

**Order Toll-Free from TOUCH Outreach Ministries
1-800-735-5865 • Order Online: www.touchusa.org**